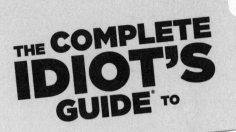

THE COMPLETE **IDIOT'S** GUIDE® TO

Grant Writing

Third Edition

by Waddy Thompson

ALPHA

A member of Penguin Group (USA) Inc.

NEWARK PUBLIC LIBRARY
121 HIGH ST.
NEWARK, NY 14513

ALPHA BOOKS

Published by the Penguin Group

Penguin Group (USA) Inc., 375 Hudson Street, New York, New York 10014, USA

Penguin Group (Canada), 90 Eglinton Avenue East, Suite 700, Toronto, Ontario M4P 2Y3, Canada (a division of Pearson Penguin Canada Inc.)

Penguin Books Ltd., 80 Strand, London WC2R 0RL, England

Penguin Ireland, 25 St. Stephen's Green, Dublin 2, Ireland (a division of Penguin Books Ltd.)

Penguin Group (Australia), 250 Camberwell Road, Camberwell, Victoria 3124, Australia (a division of Pearson Australia Group Pty. Ltd.)

Penguin Books India Pvt. Ltd., 11 Community Centre, Panchsheel Park, New Delhi—110 017, India

Penguin Group (NZ), 67 Apollo Drive, Rosedale, North Shore, Auckland 1311, New Zealand (a division of Pearson New Zealand Ltd.)

Penguin Books (South Africa) (Pty.) Ltd., 24 Sturdee Avenue, Rosebank, Johannesburg 2196, South Africa

Penguin Books Ltd., Registered Offices: 80 Strand, London WC2R 0RL, England

Copyright © 2011 by Waddy Thompson

All rights reserved. No part of this book shall be reproduced, stored in a retrieval system, or transmitted by any means, electronic, mechanical, photocopying, recording, or otherwise, without written permission from the publisher. No patent liability is assumed with respect to the use of the information contained herein. Although every precaution has been taken in the preparation of this book, the publisher and author assume no responsibility for errors or omissions. Neither is any liability assumed for damages resulting from the use of information contained herein. For information, address Alpha Books, 800 East 96th Street, Indianapolis, IN 46240.

THE COMPLETE IDIOT'S GUIDE TO and Design are registered trademarks of Penguin Group (USA) Inc.

International Standard Book Number: 978-1-61564-097-3
Library of Congress Catalog Card Number: 2010919338

13 12 11   8 7 6 5 4 3 2 1

Interpretation of the printing code: The rightmost number of the first series of numbers is the year of the book's printing; the rightmost number of the second series of numbers is the number of the book's printing. For example, a printing code of 11-1 shows that the first printing occurred in 2011.

Printed in the United States of America

Note: This publication contains the opinions and ideas of its author. It is intended to provide helpful and informative material on the subject matter covered. It is sold with the understanding that the author and publisher are not engaged in rendering professional services in the book. If the reader requires personal assistance or advice, a competent professional should be consulted.

The author and publisher specifically disclaim any responsibility for any liability, loss, or risk, personal or otherwise, which is incurred as a consequence, directly or indirectly, of the use and application of any of the contents of this book.

Most Alpha books are available at special quantity discounts for bulk purchases for sales promotions, premiums, fund-raising, or educational use. Special books, or book excerpts, can also be created to fit specific needs.

For details, write: Special Markets, Alpha Books, 375 Hudson Street, New York, NY 10014.

Publisher: *Marie Butler-Knight*

Associate Publisher: *Mike Sanders*

Executive Managing Editor: *Billy Fields*

Executive Editor: *Randy Ladenheim-Gil*

Senior Production Editor: *Kayla Dugger*

Copy Editor: *Monica Stone*

Cover Designer: *Kurt Owens*

Book Designers: *William Thomas, Rebecca Batchelor*

Indexer: *Angie Bess Martin*

Layout: *Brian Massey*

Proofreader: *John Etchison*

Contents

Appendixes

Introduction

Many people have extensive experience in writing grants and don't even know it. If you've ever asked anyone for anything in writing, you probably followed many of the procedures outlined in this book. That's all a grant proposal is.

How can you harness that power for good? I tell you exactly how in this book.

Grant writing can be a satisfying and rewarding experience, no matter if you're a volunteer or building a career. It's a great feeling when the check comes in the mail, but there's a lot to do before you can start counting the money.

Throughout the book, I refer to the other people at a nonprofit you'll interact with in the process of creating a grant proposal. Of course, if you're volunteering for a small nonprofit with no paid staff or one just being formed, you may have only yourself to rely on for all the information you need. At least you won't have other people relentlessly editing your copy!

Grant writing entails a lot more than just writing a grant. You are developing financial resources for your charity. Grant writing requires knowledge of the philanthropic field, excellent general writing skills, organizational and project management ability, and a personal touch. That's a broad range of talents and knowledge, but you'll find information on all of them here.

What's in This Book

I've divided the book into six parts:

Part 1, Getting Started, provides you with the basics about what it takes to be a good grant writer and what the process of writing a grant will be like.

Part 2, Where the Money Is, takes you behind the scenes of all the different institutions that make grants to see what makes them tick. I also provide you with a primer for getting a grant from an individual by learning what basic human emotions come into play.

Part 3, Research, or Just How Nosy Are You? guides you in satisfying your curiosity about funders and all the people associated with them, and how to use that information to win them over.

Part 4, Strategies for Success, teaches you the little tricks of the trade to warm up your prospects before you ask them for money and to get yourself organized so everything can proceed according to a plan.

Part 5, Writing the Proposal, shows you how to gather the information you need from your colleagues and put it into the form the funder wants to receive, including spelling it out in dollars and cents in the budget.

Part 6, Everything Else You Need to Know, covers what might be the most difficult part of the whole business—waiting to hear how you did. Individuals seeking grants face special challenges, which I address in a separate chapter. And for those of you who would like the "in-brief" version of grant writing or a solid summary of what you're supposed to have learned from these pages, I've ended the book with a whirlwind grant-writing course. Finally, you'll find two chapters of advice on how to go about making a living as a freelance grant writer.

The appendixes include a glossary that covers all the insider lingo; an extensive listing of reference resources, online and off; and examples of complete grants.

In addition to the many examples you'll find throughout the book, a number of useful documents and spreadsheets can be downloaded from idiotsguides.com under "Book Extras."

The Philanthropy Insider

Throughout the book, you'll find tips on different aspects of the grant business:

HOW TO SAY IT

Every business has its own way of saying things. These writing tips help you avoid sounding like an amateur.

DEFINITION

The philanthropy world has its own language. In these sidebars, you'll get a plain-English explanation about what the arcane terms really mean.

PHILANTHROPY FACT

The more you know about the grant world, the better prepared you are to take it on. These facts are meant to both clue you in and give you a perspective beyond the grants you're writing.

WORDS TO THE WISE

There are two ways of doing things in this business: the wrong way and the insider's way. These cautions help you avoid the mistakes of others (including me) and set you straight about what's expected in a variety of situations.

Acknowledgments

During the past two decades, I've been fortunate to work for a number of knowledgeable people who have gently introduced me to the philanthropic and grant-seeking world. I've learned so much from each of them, but I also have learned much from the grant writers who have worked for me. They, too, have given me insights into the process of getting a grant, while putting up with my endless editing of their documents. Special thanks go to my colleagues Leah Maddrie, Kate Taylor, and Rados Piletich, who read and gave me advice on various parts of this book.

I must also thank Theodore Berger, former executive director of the New York Foundation for the Arts (NYFA), for allowing me to include examples from NYFA grants. All examples in this book not related to NYFA are about fictional charities, and no funder referred to in any grant-writing example is intended to represent the policies and intent of any actual funder.

Finally, many thanks to my agent, Marilyn Allen, without whom this book would not exist.

Special Thanks to the Technical Reviewers

The Complete Idiot's Guide to Grant Writing, Third Edition, was reviewed by experts who double-checked the accuracy of what you'll learn here, to help us ensure that this book gives you everything you need to know about grant writing. Special thanks are extended to Nancy S. Clarke and Tess O'Dwyer.

Trademarks

All terms mentioned in this book that are known to be or are suspected of being trademarks or service marks have been appropriately capitalized. Alpha Books and Penguin Group (USA) Inc. cannot attest to the accuracy of this information. Use of a term in this book should not be regarded as affecting the validity of any trademark or service mark.

Getting Started

It's always good to get the lay of the land before beginning any endeavor. In Part 1, you discover your hidden grant-writing skills. You also learn just what grant writing entails, including what knowledge, skills, and disposition you need to bring to the practice of grant writing. A week-by-week timeline gives you a heads-up on how much time you need to allow for the often lengthy grant process.

Although everyone would like to receive a grant, institutions that make grants operate within a relatively narrow compass, usually making grants only to nonprofits. You'll learn how to you can sometimes get around that restriction.

Funders are also selective about what kinds of projects they will support, so I take you through the different types of fundable projects.

Finally, I give you a quick look at what the funder wants to see when he opens your application and how to avoid getting rejected right off the bat.

The Practice of Grant Writing

In This Chapter

- Grant writing defined
- Why grant writing is right for you
- How the economy affects grants
- What it means to be a grant writer
- Time line for success

Grant writing is one of those topics that seems very technical and esoteric, yet you probably already know more about it than you think you do. But before I go any further, let's be clear about just what grant writing is and isn't.

Grant writing is the skill or practice of asking for money in the form of a grant from a foundation, corporation, or government agency by crafting a well-considered document (the proposal) that outlines how the money will be used, what receiving the money will accomplish, and who will undertake the tasks described in the proposal.

Grant writing is *not* about writing a group of friends to get each of them to give $25 for the local library. (That sort of fundraising is called direct mail or unsolicited third-class mail, but never junk mail if you are in the business of raising money.)

Grant writing *is* about creating a proposal, which you can send to local corporations or foundations asking for several thousand dollars for the local library. On occasion, proposals will be written to individuals when a four- to seven-figure gift is being sought, and I cover that in this book, too. But for the most part, you'll be concerned with getting largish sums of money from some kind of institution or another. Grant writing is an important part of any fundraising program, which would likely include at least direct mail and special events as well.

I start off with what I think you already know and finish this chapter with the key things you need to know about the practice of grant writing. Then I show you how to pursue the technical aspects in the remaining chapters of the book.

You Already Are a Grant Writer!

If you're anything like me, when you were in college or away at summer camp, you found it easiest to remember to write home just when your wallet was getting a little thin. Believe it or not, that was your first grant-writing experience. (I hope you were successful!)

PHILANTHROPY FACT

More than 1.5 million nonprofit organizations in the United States have federal tax-exempt status, hundreds of thousands more have state tax-exempt status, and untold numbers of other groups are unincorporated.

Asking for money is never easy, but anyone can acquire the skills to ask like a professional fundraiser. This book tells you how to do that, but like so many important life lessons, you'll find you learned the basics much earlier in life. In case your memory is fuzzy on what those letters home were like, I've included a "Dear Mom and Dad" letter to refresh your memory.

Dear Mom and Dad,

Thanks so much for the check you sent a couple of weeks ago. It really came just in the nick of time so I could get all the books for the new semester.

College is great! You probably saw the basketball game on TV last weekend. It was really something to actually be there. The college has a terrific series of concerts in the Coliseum, too, with first-class bands.

There are so many things to do and see, but recently I have not been able to do and see as many things as my friends because I've been running low on funds. If you could send me an extra $100 to tide me over to the end of the month, that would really be great!

It's not that I expect to go out every night. Most of my time is still spent studying, especially for Psych 101, which is really tough, but I think is the subject I like the best. Reading the case studies has really brought home to me what great parents you are.

When do you think you'll come up for a visit? Hope it's soon, and if you could help me out with a check really soon, I'd really appreciate it.

Love,

Jack

Like Writing Mom and Dad

You can learn many things from that "Dear Mom and Dad" letter that will serve you well as a grant writer. Let's take a closer look at the letter to see some of the points of similarity.

Because Jack's letter home was not the first time he had ever asked for money, he was seeking a renewal grant. So Jack naturally started out telling his parents how he had used the last money they sent. And note that his very first word was "Thanks"—the magic word that can open so many doors. It's so important to always acknowledge past support. No one—not a parent or a funder—ever wants to be taken for granted.

Jack follows his opening by telling his parents what has been happening at school to make them feel involved and current. Every funder will want to know what significant things are happening in your organization right now, whether they're related to the specific grant or not.

Eventually Jack had to actually ask for money, which to be convincing, had to include some ideas on how he'd spend this new money. Jack's pretty vague on this, so he must be looking for *general operating support*.

DEFINITION

General operating support refers to a grant to pay for the everyday expenses all organizations have—rent, utilities, and insurance—as well as for personnel who are not involved in programs (like the grant writer). General operating support can also be used to help pay for programs, which is sometimes necessary when a program is just getting started.

Note that he does at least ask for a specific amount. People like to know what you expect of them, so always be specific in your grant proposals—don't make them guess how much the new bus will cost or how much it takes to build a website. And don't ask a funder for too much or too little. Your best guide to how much to ask for is how much the funder has given to organizations similar to yours. Check the funder's annual report or IRS return for lists of grants.

Usually, when seeking general operating support, you would make a point of covering a wide range of issues your charity addresses. Jack can assume his parents have an intimate acquaintance with his general operating needs, so he doesn't have to go into detail here.

Jack knows to end on a high note, staying positive and connecting emotionally with his parents one last time to remind them why they really want to write him that check. He isn't shy about pushing his parent's emotional buttons. (Who knows better where they are; he probably "installed" some of them!)

Jack's big advantage over you or me in writing a grant proposal is that he wrote based on a relationship built up over nearly two decades. The prospects were knowledgeable about the cause to which they were being asked to contribute. And because of the long relationship, they were predisposed to responding positively to his request.

So how do you create a level of knowledge and (hopefully) a predisposition to a positive response? In the fundraising business it's called *cultivation*, by which you develop the prospect over a period of time so the proposal arrives on the desk of someone who is well informed about your organization (if not necessarily about your project). "Cultivation before solicitation" is my favorite saw, and one everyone who works for me is tired of hearing. You don't have to hear too much more on the subject from me until Chapter 10.

 HOW TO SAY IT

The "ask" usually comes at the beginning of a proposal and is repeated at the end. Always ask for a specific amount, and with renewals, always ask for more unless you know the funder doesn't make larger grants.

Now let's use Jack's letter as a guide to write a simple—very simple—grant proposal:

Ms. Betty Smith
Executive Director
Small Town Foundation
123 Main Street
Anywhere, IL 60000

Dear Ms. Smith:

On behalf of the board and all those we serve, I would like to thank you again for Small Town Foundation's generous $5,000 gift to support our after-school activities last year.

Since we received your gift, 75 additional children have become regular participants in the activities offered at our center. You might have seen the short write-up that appeared in the local paper about us. Although this recognition was important, the looks in the eyes of our children are the true rewards.

We are writing now to ask that you renew your $5,000 gift this year. Your funds will be used to further expand the number of children we can accommodate each day by making it possible to retain an additional teacher's aide.

I would love to arrange a visit so you can see firsthand what your gift can accomplish. Please give me a call at 312-555-1212 or e-mail me at execdir@all4youth.org, and I'm sure we can find a time to meet. Your kind consideration of this proposal is greatly appreciated.

Sincerely,

Mary Stuart

Mary Stuart
Executive Director

That's a much simpler proposal than you'll ever write, but you get the point. Grant writing is no big mystery. It doesn't require a Ph.D., but you do need to know how to put the parts together, avoid amateurish pitfalls, and convince others of the importance of what you're writing about.

If you were good at writing please-send-money letters to home from college, you're going to be a great grant writer. And if you lived at home and never wrote one of these letters, well, congratulations! You probably have experience in face-to-face solicitation, which is also a good skill in fundraising.

You say you never needed money from your parents? Well, maybe you'll soon be the one making grants to your own kids. But whatever your experience, this book will take you from simple show-me-the-money letters to fully developed grant proposals.

Why Grant Writing Is the Answer

No one grows up wanting to be a grant writer (or any kind of fundraiser, for that matter). Most of us fall into it out of necessity, either as part of our jobs or because we want to raise some significant money for a cause we believe in.

You might want to write a grant proposal, for example, if …

- You can't face one more bake sale for the soccer team.

- You see your local seniors' center needs a big infusion of cash to keep a program going.

- The local library's new book budget has been slashed by the city, and a group of neighbors want to help out.

- You're on the board of a new nonprofit group that can't yet afford professional development staff.

- You're raising funds for your own arts project.

Whatever your motivation for wanting to be a grant writer, you'll want to produce a professional proposal that will withstand the scrutiny of foundation staff *and get funded!*

Despite the proliferation of new foundations in the last two decades, there are still far more organizations and individuals seeking grants than there are organizations and individuals making grants. In fact, nonprofits outnumber grantmaking foundations by about 20 to 1. Many well-known organizations have large, well-paid development staffs vying for this money, but that doesn't mean you won't be successful. Fortunately, there are foundations and other grantmakers for every size organization and every conceivable cause. Private foundations in the United States alone give away as much as $43 billion annually.

In this book, I cover everything you need to know to write a successful grant proposal. You'll learn how to research prospects, cultivate relationships within and outside your charity, develop a complete proposal in several common formats, create a budget that also tells a story, and end up with a proposal that will stand out from a foundation's slush pile.

The Stock Market and Grants

Everyone whom you might approach for a grant lives in the same economic world as you and I. This means that when times are good and the stock market is riding high, foundations have more money to give away, corporations have greater profits from which to support charities, and governments are flush with taxes. Obviously, the opposite is true when times are hard.

If your charity receives a large percentage of its income from foundations and corporations, economic downturns will dramatically affect your funding. Individuals tend to give more to the causes they most believe in during tough times, but they might drop charities in which they have less interest. Government funders generally are affected a bit later, when tax income falls. All this, of course, is a good argument for not relying too heavily on one source of funding.

Foundations are required by law to spend 5 percent of their assets each year on grants and related expenses. Few give more than that, even when their investments are earning three times that amount. After the national tragedy of September 11, 2001, occurred, many foundations did dip into their principle to make large emergency grants—that is, they gave away more than they earned on their investments in 2001, but that was an exceptional time in every regard.

A grant writer should always be aware of how the economy might be affecting those she is soliciting. In lean times, foundations tend to take on fewer new grantees, preferring to maintain their commitments to their current charities. When times are tough, one of the first things corporations eliminate is corporate giving. And because many corporate foundations are funded year by year, there's not even an endowment to fall back on. Government funding can be particularly capricious, being affected by the political agendas of those in power as well as by the economy. In 2010, states sharply reduced or eliminated support for many sectors, including social services that were already struggling to meet basic human needs.

In a slow economy, the grant writer's job becomes much more difficult. The grant writer must spend more time getting current funders to renew grants rather than sending out lots of new proposals. Just remember, though, that foundations still have to give money to someone, so it might as well be you.

The Complete Grant Writer

A grant writer is someone who is able to craft elegant, clear, concise sentences that can convey passion as well as detailed information. Often you'll be called upon to describe technical facts (for example, in a grant for a new computer network) or concepts and procedures about which you know nothing (as in a scientific proposal) or abstract concepts that lie well outside your daily life (as in a research proposal).

A good grant writer learns enough about the subject to write intelligently and make the subject comprehensible to others who have no background in the subject. The grant writer also reflects the passion and enthusiasm of the people who run the project or program to get whoever reads the proposal equally excited about the project. Don't be shy about asking program staff about their program—they'll probably be thrilled to know someone is interested in what they do.

PHILANTHROPY FACT

In response to the 2010 Haiti earthquake, American foundations contributed more than $306 million to relief efforts, compared to the $4 million going to Haiti before the quake. (Source: *Focus on Haiti: Earthquake Relief and Recovery*, The Foundation Center.)

A Diplomat

A grant writer must be a diplomat who helps the people running programs get their ideas into shape. Many people who run programs are so close to the program they can't see how to clearly explain it to someone unfamiliar with the project or organization—and many simply are just not good writers.

The grant writer takes the words from the program staff and states their ideas in plain English, without making the program staff feel belittled. The grant writer must often also be an advocate with senior staff and board members.

A Financier

A grant writer is a financially savvy person who can make numbers speak as clearly as words. Numbers can tell any story you want them to tell. Your budget should reflect the project's narrative description and include enough detail to be convincing, but not so much as to restrict the execution of the program.

Crunching the numbers and presenting the numbers are very different talents. The grant writer needs to do both, but more of the latter.

A Nosy Parker

A grant writer is also full of curiosity, willing to go to any length to ferret out information about funders to find the right match for his organization.

A grant writer is interested in people—those for whom he is trying to raise money, as well as those from whom he hopes to get the money.

A Passionate Advocate

But mostly, a grant writer needs passion for the cause at the heart of the proposal. After all, if you don't really care about your project, why should the funder?

Although grant writing might sound like a solitary activity, in the course of preparing a grant proposal, you actually interact with a wide range of people, including program and executive staff at your charity, members of your board of directors, and staff at foundations and corporations. On the other hand, it's something you can do on a part-time basis working from home.

Grant writing can be quite a lucrative profession. The positions at different charities go by a variety of names, including grants officer, institutional giving manager, foundation/corporation/government affairs manager, director of development for institutional giving, and many others.

Salaries for grant writers vary widely, according to the type of charity and the size of its budget. Generally, fundraisers at hospitals and universities make the highest salaries; social services charities tend to pay the least, with the arts somewhere in between. Expect to make from $30,000 with a small organization away from a major metropolitan area to $100,000 for writing grants and supervising others at a major institution.

If you're considering doing grant writing as a consultant, be aware that, in many states, all fundraising consultants must register with the state attorney general. In some cases, you must also register with the state in which any funder you approach is located.

If you're hiring a consultant to help with grant writing, check with your state's attorney general's office to see if registration is required, and be sure your consultant has the necessary registration (if any).

One final note on consultants: professional fundraising consultants work for a flat fee, never a percentage of what they raise. (You can learn more about being a consultant in Chapters 23 and 24.)

A Week-by-Week Guide

It's important to allow yourself enough time to prepare your grant proposal, especially your first one. The great unknown in preparing a grant is how long the internal review will take. If your executive director is a real stickler who lives to edit someone else's prose, allow additional time for review.

The following time line assumes you've spent at least several months cultivating a range of prospects so that when the right project came along, they were already primed and ready to receive your proposal.

Week 1: Most proposals you write will be for specific projects, so you'll have to get to know the ins and outs of the project before you can do anything. Allow at least a week to get information from others and digest it. You'll have time during the inevitable rewrites to continue learning and digesting.

Weeks 2 and 3: Conduct research to find the best funder matches for the project, and write or call for guidelines (if not available on the Internet). This is the most crucial stage in the proposal process. If you haven't done *all* your homework, you won't stand a chance at success.

WORDS TO THE WISE

If you need money in less than three months, you're better off approaching an individual using a board or volunteer contact. Institutions move slowly.

Week 4: Complete research, checking to see if anyone connected with your organization knows anyone connected with the funder, and review information received from funders.

Weeks 5 and 6: Write the proposal, and share it with program staff and others. Make revisions and more revisions.

Week 7: Make final edits, contact the funder when appropriate, and mail the proposal well in advance of the funder's deadline.

Week 8: Relax and wait.

Week 9: Make a follow-up call to see if the application was received.

Weeks 10 through 25 or longer: Patiently wait for news from the funder.

Weeks 12 through 52: The check arrives! General rejoicing!

As you can see, grant writing involves a lot more than just writing, but that's what makes it interesting and challenging for those of us who do it. I love learning about the new projects I raise money for, and it's so gratifying when a grant is successful and you know it was *you* who helped buy the books for the library, provided daycare for more kids, or helped people learn to read.

But what makes you eligible for a grant, and what's a reasonable grant request? You'll find out in Chapter 2.

The Least You Need to Know

- Asking Mom and Dad for money and approaching a foundation aren't all that different.
- Grant writing can produce substantial sums for your community center, soccer team, church, or beginning nonprofit.
- Grant monies for charities decline in a down economy—just like everything else—and rise when times are good.
- The grant writer's best friends are knowledge and passion.
- A good grant writer possesses diplomatic skills, financial acumen, curiosity, and passion.
- From concept to grant check can take six months to a year—or longer.

The ABCs of Grants

In This Chapter

- Grants defined
- Legal status necessary to receive a grant
- Project, operating, capital, and challenge grants
- Ways to keep your grant from being rejected out of hand

In this and the next four chapters, you learn a lot about the meaning of the word *grant* and the people and institutions that make grants. This is not just background. This is context, the *gestalt* of grant writing and grantmaking. An understanding of what lies behind the grant process is key to successful grant writing, or maybe I should say, successful grant *getting*. So let's learn some grant basics.

A Closer Look at Grants

If I send a $25 check to the local animal shelter, that could be considered a "grant" from me, but we generally think of grants as coming from institutions—whether foundations, corporations, or government agencies. *Webster's* defines the act of making a grant as "giving to a petitioner, often a subordinate or inferior, something sought that could be withheld." This is contrasted with *award*, which refers to "the granting of something merited or earned."

Historically, the word *grant* has been used in a wide variety of contexts, but in every instance, an exchange takes place. Not only does someone give away something of value, but the giver expects the recipient of the grant to do something in return. For example, when England's King Charles made land grants to the American colonists, he expected them to settle and develop the land, in turn producing tax income for the Crown. And when Jack in Chapter 1 received an extra $100 spending money, his parents expected him to stay in school and study.

The roots of modern philanthropy build on the idea of an exchange. When your charity receives a grant, it promises to perform the actions described in the proposal. Many foundations will send you a contract along with the award letter that makes clear the obligations you incur by accepting the grant—usually stated simply as doing everything in your proposal. This is a very good reason to ensure your organization can actually do everything you say it will do in your proposal. Exaggerated claims or inflated (or deflated) budgets won't help you in the end.

Today, governments recognize that the practice of philanthropy is good for everyone, and therefore give a privileged status to organizations formed for charitable purposes. In many countries, the United States included, governments exempt money given for charitable purposes from taxation.

Who Can Receive a Grant?

In common practice, terms such as *nonprofit, tax-exempt, charity,* or the more technical *501(c)(3)* are used interchangeably in the United States. They all mean that an organization has been organized for purposes other than profit and that some government agency has recognized that. Other than the few exceptions described in the following sections, only organizations recognized by some level of government as formed exclusively for charitable, nonprofit purposes can receive grants. In other countries, nongovernmental organization (NGO) designates a nonprofit organization.

Recognition by the Feds

The most commonly recognized form of tax-exempt status in the United States is the *501(c)(3) status* conferred by the Internal Revenue Service (IRS) to organizations formed for educational or charitable purposes and not to make a profit, hence a nonprofit organization. In certain cases, fraternal organizations—501(c)(8) or 501(c)(100), cemetery companies—501(c)(13), and some veterans organizations—501(c)(4) or 501(c)(19) can also receive grants. Other nonprofit organizations might not be eligible to receive tax-deductible donations such as grants.

DEFINITION

501(c)(3) status refers to the paragraph in the tax code that defines which types of organizations are recognized to be free from federal income taxes, defined as "organized and operated exclusively for religious, charitable, scientific, testing for public safety, literary, or educational purposes …."

The IRS publishes a list of nonprofit organizations. Look for *Publication 78* or find it online at irs.gov/charities and select "Search for Charities." In Canada, the equivalent tax status comes from Canadian Customs and Revenue Agency certifying Canadian Charitable Registration. See cra-arc.gc.ca/chrts-gvng.

Recognition by the State

It's also common for organizations to be recognized as tax-exempt by the state or states in which they run programs or have offices. Your organization probably has (or is seeking) state tax-exempt status as well as federal tax-exempt status because this usually carries exemption from both state income taxes and state and local sales taxes. The state agency responsible for granting tax-exempt status varies from state to state, but the office of the secretary of state or the attorney general usually handles this task.

It's not necessary to have federal tax-exempt status to have state tax-exempt status and vice versa.

Many funders will accept either federal or state nonprofit status. With every grant proposal you submit, you will usually be asked to include proof of nonprofit status. If you have federal 501(c)(3) status, you don't need to also submit evidence of state charity status.

Government Agencies, Schools, and Religious Groups

When receiving a grant for a public school or other government agency (such as a public library), the funder will assume nonprofit status applies, even though these are not 501(c)(3) organizations, and will probably not ask for proof of nonprofit status. If, however, a funder receives a proposal from a private school, it will need proof of nonprofit status. Religious institutions might include proof of nonprofit status rather than have it questioned.

Grants to Individuals

Less than 10 percent of foundations (and an even smaller percentage of corporations) will make grants to individuals. The ones that do make grants to individuals usually do so as scholarships or for research, independent study, or artistic pursuit. Government agencies also offer scholarship funds and research grants. You might also find it necessary to write grant proposals for residencies that provide room, board, and a studio, laboratory, or other facility but no cash.

The grants to individuals you as a grant writer are concerned with are all based on merit, even though some scholarships have a financial need consideration. Many government agencies and nonprofits give financial assistance based on need, but this aid requires only an application form, not a grant proposal.

Whenever money flows from one nonprofit organization to another, there's little room for the IRS to question the transaction. This is not so when money goes from a nonprofit to an individual. Additional record-keeping and rules come into play, and most funders keep life simple by not making grants to individuals.

One rule that affects grants to individuals involves *private inurnment*. This term refers to something that would benefit a person who is a close relative of or who has a relationship with a funder. For example, if your parents establish a foundation to provide scholarships to students in the health sciences and you are attending medical school, their foundation generally cannot provide you with a scholarship, although it could give your roommate one.

Chapter 22 covers research and grant proposal techniques specifically for individuals, although you'll also need to know the basics of grant writing covered in the rest of this book.

When You're Not a Nonprofit

Businesses can sometimes receive grants. Government agencies such as the Small Business Administration make grants to help businesses get started or make improvements. The procedures for these grants are the same as for nonprofit grants.

But if your group is new and doesn't yet have nonprofit status or if you're seeking funds to make a film, create a work of public art, or for your own private research, you will need a plan.

Plan A: Become a nonprofit

For projects that will take place over a period of years, you might want to consider forming a nonprofit corporation. Advantages include making you eligible for 10 times as many funding possibilities and possibly making the costs of your project exempt from sales taxes. Disadvantages include a greater burden of bookkeeping and government reporting (depending on how much money you raise) and yielding ultimate control of your work to a board of directors.

It's a complicated issue covered in a number of books and websites (good examples of which appear in Appendixes B and C), but it was worth raising the subject here so you can keep it in mind as you read further.

Plan B: Borrow Tax-Exempt Status

Fortunately, the law allows for organizations that already have tax-exempt status to accept grant money on behalf of a group (or individual) that does not have nonprofit status.

This is called *fiscal sponsorship*. It's a very common means for groups just starting out to receive tax-deductible contributions from the public—including foundation, corporate, and even government funders—while developing their programs and seeking nonprofit status. The fiscal sponsor will usually deduct a service fee from contributions it receives on your behalf, usually 5 to 10 percent, depending on how much service they provide.

DEFINITION

Fiscal sponsorship is a formal relationship between a nonprofit organization and an organization that's unincorporated, in the process of seeking nonprofit status, or an individual. The relationship is formed so the organization or person without nonprofit status has access to contributions from foundations, corporations, individuals, and government agencies.

Legally, the fiscal sponsor is responsible for the contributions made to it on your behalf, which requires a level of scrutiny and control that makes fees necessary. The services a fiscal sponsor provides can range from simply accepting funds and issuing a check to full bookkeeping and management assistance.

Individuals, especially those in the arts, also use fiscal sponsorship to raise funds to carry out a project or to provide seed money for a project. Fiscal sponsorship makes possible many, many documentary films. (Note all those credits to funders at the end of documentary films you see on public television.)

Common fiscal sponsors include nonprofit service organizations, community foundations, and other public foundations (that is, foundations that receive support from a wide section of the public rather than a single individual).

Here are some agencies providing fiscal sponsorship:

Dance Theatre Workshop
219 West 19th Street
New York, NY 10011
dancetheaterworkshop.org/programs
This service group is involved with sponsorship for dancers, musicians, performers, visual artists, and art educators.

Film Arts Foundation
145 9th Street, #101
San Francisco, CA 94103
filmarts.org (and click on "Services")
This foundation is involved with sponsorship for film projects.

Fiscal Sponsor Directory
fiscalsponsordirectory.org
National directory of fiscal sponsors created by the San Francisco Study Center.

Fractured Atlas
fracturedatlas.org
Service organization for artists, specializing in fiscal sponsorship.

New York Foundation for the Arts
155 Avenue of the Americas, 14th Floor
New York, NY 10014
nyfa.org/fs
This grantmaking public charity is involved with sponsorship for emerging arts organizations and for artist projects in all artistic disciplines.

The Rose Foundation
6008 College Avenue, Suite 10
Oakland, CA 94618
rosefdn.org/
This foundation is involved with sponsorship of environmental protection and community regeneration projects.

Third Sector New England
18 Tremont Street, Suite 700
Boston, MA 02108
tsne.org (and click on "Programs & Services")
This service organization is involved with sponsorship for community coalitions and regional or national projects that share their mission of creating healthy, sustainable communities and active democracy.

Hundreds of organizations offer fiscal sponsorship, and you'll probably find there's more than one in your community. When considering an organization to sponsor you, be sure to check them out. Talk to someone whom they have sponsored, and take a look at their audited financial statements for the last three years to see if they're financially stable.

Ask an accountant to review the financial statements with you because these are difficult to understand if you're not used to reading them. It doesn't happen often, but nonprofits have been known to go out of business having spent not only all of their funds but also those of the groups they were sponsoring.

For more information, you might want to read *Fiscal Sponsorship: 6 Ways to Do It Right*, now in its second edition, by Gregory L. Colvin (Study Center Press, 2006) or consult the guide to fiscal sponsorship on the Foundation Center's website.

What Can You Raise Money For?

No matter what you want to raise money for, there's probably a funder out there interested in making a grant for it. When you begin your research into your potential funders, you'll need to keep in mind the broad categories funders use to describe the kind of support they will give.

WORDS TO THE WISE

Never put all your eggs in one basket. Apply to several funders at the same time for your project. What, you ask, will happen if they all come through? You should be so lucky to have such a problem, but if you do, you can always expand the scope of the project or ask one of the funders to allow you to use their grant to extend the project for a longer period of time.

Project Support

By far the most common type of grant is made to support a particular project, as opposed to operating, capital, and challenge grants, which I describe in the following sections. Fortunately, a clever grant writer can make almost any need into a project.

Sometimes the difference between a project and a capital grant lies in how you say it. A small capital project can easily be pitched as a project. Avoid using the word *capital* in the proposal if the funder doesn't fund capital projects. Emphasize the short-term rather than the long-term benefits of the project.

Funders like projects because projects have a defined beginning and end. This makes it easy to judge if a project has been successful. Funders are wary of a charity coming back again and again expecting support for the same thing. Although renewal grants are fairly common, the funder will almost always make it clear in your grant letter that their grant does not imply any promise of future funding.

Here are some samples that show the wide range of project grants (also called *program grants*) I have been successful with over the years:

$10,000 received from a community foundation to provide after-school arts programming to children in a homeless shelter. The grant paid for a writer and a musician to work with the kids, transportation from the homeless shelter in which they lived to the after-school facility, and materials for use in the program.

$25,000 received from a corporate foundation toward the purchase of new computer equipment. The remaining $40,000 for this project was raised mostly from members of the organization's board of directors. The grant paid for hardware, software, and consultants to do the installation. Note that some foundations will pay for software but not hardware and vice versa. We fortunately found one that did not make a distinction.

$50,000 received from a corporate foundation to expand an internship program over a two-year period. With unemployment at record levels, the corporation was interested in helping people change careers by gaining experience in areas for which their skills were transferable but in which they lacked experience. The grant paid for modest stipends to the interns and for mini-seminars to further develop skills needed in a nonprofit arts organization.

$75,000 received to design a new website and announce it to the public. The grant covered the fees of the web designers and programmers and advertisements to announce the new site, as well as paid for some of the time of regular staff who worked on it.

WORDS TO THE WISE

One of the greatest challenges for a grant writer today is writing a grant proposal for a highly technical subject such as website design or computer networks. Try to integrate definitions into a sentence in a way that does not seem like you're talking down to the reader. Note the subtle difference between "25,000 different people, or unique users, visited our website in January" and "25,000 unique users, or different people, visited our website in January." Placing the tech term second indicates that you, like the reader, are more comfortable with the plain language description.

$100,000 received for a museum to carry out a pilot program to remain open an additional evening each week and a publicity campaign to let the public know about the new hours. Funders love pilot programs—that is, programs that can be continued or used as an example for similar programs elsewhere. The grant paid for placement of newspaper ads and partly subsidized the cost of remaining open. This grant was one of several for this program. In this case it really paid off: 15 years later, the museum is still open and free to the public on Friday evenings.

$170,000 received to provide information services. This grant covered staff salaries to do research to maintain a database of opportunities for artists and to provide personal assistance by phone and e-mail. The grant also covered office expenses incurred by these staff members.

$250,000 received to increase the circulation of a magazine for writers that provides career advice and listings of opportunities. The grant paid for a large direct-mail campaign that would allow testing different approaches and using different designs to see which would be the most successful in attracting new subscribers. This was attractive to funders because it served a dual purpose: it increased the number of writers who were served by the publication, and it increased the *earned income* for the organization, thus making it less dependent on grants in the future.

DEFINITION

Grants that increase **earned income,** that is, income not dependent on grants, are popular with funders because more earned income means less dependence on grants. Earned income can come from service fees, products sold, or even interest income.

Each of these grants was restricted to the purpose outlined in the proposal or grant contract. We couldn't change our minds and spend on something else without the funder's permission.

But what about all those day-to-day expenses that aren't part of a particular project? That brings us to general operating support.

Operating Support

The most valuable grant you can receive is for general operating support (known popularly in the business as GOS). You can use this support for basically anything and everything your organization needs to function, including programs, staff salaries (including administrators and fundraisers who are not covered by project grants), rent, utilities, and office supplies.

Because every funder has these same kinds of expenses, you would think they would see the need to make grants to cover them, but that isn't the case. Consequently, when you find a GOS funder, treasure them, cultivate them, and appreciate them every day.

Funders that provide GOS understand what you do and appreciate its intrinsic value to those you serve. In the best of all possible worlds, these funders will support you over a period of years. But never take your GOS funders for granted. All of them will eventually move on to help other groups.

Many GOS grants will be quite small (as little as $1,000), requiring you to find many of them to pay the basic expenses. This is not necessarily a bad thing—it's easier to replace two $1,000 funders than to replace one $10,000 funder. Spend some time every month looking for new GOS supporters.

Capital Support

Grants to help pay for a new building are the typical capital grant, which is why capital grants are also referred to as *bricks-and-mortar grants*. Capital grants, like capital expenses, cover a wider range of needs. Fewer funders make capital grants than make project grants. There are, however, a few major funders that *only* make capital grants.

Capital expenses are usually defined as those that pay for something that will serve the charity over a period of time, from the 50- to 100-year life of a building to three years for computer equipment. Renovations of an existing space and major purchases such as buses or automobiles are also typical capital grant opportunities.

In the previous list of successful grant proposals, you'll remember a project grant for computer equipment. This could have been considered a capital grant, but the scale of the project (less than $100,000 at an organization with a $12 million budget) made it more of a project. "Scale" will depend on your organization's budget and the relative size of the project.

Capital projects are also funded by program-related investments (PRIs). These are usually loans at below-market rates (sometimes at 0 percent interest). In other cases, PRIs will be made to a nonprofit to develop a program that will create earned income through sale of a service or product. Rather than simply repaying the loans, the nonprofit might pay a percentage of the profits to the foundation, just as a for-profit corporation pays dividends to stockholders. Only a small percent of foundations make PRIs.

There's a natural attraction to helping bring about something as tangible as a building. The funder and the entire community will actually see what you've accomplished. Never underestimate the value of naming something—anything—for a donor. You don't have to put up a building to cash in on naming opportunities. You can name the coffee machine or new television for the recreation room. Although a number of donors shy away from naming, others respond well to the extra motivation.

Capital grants can also be used to build an endowment to support a particular program or your operations. Some foundations specialize in making endowment grants, which are frequently in the form of challenge grants.

Challenge Grants

Funders in general do not like to be the only ones supporting anything, whether it's a project or capital expenditure. A challenge grant allows a funder to ensure you pursue a broad base of support. The funder provides only partial support for your project and challenges you to find the other funds by withholding the payment of their grant until you prove to them that you have raised other money.

Some funders particularly like to be part of challenges, either as the one making the challenge or by helping to match or fulfill the challenge. A challenge grant can also be a means of encouraging your regular individual contributors (especially board members) to make additional gifts.

Typically, a challenge grant requires you to raise a proportionate amount of money, either matching the challenge grant equally (a one-to-one match) or greater (a two-to-one or even three-to-one match). With a three-to-one match, the challenger promises to give you, for example, $25,000 if you raise an additional $75,000.

The $25,000 grant for computer equipment mentioned earlier was an interesting match—the grant was conditional on our raising the "additional funds to complete the project." This created a wide-open matching situation because we could "make the match" by finding cheaper equipment as well as by raising additional funds, which is exactly how it worked out.

> **WORDS TO THE WISE**
>
> What happens if you are unable to raise the matching funds required by a challenge grant? If you can find a way to still complete the project (even if it's a scaled-down version), go back to the original challenger with a revised plan. Chances are they'll still give you the grant. Government agencies, however, are usually not allowed to be so accommodating.

Large capital projects commonly include challenge grants to stimulate both additional giving from current contributors, as well as your resolve to find a number of new ones.

When accepting a challenge grant, be sure you understand all the implications of the challenge, including how many dollars you must raise for the match, the time period you have to raise it, and from whom you must raise the money. The last condition might seem strange. After all, money is money. But if a funder thinks you have too few donors to support your new building, for example, they might require that funds come from new donors. Challenge grants help you raise more money, even though all the conditions can sometimes make them seem more trouble than they're worth.

What Funders Look For

It's unfortunate, but I've heard on more than one occasion that funders first look for a reason why they should *not* fund a proposal. Wow! But yes, that's how tough this business can be.

With the huge number of proposals funders receive and the limited staff they have to review proposals, they need to do whatever they can to narrow the field of applicants as quickly as possible. This brings me to the number one rule of grant writing: *follow instructions*. If they ask for three copies on yellow recycled paper in 13-point type, paper-clipped singly and then clipped together, do it. If they are 25 years behind the times and have an application you must type on a typewriter, do it. If they restrict the number of pages or even the number of words, do it.

WORDS TO THE WISE

It might sound like grade school, but failure to follow instructions and lack of study (research) doom many proposals before they even reach a foundation board.

Funders next look for a match between their funding interests and your proposal. Too often, grant writers send out proposals to a large number of funders, thinking that at least one will be successful. Wrong. Grant writing is not about luck and multiple submissions. It's about research and focused writing. Not only will sending a proposal to a funder who does not fund your type of project result in a rejection now, but when you later have a project that does meet their interests, they'll remember you as the one who didn't do their research the previous time. So the second rule of grant writing is: *do your research*.

When you've passed these two hurdles (which aren't that hard to cross), the funder will likely give your proposal serious consideration. The funder will, of course, also check to be sure you are a nonprofit (or have a fiscal sponsor) and fall within any other restrictions they have (a geographic area being the most common other restriction).

I discuss the other things a funder looks for when I cover the parts of a proposal, beginning in Chapter 13. For a peek inside the process foundations use to screen proposals, read Martin Teitel's book *Thank You for Submitting Your Proposal* (Emerson and Church, 2006).

The Least You Need to Know

- Grants can come from foundations, corporations, or government agencies.
- A nonprofit status or a fiscal sponsor are required to receive most grants.
- Individuals can also receive grants, but from a limited number of funders.
- Grants are awarded for projects, general operating expenses, a capital project (such as a new building or major piece of equipment), or for an endowment fund.
- Follow each funder's instructions, no matter how trivial they might seem or how much they restrict your creativity.
- Approach only those funders whose interests could reasonably include your project.

Where the Money Is

Philanthropic institutions and individuals donate billions of dollars every year. Part 2 looks at each source of grant money and takes a peek behind the scenes at what motivates each type of funder to give away its money.

I look at foundations—large and small, family run and professionally staffed, community and commercial—and their similarities and differences. I break down corporations' many ways of making grants so you'll know which door to knock on. And I give you a tour of government agencies and show you how to get back some of your tax dollars, either by performing a service for the government or by getting money for your project! I also take a look at grants from individuals and the different ways to approach them.

Not only do you have to know what makes each type of funder tick to unlock their vast treasuries, you also need to know what each will expect from you after you have their money, so I take a look at how acceptance of a grant obligates you and your nonprofit.

A Foundation Primer

In This Chapter

- What makes a foundation a foundation
- How the type of foundation influences your approach
- When a foundation is not a foundation
- Venture philanthropy: friend or foe?
- How to read IRS Form 990-PF for foundations

Foundations have been around since the early seventeenth century, when they were largely associated with religious institutions. When we think of a foundation today, the picture that most likely comes to mind includes those set up by the great industrialists of the late nineteenth and early twentieth centuries, such as Andrew Carnegie, Henry Ford, and John D. Rockefeller. Each, in his way, saw philanthropy as a way to right society's wrongs.

Andrew Carnegie, in particular, was the very picture of the American philanthropist. In his book *The Gospel of Wealth* (1889), Carnegie advocated that the rich have a moral obligation to give away their fortunes. His philanthropy during his lifetime was wide-ranging, resulting in New York City's Carnegie Hall, The Carnegie (a group of museums, a concert hall, and a library in Pittsburgh), Carnegie Mellon University, more than 2,000 public libraries throughout the English-speaking world, and several foundations that still bear his name. In 2009, the Carnegie Corporation of New York (the only one of his philanthropies that's a grantmaking organization) had assets of $2.4 billion and made around $101 million in grants. His other six U.S. foundations are concerned with ethics and international affairs, recognizing heroic individuals, and educational policies.

Toward the end of the twentieth century, history seemed to be repeating itself when the titans of the computer world set up foundations bearing their names that quickly took their places among the world's largest. Think Gates, Allen, Hewlett, and Packard.

The 1913 law that established the income tax gave the creation of foundations a boost and at the same time exempted organizations that were formed solely for charitable purposes.

The super-rich industrialists weren't the only ones starting foundations in the early twentieth century. Around the same time, the first community foundation was founded in Cleveland, Ohio. The community foundation drew on the wealth of a number of donors who pooled their funds for the support and betterment of their community.

Foundations are usually set up to exist forever. A surprising number of donors, however, establish their foundations with a "sunset clause" that requires their foundations to go out of business at a predetermined time, usually a set number of years after the founder dies. Donors include sunset clauses, at least in part, out of a desire to have their money given away only by people who knew them (or people who knew people who knew them). In this way, they believe their money will more likely be used for purposes they would have approved of.

In the philanthropy business, this is called "funding out" because the foundation gives away all its money, interest, and principle. This frequently results in a number of very large grants, which can be a boon to charities. If your organization is not already one of their grantees, however, don't expect to be part of the going-out-of-business bonanza. When they're getting ready to shut the doors, foundations usually won't accept new causes or charities. They will, however, likely be making large grants to their current grantees to stabilize programs they had previously supported.

The Types of Foundations

Foundations today range from small foundations with total assets of $500,000 or even less to the Bill and Melinda Gates Foundation with assets in 2009 of $34 billion, making it the nation's largest. Most foundations fall well in the middle of this dramatic spread. We can divide foundations into several categories; an understanding of each will help you in researching prospects and focusing your grant proposal.

PHILANTHROPY FACT

According to the Foundation Center's helpful FC stats, in 2008, health captured the greatest share of foundation grants (23 percent), with education coming in second (22 percent), followed by human services and the arts (tied at 13 percent each), public affairs (10 percent), and the environment and animals (9 percent). (Source: *FC Stats—Grants,* The Foundation Center, 2008.)

Typical Foundations

Statistically, it's hard to justify any model as a typical foundation, but I can describe the type of foundation you most often will encounter in your work as a grant writer.

One of these foundations will have been founded a number of years ago by a single wealthy individual, legally making it a private foundation. The individual's name, or that of a close relative, is probably also the name of the foundation. This person might or might not still be living, but even if he or she is, some people not related to the founder might serve on the board of trustees. Usually, the longer the founder is deceased, the greater the number of nonrelatives on the board.

The foundation probably employs a professional staff of 5 to 200 program officers, assistants, and executive staff. The board of trustees meets several times a year to consider grant proposals. A program officer presents the proposals to the board after carefully screening them according to the foundation's guidelines and interests.

The philanthropy or trusts department of banks or lawyers administer many smaller foundations, in which case the banks' or lawyers' employees serve as the foundation staff.

Foundations fitting this very general description will be the easiest for you to learn about and approach for a number of reasons. They publish guidelines. They will at least look at any application that comes through the door. And they have professional staff who can guide you.

Here are a few examples of my so-called typical foundations:

The Dana Foundation
745 Fifth Avenue, Suite 900
New York, NY 10151
dana.org
This foundation's principal interests are in improved teaching of the performing arts in public schools and in health, particularly neuroscience and immunology. It employs nearly 46 people. Grants: $20 million in 2008.

The James Irvine Foundation
575 Market Street, Suite 3400
San Francisco, CA 94105
irvine.org
This foundation gives in California only, primarily for the arts; higher education; workforce development; civic culture; sustainable communities; and children, youth, and families. It has 41 employees. Grants: $69 million estimated in 2008.

The Joyce Foundation
70 West Madison Street, Suite 2750
Chicago, IL 60602
joycefdn.org
This foundation makes grants for urban issues in Chicago; improvement of schools in Chicago, Cleveland, Detroit, and Milwaukee; poverty in the Midwest; the natural environment of the Great Lakes; election finance reform; and gun control. It also makes grants to individuals whose work falls within these areas. It has 24 staff members. Grants: $36 million in 2009.

Robert W. Woodruff Foundation, Inc.
50 Hurt Plaza, Suite 1200
Atlanta, GA 30303
woodruff.org
Interests of this foundation include kindergarten through college education; health care and education; human services, particularly for children; economic development; art and cultural activities; and the environment. It prefers one-time capital projects of established charities. Its staff consists of 12 people who also manage several other foundations. Grants: $106 million in 2009.

The Rockefeller Foundation
420 Fifth Avenue
New York, NY 10018-2702
rockfound.org
This foundation's wide-ranging interests include the arts; civil society; feeding and employing the poor; medical research, training, and distribution of services; revitalization of the African continent; and more. It also runs a conference center in Italy for scholars, scientists, artists, writers, policymakers, and others to conduct creative and scholarly work. Around 173 people manage these programs. Grants: $138 million in 2008.

W. K. Kellogg Foundation
1 Michigan Avenue East
Battle Creek, MI 49017-4058
wkkf.org
This foundation's primary interests lie in health, food systems, and rural development especially in Latin America and Southern Africa, youth and education, and philanthropy and voluntarism. They also make special grants in their local community. They have 130 employees. Grants: $244 million in 2009.

> **WORDS TO THE WISE**
>
> Foundations tend to fund locally, but don't overlook funders outside your area. For example, the Jerome Foundation in Minneapolis makes grants in Minnesota and in New York City. The better foundation directories will have an index of geographic interest to cross-check against office locations. When searching online databases, search by the location of the recipient as well as the funder.

Although these are all very large foundations, their range of interests is not atypical nor is the way they limit their grantmaking to organizations in specific geographic areas. As with all funders, you must do your homework to be sure your grant proposal meets all their restrictions.

Family Foundations

A family foundation is one in which the majority of trustees (frequently all) are related to the foundation's founder. Most foundations begin as family foundations, but here we're talking about those that are still governed by the family that founded them. The Council on Foundations estimates that two fifths of all private and community foundations are run by families. These foundations account for 43 percent of all foundation giving.

Many family foundations have few or no paid staff and depend on family members volunteering their time. Because the volume of applications can easily overwhelm these volunteers, be sure only to approach them (1) if they state they will accept unsolicited proposals and (2) when you're certain your organization fits their requirements and you're ready to submit a proposal.

As with any family undertaking, family dynamics frequently come into play at these foundations. At some, the "I'll vote to make a grant to your library if you'll vote to support my hospital" interaction can make for seemingly erratic grantmaking. This makes your research that much harder. On the positive side, if you or someone on your board knows one of the family foundation's trustees, that trustee will likely have enough sway to get your grant approved.

If you notice very specific and seemingly erratic geographic restrictions, you'll probably find that family members live in each of those locations. Your research may be able to pinpoint who lives where, allowing you to then discover that family member's local giving preferences, which in turn will help you focus your proposal.

PHILANTHROPY FACT

Family foundations are among the largest foundations in the United States; the Bill and Melinda Gates Foundation is the nation's largest of any kind. The top five family foundations contribute upward of $3.2 billion annually and include families such as the Packards (as in Hewlett-Packard) and Microsoft's Gates, which accounts for $2 billion of that amount.

The changing of the generations at a family foundation can result in a sharp change in funding priorities. It's only natural that the younger generation will want to differentiate itself from its parent's grantmaking.

When researching foundations, note the surnames of the trustees, if the founder is living, and if he or she is also a trustee. You might have to do a little detective work because surnames might have changed with marriages.

If it appears that you're dealing with a family foundation, be prepared to …

- Forget about applying to one if they do not accept unsolicited proposals, unless you can …

- Find a personal connection with a trustee.

- Look carefully at the *most recent* grant awards to see how they match (or don't) any published guidelines.

Here are a few examples of the larger family foundations:

The Brown Foundation, Inc.
2217 Welch Avenue
Houston, TX 77019
brownfoundation.org
The Brown Foundation, Inc., supports public primary and secondary education in Texas, services for children, and the visual and performing arts. It has eight people on staff. Grants: $64 million in 2007.

The Heinz Endowments
30 Dominion Tower
625 Liberty Avenue
Pittsburgh, PA 15222-3115
heinz.org
Its mission is "to help the region of southwestern Pennsylvania thrive as a whole community—economically, ecologically, educationally, and culturally—while advancing the state of knowledge and practice in the fields in which it works." The foundation is run by a staff of 32, and it gave away $65 million in 2008.

The Walton Family Foundation, Inc.
PO Box 2030
Bentonville, AR 72712
waltonfamilyfoundation.org
Walmart may be an international company, but the Walton family practices most of its philanthropy locally to support reform in K–12 education and the environment—especially marine and freshwater conservation—in the delta region of Arkansas and Mississippi, and northwest Arkansas. Six staff members helped the family distribute $168 million in 2008.

Community Foundations

The United States has more than 700 community foundations, and Canada has 174, serving virtually every geographical area. These foundations collectively make grants of as much as $4.5 billion annually, making them an important source to consider for your proposal. Community foundations are considered public foundations because they actively solicit support from a wide range of the public. This is in contrast to the private foundations discussed in the previous two sections, which receive support from one or two individuals.

Community foundations bring philanthropy within the grasp of those who are comfortably well-off but unable to put millions into a private foundation. This is not to say that immensely wealthy people do not contribute to community foundations; many do, establishing funds at a community foundation in addition to their private foundations. The concentration of technology millionaires in Silicon Valley have made the Silicon Valley Community Foundation among the largest in the United States.

A chief characteristic of a community foundation is the many funds that have been entrusted to it, each established by a different donor to benefit some aspect of life in that particular community. The New York Community Trust, for example, has some 2,000 different funds.

So how do you go about deciding which of those 2,000 funds to apply to? You don't. You cannot apply directly to most of them. Although administered by the community foundation, the donors have retained the right to advise the foundation on what grants to make. Legally, the final decision rests with the community foundation, but donor recommendations are usually followed when they fall within the guidelines of the community foundation. Theoretically, you could solicit these donors as individuals, but finding their names will be difficult. Other funds at community foundations might issue a *request for proposal* (*RFP*) or have formal guidelines.

DEFINITION

A **request for proposal** (**RFP**) is a means funders employ to encourage proposals for a program established by the funder. In many cases, an RFP is no different from the guidelines a funder issues for grants. With the RFP, the funder is being proactive in soliciting proposals, perhaps for a new initiative or for a program that's not been receiving good proposals. The Foundation Center maintains a free, current national list of RFPs on its website at foundationcenter.org, which they'll also e-mail you weekly for free.

You can gain access to the funds without donor advisors with one application—you simply apply to the community foundation itself, after first researching its areas of interest, of course. If it finds your proposal both worthy of funding and meeting the restrictions established by a particular fund's donor, your grant letter will tell you that you have received a grant "from the Betty F. and Henry S. Smith Fund of the Community Trust." (And yes, if you get a grant from them, you have to use the whole long name in all acknowledgments and donor listings.) Not every grant from a community foundation will be from a specific fund. It likely will also maintain a general endowment from which it makes grants.

If a community foundation is on your prospect list …

- Research to see if any of your potential individual donors or one of their family members has established a donor-advised fund.

- Check to see if the community foundation solicits proposals through RFPs.

- Only apply to a specific fund at a community foundation if its guidelines say to do so.

- Only apply to a community foundation in your area. It isn't interested in work you might do elsewhere, and community foundations in other areas might be unable to fund you, even for a program that takes place in its community.

Operating Foundations

An operating foundation may make grants, but grantmaking is a small part of what it does. An operating foundation can be private or public. It usually runs one or more research or service programs that are its primary reason for existing. For the most part, these will not be good prospects because they do limited grantmaking and have a narrow range of interests. But if their interests match yours, go for it.

Here are a few examples of what you can expect operating foundations to look like:

KnowledgeWorks Foundation
One West Fourth Street
Cincinnati, OH 45202
kwfdn.org
Educational initiatives in Ohio are the sole concerns of this foundation, which does make grants. Grants: $4.5 million, but this was a mere 16 percent of what it spent on programs in 2009.

Russell Sage Foundation
112 East 64th Street
New York, NY 10021
russellsage.org
This foundation is devoted to research in the social sciences, supporting scholars who study at its facility or at other institutions. It also publishes books and holds seminars. Grants: $3.9 million in 2009.

Commercial Foundations

How can there be a "commercial foundation"? Well, technically there can't be, but I'm using this term to identify and distinguish one of the most dramatic trends in funding in the last decade.

PHILANTHROPY FACT

All foundations do not have *foundation* in their name. Some might use the designation *fund* or *trust* or *charitable trust,* but others call themselves *corporations,* like the Carnegie Corporation of New York, mentioned at the beginning of this chapter.

The very wealthy have always had access to professionals to manage their philanthropy through the trust departments at their banks. This assistance, however, usually came only to those with seven-figure (or higher) deposits at the bank. In 1992, Fidelity Investments Corporation realized that many of its clients (both middle class and beyond) would be interested in a way to manage their philanthropy just like they managed their other investments. The result was the Fidelity Charitable Gift Fund. (Which shouldn't be confused with the Fidelity Foundation, fidelityfoundation.org, which is the company foundation that makes grants only in areas where it has a major presence to a wide range of nonprofits.)

The *Chronicle of Philanthropy*'s 2009 ranking of the largest charities by total donations received showed that the Fidelity Charitable Gift Fund was the third-largest charity in the United States, receiving $1.6 billion in contributions, just $200 million behind the Salvation Army. The United Way Worldwide was the largest with $4 billion in donations.

Needless to say, every other investment bank took notice, and today dozens if not hundreds of institutions operate in the same way. Legally, these are 501(c)(3) nonprofits, not foundations at all, even though without any programs and vast reserves of money, they certainly look like foundations.

Don't get excited by all that money in the gift funds operated by commercial financial institutions. You can't apply for a grant. If one of its investors … I mean, donors … decides to make a grant to your charity, you'll receive a check, possibly accompanied by a letter identifying the donor, or possibly not, because the gift funds allow donors to give anonymously. The commercial gift fund administrators do not need to receive your newsletters or anything else beyond the acknowledgment letter required by IRS regulations because they do not direct the grantmaking.

Foundations in Name Only

There's no legal definition for a foundation. Even the IRS defines a foundation by what it is *not*. For example, a private foundation is defined as one that does not receive its funds from a wide segment of the public. Some organizations with the word *foundation* in their name aren't foundations as we understand them.

They and other nonprofits that make grants using funds they've raised are called Grantmaking Public Charities by the Foundation Center to distinguish them from private, corporate, or public foundations. Examples include the Foundation for AIDS Research and the Actors Fund of America. The Foundation Center and other funder directory resources include many of them in their publications and databases. Community foundations and local service organizations might be able to point you to others.

Venture Philanthropy

The hot topic at the end of the twentieth century was *venture philanthropy*, which was used in relation to both foundation and corporate giving. The vogue term was coined possibly as long ago as 1984 to denote the source of much of this new phil-anthropic money (venture capitalists who were making a killing in the stock market) and the way they approached their philanthropy (supposedly just like they did their businesses).

HOW TO SAY IT

Strunk & White's admonition in *The Elements of Style,* "Do not be tempted by a twenty-dollar word when there is a ten-center handy, ready, and able," could have been written with venture philanthropists in mind. Shed all your jargon, and never say anything that could be viewed as talking down to your funders.

Venture philanthropy typically has these characteristics:

- Venture philanthropists seek involvement with the nonprofits they fund, not necessarily as board members or trustees, but as a source of management and technical assistance.

- They provide support over a period of years. Just as a business needs time to grow, so do nonprofits—something we can all agree on.

- They expect accountability beyond annual progress reports, making fulfill-ment of specific goals and frequent reporting essential.

- Venture philanthropists expect you to plan from the beginning of their sup-port how you will continue the program after their support ends.

- They are likely to use the Internet to research charities that address particu-lar problems.

If you apply to a foundation that practices venture philanthropy (and frequently they'll say so if they do), be prepared for the higher level of involvement and for thinking of your grant proposal as a business plan. Also expect to provide some kind of ROI (return on investment), whether that's a social return (through improved services), a financial return (when your charity performs more efficiently), or even an emotional return (warm-and-fuzzy feelings), the venture philanthropist expects something back—for the charity as much as for himself.

Financial transparency is key when engaging venture philanthropists. Have your 990 tax return ready to give them, and be sure the information on top staff salaries is included. High staff salaries won't bother them: they expect highly skilled people to be paid well. They will expect full financial disclosure. Don't be afraid to post your audited financial statement and 990 form on your website for them to find on their own.

Venture philanthropists have been successful in business and believe they can be successful in other areas (like philanthropy). Provide them with an opportunity for success.

The novelty of venture philanthropy has certainly cooled a bit these days. Some venture philanthropy foundations, however, continue to function and function well, such as the Robin Hood Foundation in New York City (robinhood.org).

Corporate Foundations

Corporate foundations are legally no different from other private foundations. They must spend the same portion of their total assets each year and report their financial dealings to the IRS. I discuss corporate foundations in full in Chapter 4.

Foundations as the IRS Sees Them

Every foundation must complete an annual "information return" for the IRS, which holds a wealth of information for the grant seeker. Called the 990-PF form (*PF* stands for "private foundation"), this form can be found easily. Both the Foundation Center (foundationcenter.org) and GuideStar (guidestar.org) websites provide access to this form as a public service, as do other charity associations and, on occasion, foundations themselves.

PHILANTHROPY FACT

Every foundation must file an IRS informational return (990-PF), but some nonprofits don't have to. Nonprofits with an income of $25,000 or less and most religious organizations are not required to file the 990 form. Also, foundations must reveal the names of their donors and how much was given, but other nonprofits are allowed to keep that information confidential.

Why do you want to look at their IRS returns? After all, they pay no taxes, and it's just an informational return. Are you kidding? There's gold in those forms! For instance, you can find …

- If the foundation received any contributions during the year (which is not uncommon for young foundations and for corporate foundations) and who made them.

- The foundation's total assets, 5 percent of which they must spend on programs—including grants—each year.

- Salaries of the top-level staff and/or board. (Okay, this is interesting just because I'm nosy, but aren't you curious, too?)

- A complete list of trustees (occasionally with home or business addresses).

- A list of each and every grant they made.

- And sometimes, a statement of what they give grants for.

The information in the IRS returns might be more complete and up-to-date than the listings in some directories, even though the IRS return might be 18 months old.

Because looking at the 990-PF is such an important part of research, let's look at some examples and take some time to go through it together. (I've blacked out the name and other identifiers of this large foundation. Even though the 990s are part of the public record, some foundations still get sensitive about revealing themselves, and who knows, I might send them a proposal one day.)

WORDS TO THE WISE

In 2008, the IRS redesigned the 990 form, so if you're looking at older forms, the information described here will be in different sections.

The first page resembles your own IRS return. It starts out asking for name, address, and tax ID number. The address here will be the foundation's legal address, which might be different from the address used for grant applications. Cross-check with other references before mailing anything to this address.

efile GRAPHIC print - DO NOT PROCESS	As Filed Data -	DLN: 93491320005329

Form 990-PF

Return of Private Foundation
or Section 4947(a)(1) Nonexempt Charitable Trust
Treated as a Private Foundation

OMB No 1545-0052

2008

Department of the Treasury
Internal Revenue Service

Note: The foundation may be able to use a copy of this return to satisfy state reporting requirements

For calendar year 2008 , or tax year beginning 01-01-2008 and ending 12-31-2008 ——————— Note fiscal year

G Check all that apply ☐ Initial return ☐ Final return ☐ Amended return ☐ Address change ☐ Name change

Use the IRS label. Otherwise, print or type. See Specific Instructions.

Name of foundation ▆▆▆▆▆▆▆

Number and street (or P O box number if mail is not delivered to street address) ▆▆▆ Room/suite

City or town, state, and ZIP code
NEW YORK, NY ▆▆▆▆▆

A Employer identification number
13-▆▆▆▆▆

B Telephone number (see the instructions)
(212) ▆▆▆▆▆

C If exemption application is pending, check here ▶ ☐

D 1. Foreign organizations, check here ▶ ☐

2. Foreign organizations meeting the 85% test, check here and attach computation ▶ ☐

H Check type of organization ☑ Section 501(c)(3) exempt private foundation
☐ Section 4947(a)(1) nonexempt charitable trust ☐ Other taxable private foundation

E If private foundation status was terminated under section 507(b)(1)(A), check here ▶ ☐

I Fair market value of all assets at end of year (from Part II, col. (c), line 16) ▶ $ 3,053,944,733

J Accounting method ☐ Cash ☑ Accrual
☐ Other (specify)
(Part I, column (d) must be on cash basis.)

F If the foundation is in a 60-month termination under section 507(b)(1)(B), check here ▶ ☐

Part I Analysis of Revenue and Expenses (The total of amounts in columns (b), (c), and (d) may not necessarily equal the amounts in column (a) (see the instructions))

		(a) Revenue and expenses per books	(b) Net investment income	(c) Adjusted net income	(d) Disbursements for charitable purposes (cash basis only)
1	Contributions, gifts, grants, etc , received (attach schedule)					— No donations received
2	Check ▶ ☑ if the foundation is **not** required to attach Sch B				
3	Interest on savings and temporary cash investments	2,696,532	2,696,532		
4	Dividends and interest from securities	39,703,701	73,017,996		
5a	Gross rents	556,950	556,950		
b	Net rental income or (loss) _____ 556,950				
6a	Net gain or (loss) from sale of assets not on line 10	44,865,000			
b	Gross sales price for all assets on line 6a 1,571,369,183				
7	Capital gain net income (from Part IV, line 2)		465,506		
8	Net short-term capital gain				
9	Income modifications				
10a	Gross sales less returns and allowances				
b	Less Cost of goods sold				
c	Gross profit or (loss) (attach schedule)				
11	Other income (attach schedule)	-685,025	5,639,148		
12	**Total.** Add lines 1 through 11	87,137,158	82,376,132		
13	Compensation of officers, directors, trustees, etc	3,936,131	1,050,866		2,885,265
14	Other employee salaries and wages	12,947,818	2,441,372		10,021,874
15	Pension plans, employee benefits	6,882,932	509,418		6,193,739
16a	Legal fees (attach schedule)	1,261,572	598,076		620,496
b	Accounting fees (attach schedule)	383,695	191,137		249,434
c	Other professional fees (attach schedule)	11,892,013	7,304,454		4,632,451
17	Interest	1,262,954	4,484,624		1,187,140
18	Taxes (attach schedule) (see the instructions)	861,858			
19	Depreciation (attach schedule) and depletion	2,501,899	82,463		
20	Occupancy	2,501,899	197,376		2,554,424
21	Travel, conferences, and meetings	3,892,492	247,173		3,688,390
22	Printing and publications	667,439	71,560		717,314
23	Other expenses (attach schedule)	3,755,422	26,401,994		4,210,655
24	**Total operating and administrative expenses.** Add lines 13 through 23	51,374,311	43,580,513	0	36,961,182
25	Contributions, gifts, grants paid	143,868,988			137,741,403	— Total grants made
26	**Total expenses and disbursements.** Add lines 24 and 25	195,243,299	43,580,513	0	174,702,585
27	Subtract line 26 from line 12				
a	**Excess of revenue over expenses and disbursements**	-108,106,141			
b	Net investment income (if negative, enter -0-)		38,795,619		
c	Adjusted net income (if negative, enter -0-)			0	

For Privacy Act and Paperwork Reduction Act Notice, see the instructions.   Cat No 11289X   Form **990-PF** (2008)

This foundation's 990-PF is typical of those for most foundations. This is a large foundation, and the complete return contains 167 pages.

Form 990PF Part XV Line 3a - Grants and Contributions Paid During the Year

Recipient Name and address (home or business)	If recipient is an individual, show any relationship to any foundation manager or substantial contributor	Foundation status of recipient	Purpose of grant or contribution	Amount
Paid during the year				
DUKE UNIVERSITY PO BOX 90001 DURHAM, NC 277080340	n/a	501 (C)(3) PUBL CHAR	TO STRENGTHEN HEALTH SYSTEMS IN DEVELOPING COUNTRIES	150,000
DUKE UNIVERSITY PO BOX 90118 DURHAM, NC 27708	n/a	PUBLIC CHARITY	matching gift	22,951
ECONOMIC POLICY INSTITUTE 1333 H STREET NW SUITE 300 EAST TOWER WASHINGTON, DC 20005	n/a	501 (C)(3) PUBL CHAR	TO ENSURE GREATER ECONOMIC SECURITY IN RETIREMENT FOR ALL U S WORKERS	289,000
EDU AND RSRCH FND EE BEN RSRCH INST 1100 13TH STEET NW SUITE 878 WASHINGTON, DC 20005	n/a	501 (C)(3) PUBL CHAR	TO STUDY BEHAVIORS OF AMERICAN WORKERS AND RETIREES AROUND FINANCES	7,500

On the first line below the heading, the foundation will fill in dates of its fiscal year. This foundation apparently uses the calendar year because no dates appear here. Knowing the fiscal year can guide you as to when to apply. Frequently, foundations (especially corporate ones) budget a set amount for grants for the year (and most do operate on a calendar year). If you apply late in the year, less money will be available.

After the address, the form asks for any income received during the past year. A number of foundations receive additional income from their donor(s), and corporate foundations frequently receive a major donation from the company each year. This explains how (as noted in Foundation Center directory summaries) it's possible for a foundation with $100,000 in assets to make $2,000,000 in grants. Its expenses are summarized, and it ends with net income, after detailing income from investments and expenses.

The rest of the form definitely does not resemble your IRS return. Section VIII asks for a list of its board of trustees and for how much anyone was paid. This will probably be on an attached schedule. Part IX-B lets you know if this foundation makes program-related investments (PRIs).

Part XV should contain a list of the grants it has made, but usually these appear in an attached sheet because most foundations make more grants than would fit on the page. This section should also tell you the purposes for which the grants were made. This foundation gave a brief description for each of hundreds of grants, a few of which are listed.

Sometimes, trustee addresses will be given (business or even home addresses). The addresses help you identify if the John Jones who is a trustee is the same one as on your mailing list or the one who went to college with your board president. A business address can help you discover connections; for instance, if one of your board members works at the same law firm, or knows someone who does, you've found your connection.

> **WORDS TO THE WISE**
>
> Although some foundations give the trustees' home addresses, don't use this information to contact them or even send them a newsletter. You don't want them to feel you've invaded their privacy, especially because you'll soon be asking them for money. And mail sent to a trustee at his or her business address will probably be treated as junk mail, so don't waste your stamp.

The Least You Need to Know

- The way a foundation is set up and managed should influence your approach.
- Large, long-established foundations are generally more open to your approaching them than those still controlled by the founder or the founder's family.
- Charitable gift funds run by financial institutions are not foundations and not places to which you can submit a proposal.
- Operating foundations have limited grantmaking programs, and prefer to run their own programs.
- Many nonprofit organizations, some calling themselves foundations, also make grants to other nonprofits and to individuals.
- A grant from a venture philanthropist might bring with it technical support, involvement by the funder, a long-time commitment, and greater reporting requirements.
- A foundation's 990-PF report to the IRS gives you information on the grants it awarded, its trustees, and contributions it received.

A Corporation Primer

In This Chapter

- Why corporations give away their money
- Sponsorships versus grants
- Parts of a sponsorship proposal
- Corporate donations other than cash
- Which corporate door to knock on first

On the face of it, it might seem strange for a corporation to give away some of its profits. After all, a public corporation operates to make money for its stockholders. Corporate philanthropy still remains controversial at some companies for this reason. Corporations, even those with supportive boards and stockholders, must justify their philanthropic expenses as good for the bottom line. This is why, when all is said and done, corporate philanthropy is about public relations and marketing the company's name and products to some degree.

Corporations give money to charities to …

- Improve employee morale by supporting charities the employees care about.
- Improve the company's public image as good corporate citizens by supporting charities that serve the public.
- Improve the company's image with stockholders by burnishing their public image.
- Make the communities where they operate better places to live and work.

Formal corporate giving has only been active in a substantive way since 1935, when the tax laws were structured to permit (and encourage) greater corporate giving. Since then, corporate giving has become an important part of funding for charities of all kinds. According to the AAFRC Trust for Philanthropy's *Giving USA* report, corporations in 2009 gave away some $14.1 billion. An enormous part of that was in-kind donations (free stuff), principally pharmaceuticals donated by manufacturers. Health and human services captured the largest share of corporate giving, followed closely by education. Environmental causes came in last with only 2.5 percent.

Corporations give their money away through a variety of mechanisms based on how the company's structured and what it wants to accomplish through charitable giving. In this chapter, we look at corporate foundations, giving programs, matching gifts, sponsorships, and in-kind gifts.

Corporate Foundations

Corporate foundations usually don't have huge endowments. Instead, the relatively small income for grants produced by the endowment is supplemented (sometimes to the tune of seven figures!) by an annual donation to the foundation by the company. This gives the company the flexibility of making fewer grants in lean years and more grants when business is booming.

Ostensibly, the foundation is independent of the corporation. A corporate foundation is subject to the same laws prohibiting self-dealing and minimum grants made from their assets as is a private foundation. This isn't to say that the mission of a corporate foundation is ever far from that of its company. The board of the foundation is usually composed of high-ranking executives from the company, and its policies reflect the public image the company seeks to project.

PHILANTHROPY FACT

The nonprofit community lobbies corporations to commit to donating 2 percent of net income, although few contribute at this level. Minneapolis, however, started a 5 percent club in 1976 made up of companies pledged to giving at that level. Today it's called Minnesota Keystone, and it includes a 2 percent and a 5 percent club. The latter boasts more than 150 members, including major U.S. companies such as Target, General Mills, the Minnesota Twins, and the Minnesota Vikings.

Corporate foundations cannot receive tangible benefits in exchange for a grant, just like private foundations. But even a simple acknowledgment such as "This program has been brought to you by Local Widget Company, supplying the community with widgets for 30 years" has a great public relations value. Thus, even an independent company foundation can further the goals of better PR for the company.

To concentrate their influence where it will do them the most good, all but the largest corporate foundations fund only in geographic areas where they operate. Corporations that fund nationally operate nationally, such as Target, Bank of America, and Ben & Jerry's.

Many of the larger corporate foundations have developed programs to carry their brand name forward in a targeted manner they could not achieve with individual grants. For example, Target sponsors free admission to museums across the country.

Cashing In on Trouble

One of the more cynical (yet effective) means of targeting corporate philanthropy is to look for companies that have a public relations problem. After BP dumped millions of gallons of oil along the Gulf Coast, any environmental group that had asked for a contribution probably would have received it, but few would have wanted to associate themselves with BP at that time. Many corporations take a proactive position and focus their grantmaking on areas of potential controversy or ongoing PR problems. Several oil companies (even those without major ecological disasters to their credit) focus their grantmaking on environmental causes. Tobacco companies are among the most generous corporate sponsors, and they love to support dance and sports— activities requiring great stamina and lung capacity.

If you consider applying to a corporation in trouble, be sure your executive director and your board know about it before you get started. You don't want to create your own public relations nightmare by accepting money that would work against your charity's image.

Don't Be Led Astray

Grant writers make one of their most common errors in targeting corporate philanthropy by assuming a corporation makes grants in an area parallel to its own business. It can happen, but just as often doesn't. For example, AT&T Foundation doesn't fund technology, but instead concentrates on education, specifically decreasing high school dropout rates. Likewise, Gulfstream Aerospace Corporation Contributions Program doesn't fund science or engineering. It prefers to support historic preservation (a popular topic in its home city of Savannah, Georgia), arts, and education.

Always check carefully in a directory of funders or on the company's website to find out what a corporation will fund. Don't waste their time and yours trying to stretch the limits of their guidelines.

FOUNDATION CENTER
Knowledge to build on.

NATIONAL DIRECTORY OF CORPORATE GIVING

SAMPLE ENTRY

For a complete listing of data elements, see "How to Use the National Directory of Corporate Giving". Please refer to the actual entry to view the information for this company in its entirety.

Entry number	**2688**
Company name and address	**Progress Energy, Inc.** (formerly CP&L Energy, Inc.) 410 S. Wilmington St. Raleigh, NC 27601 (919) 546-6111

Company URL: http://www.progress-energy.com
Establishment information: Established in 2000.

Company ticker symbol and exchange
Company type: Public company
Company ticker symbol and exchange: PGN/NYSE

Business activities
Business activities: Operates public utility holding company; generates, transmits, and distributes electricity.
Business type (SIC): Electric services; holding company

Corporate financial information including Fortune and Forbes ratings
Financial profile for 2006: Number of employees, 11,000; assets, $25,701,000,000; sales volume, $10,702,000,000
Fortune 500 ranking: 2006—238th in revenues, 271st in profits, and 146th in assets
Forbes 2000 ranking: 2006—677th in sales, 734th in profits, and 545th in assets

Corporate officers
Corporate officer: Robert B. McGehee, Chair., Pres., and C.E.O.

Corporate board of directors
Board of directors: Robert B. McGehee, Chair.; Edwin B. Borden; James E. Bostic, Jr.; David L. Burner

Company subsidiaries
Subsidiaries: Carolina Power & Light Company, Raleigh, NC; Florida Power Corp., St. Petersburg, FL

Giving statement
Giving statement: Giving through the Progress Energy, Inc. Corporate Giving Program and the Progress Energy Foundation, Inc.

Corporate giving program name and address
Progress Energy, Inc. Corporate Giving Program
(formerly CP&L Corporate Giving Program)
P.O. Box 1551, M.C. PEB-14A
Raleigh, NC 27602-1551
URL: http://www.progress-energy.com/community/index.asp

Corporate giving program financial information
Contact: Kellan Moore Chapin, Contribs. Specialist
Financial data (yr. ended 12/31/05): Total giving, $4,752,718, including $4,159,135 for 1,975 grants (high: $25,000; low: $250; average: $5,000– $10,000) and $593,583 for 795 employee matching gifts.
Purpose and activities: As a complement to its foundation, Progress Energy also makes charitable contributions to nonprofit organizations directly. Support is given primarily in areas of company operations.
Fields of interest: Education; Environment; Economic development.

Types of support offered
Type of support: Conferences/seminars; Continuing support; Employee matching gifts
Geographic limitations: Giving primarily in areas of company operations in FL, NC, and SC.
Support limitations: No support for religious, fraternal, veterans', or labor organizations or individual K-12 schools. No grants to individuals, or for advertising, memberships, or athletic activities.

Printed materials available from the company
Publications: Application guidelines.

Application information
Application information: The Corporate Communications Department handles giving. The company has a staff that only handles contributions. A contributions committee reviews all requests of over $10,000. Application form required. Applicants should submit the following:
1) detailed description of project and amount of funding requested
Initial approach: Complete online application form
Committee meeting date(s): As needed
Deadline(s): None
Final notification: Following review
Administrators: Kellan Moore Chapin, Contribs. Specialist; Mary Woodley Dicus, Mgr., Corp. Community Rels.

Staff
Number of staff: 4 part-time support.

Progress Energy Foundation, Inc.
(formerly CP&L Foundation, Inc.)
P.O. Box 2591
Raleigh, NC 27602-2591 Fax: (919) 546-4338
E-mail: kellan.chapin@pgnmail.com; URL: http://www.progress-energy.com/community/foundation/grantguidelines.asp

Establishment data
Establishment information: Established in 1990 in NC.
Donors: Carolina Power & Light Co.; Progress Energy, Inc.; Florida Progress Corp.
Contact: Kellan Moore Chapin, Contribs. Specialist

Foundation financial information
Financial data (yr. ended 12/31/05): Assets, $102,333 (M); gifts received, $7,503,000; expenditures, $7,479,227; qualifying distributions, $7,475,797; giving activities include $7,473,797 for 205 grants (high: $500,000; low: $165; average: $10,000–$110,000).

Areas of foundation giving
Purpose and activities: The foundation supports organizations involved with education, the environment, and economic development.
Fields of interest: Elementary/secondary education; Higher education; Teacher school/ education
Programs:
Economic Development: The foundation supports programs designed to advance the company's economic development plans.
Environment: The foundation supports programs designed to protect the natural resources in Progress Energy's service area.
Type of support: Annual campaigns; Conferences/seminars; Continuing support.

Specific limitations to giving
Geographic limitations: Giving primarily in areas of company operations in FL, NC, and SC.
Support limitations: No support for fraternal, veterans', or labor organizations, athletic teams, religious organizations not of direct benefit to the entire community, or individual K-12 schools. No grants to individuals, or for memberships or courtesy advertising.
Publications: Annual report; Application guidelines; Grants list.
Application information: Application form required. Applicants should submit the following:
1) statement of problem project will address
Initial approach: Complete online application form
Board meeting date(s): Quarterly
Deadline(s): Feb. 1, May 1, Aug. 1, and Nov. 1
Final notification: Within 2 weeks following board meetings

Foundation officers, trustees, or members of other governing bodies
Officers and Directors:* Robert B. McGehee*
Trustee: Wachovia Bank, N.A.

IRS identification number
EIN: 561720636

Selected grants
Selected grants: The following grants were reported in 2005.
$500,000 to Wake Forest University, Winston-Salem, NC. For general support.
$393,146 to United Way, Triangle, Research Triangle Park, NC. For general support.

SYMBOLS

† Indicates individual is deceased.
(L) Ledger value of assets.
(M) Market value of assets.
* Officer is also a trustee or director.

A sample listing from the National Directory of Corporate Giving. *It provides information on the corporation and its foundation. The geographic restriction to areas where it does business is a common one.*
(*National Directory of Corporate Giving,* David Clark, ed. New York: The Foundation Center, August 2009.)

Corporate Foundations Versus Contributions Office

In a number of cases, the company foundation administers limited program areas, leaving other giving to the corporate contributions office. Every company that has two means of giving divides responsibilities for different reasons, but two generalizations might help you in researching them.

First, companies that make significant in-kind donations of services or products usually do so through the contributions office. If you're not sure if a company donates products, you might phone the foundation to ask about it, but they will in all likelihood refer you to another office.

Also, although grants made through the foundation must be listed in the foundation's IRS return, which is open to public inspection, contributions made through the contributions office do not have the same reporting requirements. This makes it easier for a corporation to support a cause that's controversial or does not fit within its foundation's guidelines.

WORDS TO THE WISE

It's rare for a corporation to make charitable grants where they don't have a corporate presence. To do so would violate the entire community relations angle of corporate giving. Take a look at the business pages in your local paper to see what companies are active in your area—and which are doing well financially—as you start your corporate prospect list.

Local Versus National Giving

Some companies make grants through their foundations or contributions office for national programs but make grants for local organizations through their branch offices or stores. Walmart, for example, has a national giving program but also makes grants and in-kind gifts through its local stores. This can definitely work to your advantage because the manager of a store in your community will likely have a better understanding of the needs in your town and might even be familiar with your charity.

Corporate Matching Gifts

As I mentioned earlier in this chapter, one reason corporations give is to improve employee morale. One way of doing this is to allow employees to have some say in which charities receive grants. Rather than influence the major grantmaking activities of the corporation, many companies match the contributions made to charities by an employee (and in some cases, those made by the spouse of an employee or a member of the corporate board of directors).

Mostly, they match dollar for dollar, but some go as high as three to one. You apply for these grants by completing a simple form (supplied by the donor) and enclosing proof of nonprofit status after you've received a contribution from someone associated with the corporation. You don't even have to do a cover letter, much less a proposal.

The Council for the Advancement and Support of Education (CASE; case.org) maintains the most complete and up-to-date information on corporate matching gift programs. This isn't surprising because more corporations match gifts to educational institutions than to any other sector. You can purchase a directory from them, or you can buy brochures listing all the companies to distribute to your constituents.

Corporate Grants Versus Sponsorship

Corporate sponsorship drops the aura of doing good and gets down to an exchange of benefits between the corporation and a charity—cash (or goods) for positive PR and some marketing opportunities. There's big money in sponsorship: the IEG (International Events Group) tracks billions in sponsorships worldwide.

In the past, the marketing opportunities nonprofits offered usually consisted of various forms of acknowledgment of the corporation's support: its logo on brochures, in ads, and on its website. These days, corporations crave "brand experiences" that allow consumers to see and touch their product in some way. Can you let your constituents sample the sponsor's products? Does your nonprofit use the sponsor's product or services? If so, how can you let your constituents take part in that experience?

A corporate sponsorship proposal bears little resemblance to a grant proposal. The sponsorship proposal's focus will be on the demographics of your constituents (age, income, occupation, home location, and buying habits, if you know them) rather than on the details of your programs. Rather than smoothly flowing prose, the sponsorship proposal uses bullet points to highlight the PR and marketing opportunities you offer.

HOW TO SAY IT

The first three sentences of your sponsorship pitch letter should include (1) your big idea and (2) why you've approached this specific company with your idea. Leave those out, and they'll read no further.

If you cannot describe the people your organization serves in demographic terms, you probably will be unsuccessful seeking sponsorships. You can survey your constituents to gather this information, or you can get general information on your local population from the U.S. Bureau of the Census (census.gov). Its website can give you a lot of what you'll need based on city, county, or even city block, and the information is free.

To give you a more concrete idea of what a sponsorship proposal looks like, here's a list of its parts:

- One-page cover letter summarizing first, the benefits to the corporation; secondly, your project; and finally, a price range for sponsorship—never an exact price.

- One-page summary of benefits to the corporation and audience or constituent demographics.

- One-page summary of the sponsorship opportunity, such as dates, location, attendance, expected media coverage—everything you would include on an invitation and on a press fact sheet.

- Samples of press and reports from your own publications of similar past projects.

- Sample brochures from past events showing prominent sponsor credit.

Do not include books, an annual report, or videotapes. The idea is to sell the corporation on your charity with the fewest possible words and pictures.

If you approach a major corporation for sponsorship, it's quite likely you'll be directed to its online application. These forms can be very specific about some things, while asking nothing about what's really special about your sponsorship opportunity. For examples, go to sponsorport.com/customers/index.aspx, where you'll find information for a wide variety of companies. Many times, you'll make your first approach by e-mail. Keep it very short and to the point. Try not to make it longer than one screen, and make the subject line focus on what the company has to gain, not what your organization needs. (You can include background information as an attachment when inquiring by e-mail.)

Pay very close attention to the company's guidelines and interests when completing one of these online forms. The first review may well be by a computer, which has been programmed to search for certain key words before passing it on to a human for further review. So if the corporation supports programs serving "at-risk youth," be sure to use that exact phrase several times in your project description. (This is an exception to the use of jargon discussed in Chapter 14.)

You'll find a template for a complete corporate sponsorship proposal in Appendix F, but here's an example of a fact sheet that lists the benefits to the corporate sponsor and the demographics of the charity's audience.

Benefits to *Anytown Daily News* as Exclusive Media Sponsor of AIDS Ride 2011:

- Exposure to the 2,000 people either participating in or attending the start and finish of the AIDS Ride 2011.

- Exposure to the 4,000 supporters of Community AIDS Services through the monthly newsletter.

- Prominent acknowledgment in all press releases, advertisements, and mailings associated with the AIDS Ride 2011.

- Distribution of free copies of *Anytown Daily News* at the event.

- Celebrity participation is likely to draw significant press attention.

- Status as sole media sponsor excludes any competitors from participating.

- Opportunity to be associated in the minds of all who hear of the event with the local agency that has done more than any other in Anytown to provide services to people living with HIV or AIDS.

Audience Demographics:

- Riders: average age 31, 60 percent male, household income between $40,000 and $55,000, college degree or higher

- Start and finish line audience: average age 29, 70 percent female, household income between $40,000 and $55,000, some college

- Supporters of Community AIDS Services: average age 42, 65 percent female, household income $55,000 to $75,000, some college

You'd think that sponsorships would not be tax-deductible, but that's not the case. As a grant writer who will be crafting sponsorship proposals, you need to understand what benefits are and aren't tax-deductible. Even though the corporation's decision to sponsor you will be based on market factors, being able to remind them that all or part will be tax-deductible sweetens the deal.

Tax-deductibility of contributions is a complex subject. The examples given here are not meant to be applicable to any other situations. Always check with your accountant or lawyer to help you determine whether gifts are tax-deductible or not.

Because neither you (probably) nor I (certainly) are tax experts, we can breathe a sigh of relief that in the end, it's up to the corporation to defend whether a sponsorship fee is tax-deductible. Your responsibility is to clearly state in any contract, agreement, or proposal exactly what benefits the corporation will receive. Benefits that might affect tax-deductibility include …

- Exclusivity: Will they be the exclusive sponsor, denying their competition from sponsoring your event, too?

- Product visibility: Will they be able to distribute product samples or information about their products at your event?

- Advertising: Do they receive free advertising space in your publications that you normally charge for?

Tax-deductibility aside, as the grant writer, you need to determine which office at the corporation will be most interested in your proposal. To do this, contact the sponsorship or marketing office if you can offer significant public relations opportunities to the corporation in exchange for the money. Regardless of how much ends up being tax-deductible, this will be considered a sponsorship. Or contact the foundation or contributions office if you can offer nothing more than a polite acknowledgment of the money.

Free Stuff and Free Consulting

Corporations also make the products they manufacture or sell available to nonprofits at no charge. Giving you $2,000 worth of soup (retail value) costs the corporation less than giving you a $2,000 grant. When you receive goods or services instead of a grant, this is known as an in-kind gift. You sometimes have to write a proposal for an in-kind gift just as you would for a cash grant.

Many corporations make their products available to nonprofits through a third-party distributor. The best known of these groups is Gifts In Kind International, which has branches across the country. Virtually anything you can think of is in that catalog. Companies donating through them include Office Depot, IBM, Dell, The Gap, and

Nike. Check the Gifts In Kind website (giftsinkind.org) to find the affiliate in your area. Other than the simple online membership application form, you won't need to submit a proposal when ordering products directly through them.

> **PHILANTHROPY FACT**
>
> Microsoft and several other technology companies make their products available at a deep discount through a San Francisco–based organization called Tech Soup (techsoup.org).

You can also apply to some corporations for a free consultant to work with you, typically on finance or technology issues, because businesses and nonprofits have these issues in common. Their companies might pay these volunteers their regular salary while they work for you.

An employee loan program provides really great community relations for the corporation because it literally puts a human face on their philanthropy. The nonprofit receives help from a highly qualified consultant at no cost. Talk about a win-win situation! Companies handle this in different ways. On Qualcomm's website (qualcomm.com/community), you can complete a simple form to find a volunteer. The Gap allows employees up to five hours each month to do volunteer work on company time.

As an extra bonus, some companies will only make grants to charities if they have an employee who volunteers with the charity. This could be one of your board members, someone providing technical assistance, or a volunteer in your soup kitchen. The Gap will make a donation for every 15 hours one of its employees puts in as a volunteer. AT&T's corporate contributions office will make a small grant to every organization that has an employee as a volunteer.

In-kind gifts can be a significant resource for your charity. To benefit your ongoing relationship with the corporation, send a thank you letter immediately and a follow-up letter a few months later to tell them exactly how you used the product. Acknowledge in-kind contributors in all your donor lists, in a ranking of equivalent value to other donors or in a separate list of in-kind donors.

And the Letter Gets Sent Where?

So with all these company divisions competing to give their money to you, how do you decide where to send your proposal? Read everything you can about what each office supports. More and more, company websites offer information that will help you direct your proposal to the right office. Also try calling someone at the division that looks most promising to discuss your project. If he isn't the correct person to speak to, he might be able (and willing) to direct you to the person or division most likely to be able to help you.

If you think you can offer substantial benefits, I'd start with the sponsorship office. If they invite a proposal, you'll probably hear back from them within a few weeks if they're interested. In contrast, foundations tend to move more slowly because committees or boards make the decisions, possibly taking months for a response.

WORDS TO THE WISE

Getting someone to advise you isn't always easy, but don't let your frustration tempt you to send a proposal to more than one office at the same company. Even if you don't tell them you're approaching different offices, they might find out, and they will resent your wasting their time. And remember that a grant proposal is not appropriate for a sponsorship office anyway.

Here are examples of some large corporations and how they part with their cash:

American Express Foundation
American Express Company
World Financial Center
New York, NY 10285
home3.americanexpress.com/corp/giving_back.asp
This corporate site provides clear directions on how to apply, areas it funds, and grants it has made. Depending on your location, you may need to submit your application to a regional office. It made $20 million in grants in 2004.

The Gap Foundation
2 Folsom Street
San Francisco, CA 94105
gapinc.com
Most of the foundation's grantmaking is aimed at programs that assist young people, although it also makes some grants in health, human services, the arts, and the environment. Grants are made "worldwide," according to its website. Grants: $3.1 million in 2009.

Walmart Foundation
702 S.W. 8th Street, Department 8687, # 0555
Bentonville, AR 72716-0555
walmartfoundation.org
The foundation makes grants nationally and focuses on education, health, and employment. It emphasizes aid to military veterans. It made grants of $217 million in 2009.

> **WORDS TO THE WISE**
>
> If you're working for a grassroots community organization, it's unlikely that you'll be able to get a large grant from a major corporation on your first try. You might possibly get an in-kind donation (for example, T-shirts from a local outlet of The Gap) and build on that contact to lead to a cash contribution or volunteer assistance the next year.

Corporate philanthropy has become an important element in the support of all kinds of charities, although it still remains controversial to stockholders focused on the bottom line and to nervous charity board members who fear corporate associations will taint the charity's image.

But corporate giving is not the only source of funding that can raise eyebrows. Even though we expect our government agencies to support health and education, other causes (such as the arts) can create an animated discussion at any dinner party. We look at public funding in the next chapter.

The Least You Need to Know

- Corporate giving is done to enhance the company's reputation with employees, stockholders, and the community.
- In all corporate proposals, describe how you will recognize the grant or sponsorship. Be creative.
- Some corporations make grants nationally but also give away money through their local operations.
- The degree of recognition and benefits you can provide to the company helps determine if you should seek a grant or a sponsorship.
- Many corporations make donations of their products, either directly or through organizations like Gifts In Kind International and Tech Soup.
- Never approach different offices at the same corporation at the same time. Do approach rival corporations at the same time.

A Government Primer

In This Chapter

- Finding grants at state and local levels
- Types of federal grants
- Differences between government agencies and other funders
- Including operating costs in a government proposal
- Turning political capital into cash

Governments at the local, state, and federal levels make grants to nonprofit organizations to carry out programs that benefit the welfare of the community. They also support research in virtually every area and artistic endeavor. In some ways, getting a grant from a government agency is easier for the grant writer than from any other source.

Applications for government grants always involve completing forms, which can be easier than constructing a proposal.

The applications limit space for the description of your program. This not only forces you to get to the essence of a program (which benefits all your foundation and corporate proposals), but it also prevents everyone at your charity who reviews your edits from adding on (and on and on) to it. I love telling people editing my government proposals that for every word they want to add, they must suggest a word to cut. This takes great discipline for all concerned.

You don't have to rely just on websites and directories to learn about government grants. You'll find it useful to establish contacts with your elected representatives' staffs. They might hear of a grant opportunity that has just come out or that you might have overlooked. The better educated you keep them about your charity and its programs, the better they can represent you by supporting legislation that will help your cause, too. Put your elected representatives on your mailing list, and that means home offices as well as legislative offices.

Governments support nonprofits (and occasionally individuals and businesses) through grants, Requests for Proposals (RFPs), and the distribution of "earmarks"— politely known as special allocations. Let's take a look at each.

Grants

There are many and varied government grants, and almost as many Internet sites where you can search for them. Keeping up-to-date on government support at all levels is important because new programs become available all the time. And don't wait until the last minute to start a government application. Many agencies require you to prequalify before you can apply by filing forms with particular agencies. The preapplication procedure for federal grants can take several weeks for approvals.

State and Local Grants

Finding local and state grant opportunities might be as easy as going to one of their websites and searching for "grants." A handy website for locating state and local government agencies is statelocalgov.net. The resources you'll find on different official state websites vary greatly. At minimum, you should find access to the websites of state agencies and in many cases county and city government sites as well.

PHILANTHROPY FACT

An Internet search will turn up dozens of vendors claiming to get government grants for you for a fee of a few hundred dollars. At most, you will receive a list of grant opportunities you could have easily found yourself. So beware of anything that sounds too easy—in the grant world as in any other.

On the Illinois site (illinois.gov), a search for "grants" returned more than 7,000 links! Although you'll never get through all of them, this might still be easier to deal with than the different ways each state agency organizes its information. The links included a number of actual grant programs as well as a grant proposal a local fire department used to get a grant for new equipment and had posted for other fire departments to copy. There were also links to listings of nongovernmental grant resources various agencies (for example, the libraries) had put together.

The Oregon state website (oregon.gov) came back with more than 45,000 links when I searched for "grants." Noticing a number of listings for "watershed" grants, I went to the agency listings and under the watershed department also found the details on grant programs for watershed restoration.

On the Texas site (texas.gov), a search for "grants" returned 45 million links(!), but after the 200th link, the results were not relevant.

When reading about a grant opportunity, always jump down to the eligibility requirements, especially when looking for government grants. Many of these grants are made only to other government agencies, so save yourself some reading time by checking one of the shortest sections first.

Even if your web searches prove successful, you'll also want to be in contact with the agencies that most closely reflect your charity's purpose, whether that's child welfare, education, senior services, the arts, or prison reform. Ask the agency to put you on its mailing list for any grants or RPFs that come up. It can also pay to look outside your sector because services for at-risk youth, for example, could be provided by an educational organization, a health service, or even an arts group.

Although the following section on federal grants dwarfs the preceding section on state and local grants, this doesn't mean the federal government will be the primary source of public money for your charity. Local and state programs are so varied, it would be impossible to give specifics on any programs or agencies here. Much of what you need to know about the ins and outs of federal grants applies equally to local and state grants, so please read on.

Federal Grants

Federal grants come in two flavors: *formula* and *project*.

Formula grants essentially reimburse your charity after you perform a service. Local or state agencies might offer their own form of formula grants. Formula grants are awarded based on your charity's ability to provide a service and a mathematical formula that, for example, might multiply the number of your clients by the average cost of providing a service in your city by some percentage the government has decided upon. Note that the majority of formula grants are restricted to other government agencies.

Project grants, on the other hand, are competitive. Your application will be judged against every other application from across the country. Examples include grants to help preserve America's jazz heritage, grants to operate or plan public service programs, and community projects to provide high-quality food to low-income families. In a random check, 64 project grant RFPs had been posted in the past 14 days alone.

A lot of competition exists for project grants. If you're grant writing for an organization that's been around for less than three years or has a very small staff and budget, you probably shouldn't waste your time seeking a federal project grant. If, however, you believe your charity might be able to compete nationally, by all means apply.

Many federal grants require that their grant be no more than half the project's cost, meaning you have to raise the remainder elsewhere—and not from another federal agency, which isn't allowed. Also remember that you might not get as much as you asked for, so be prepared to present a scaled-down program if necessary.

The main site for searching for federal grants is (what else) grants.gov. This site provides listings of all grant opportunities in all agencies, as well as instructions for the lengthy, multileveled process you must follow to apply for grants online—the only option in many cases. Checking websites of the specific agency that deals with the same issue as your charity might be easier, but by using grants.gov, you'll be less likely to miss a funding opportunity offered by more than the obvious agencies.

PHILANTHROPY FACT

In mid-2010, the *Catalog of Federal Domestic Assistance* listed 413 grant opportunities in health, 225 in agriculture, and 172 in education.

You can also research federal grants in the Catalog of Federal and Domestic Assistance (cfda.gov). This site even offers a guide to writing government grants written in classic "bureaucratese." Look up grants by category (for example, agriculture, health, or environmental quality) or by whom your project will serve (for example, youth, senior citizens, or the mentally ill). The General Info section provides a user-friendly guide to seeking federal grants.

If you're really convinced that there's gold for you in the federal grant coffers, you can also check the daily Federal Register online at gpoaccess.gov/fr/index.html, order a print version, or use the one at your local library. Information on new grant programs appears here first, but you'll have to sort through dozens or hundreds of meeting notices and legislative details to find them. This will be a fruitless labor for most charities. Another useful federal site is FirstGov (firstgov.gov), the U.S. government's official web portal.

Here are a very few of the federal agencies that make grants and their contact information:

Federal Emergency Management Association
500 C Street S.W.
Washington, DC 20472
fema.gov
FEMA assists in recovery from natural disasters such as floods and hurricanes, and unnatural disasters like terrorist attacks. FEMA has an office in every state, the addresses of which you can find on its website.

National Endowment for the Arts
1100 Pennsylvania Avenue N.W.
Washington, DC 20506
arts.gov
The NEA mostly makes grants to arts organizations, although writers and folk artists can get grants, too.

National Endowment for the Humanities
1100 Pennsylvania Avenue N.W.
Washington, DC 20506
neh.gov
The NEH gives grants for research, education, preservation, and public programs in the humanities.

National Science Foundation
4201 Wilson Boulevard
Arlington, VA 22230
nsf.gov
The NSF is a portal for locating government grants in science and engineering. It provides 20 percent of federal research support to academic institutions.

Small Business Administration
409 Third Street S.W.
Washington, DC 20416
sbaonline.sba.gov
The SBA makes loans to for-profit businesses but offers limited grant programs to nonprofits and other levels of government to provide technical assistance to small businesses.

U.S. Department of Education

400 Maryland Avenue S.W.
Washington, DC 20202
ed.gov/index.jsp
The U.S. Department of Education gives a wide variety of grants, mostly to schools, sometimes to nonprofits in partnership with a school, and sometimes to nonprofits all by themselves.

U.S. Department of Health and Human Services

200 Independence Avenue S.W.
Washington, DC 20201
dhhs.gov
This is the government's biggest grant maker.

U.S. Environmental Protection Agency

1200 Pennsylvania Avenue N.W.
Washington, DC 20460
epa.gov
The EPA's grants assist communities with environmental issues and environment-friendly development.

> **WORDS TO THE WISE**
>
> When you receive the verdict on your government grant, call the program officer to get the comments of the people who evaluated your proposal. The comments are just as helpful when you're successful as when you aren't. The Freedom of Information Act requires them to give you this information, which is critical for preparing your next grant application. Some agencies will require you to request the comments in writing; others will share them with you over the phone.

After you've found a grant program that seems to be a match for your charity, give the guidelines and application materials a thorough read. Afterward (and only afterward), don't be shy about calling for answers to any questions you might have. These civil servants have always been more than civil anytime I've needed help. A two-minute call can save you hours of work. Don't be surprised if you get an answering machine. Budget cutbacks mean fewer staff, but they will call you back.

Most government grant applications begin by asking for basic information about your charity, including when it was founded, tax status, employer I.D. (like a Social Security number, but for a corporation), budget size, mission, and a short statement about your project. The example of a government grant in Appendix G includes a cover page similar to those found with many federal grant applications.

Virtually all government applications are now accepted online only, although a few local ones may provide a downloadable form for you to complete. (I review online applications in Chapter 19.)

Covering the Bottom Line

Normally, federal grants and contracts allow little or no overhead, called *indirect costs*. If you plan to work with government agencies on a number of projects, you should apply for an *indirect rate*. An indirect rate is the percentage of your general operations you can consider part of the project budget without itemizing it.

The process for obtaining an indirect rate is a lot of work, but after it's established, you can use it with other federal agencies. You can find instructions for establishing an indirect rate in every RFP or grant application. The process takes some time and will involve some back-and-forth with the agency, so begin the application procedure several months before the application deadline.

When it's completed, you'll receive a "negotiated rate agreement" form. A copy of this is all you'll need when applying to other agencies.

Spend Now, Get Paid Later

Most federal programs will only reimburse you for actual expenses after they've been paid (or for only a very short time in advance). If cash flow is a chronic problem at your charity, talk with your finance person to be sure this won't create a hardship for your group. This is 180 degrees from the foundation or corporation practice of giving you all the money up front.

RFPs and Contracts

The forms for applying for government grants and RFPs can look very much alike, so what's the difference?

- Grants offer greater opportunity to get your charity's project funded.
- RFPs offer your charity an opportunity to carry out a government program.

If you're lucky, you'll have a program that parallels one the government is anxious to have carried out. But mostly, you'll find yourself applying for RFPs that lie somewhere in between: projects that will help your charity serve its constituents, even if the program isn't exactly one your program staff would have designed.

WORDS TO THE WISE

RFPs are not just issued for your charity to perform a service to the public. They're also issued to provide a service for the government, such as creating a manual or other product the government can use or offer to other charities. There's some prestige in performing these services, but don't expect to make a lot of money performing them. Despite what you might think about government spending, some agencies are very good at keeping out overhead beyond your official indirect rate.

A successful response to an RFP results in a contract to perform the services described in your proposal. It will include a restatement (and possible revision) of the budget, a time line you must follow, and the name of the person at the government agency to whom your program leader will report.

It's Never Free Money

Government grants come with a number of requirements and certifications you should be aware of from the beginning.

Government grants create an obligation to keep your financial records in great detail. Be sure your financial people are aware of the requirements. Government audits do occur—by agencies and the IRS—so keep your budgets very realistic.

You will probably have to sign drug-free workplace and employment nondiscrimination statements and certify that you do not supply aid to terrorists. (Some private funders have also started asking for the latter.)

You might have to certify that your office and/or the facility where the project will take place meet the minimum requirements of the Americans with Disabilities Act (ADA compliance).

You'll probably be asked for ethnic and other demographic information on your board, staff, and constituents, which you probably won't have because federal law prohibits you to collect some of it. But they still ask for it. (You can always check "general population" on the application.)

Who You Really Know: Earmarks

The most controversial means of government's distribution of wealth is through member items, also known as special appropriations or earmarks. Typically, a member of a legislature (from the U.S. Congress to your local city council, and mayors and other executives, too) adds an appropriation for your charity to a bill that's under consideration. Depending on his or her influence and the other machinations that go on in any legislature, this might get approved along with the bill.

These special allocations are common enough that your legislator probably has forms for you to complete and a staff member who deals with them. In addition to a short questionnaire, you'll probably be asked for a summary of the project and maybe a budget.

Although large capital projects get funded this way, many community groups depend on these appropriations from city and state officials to survive.

PHILANTHROPY FACT

If you plan to seek a special allocation at any level of government, immediately contact the official's staff for guidance on any restrictions, the amount of money you should ask for, and the date when your request must be in. Legislative calendars have their own logic, and if you're a day late, you'll be more than a dollar short.

Naturally, it will help if someone at your charity knows a legislator really well to get attention for this kind of action. Be aware that when you seek a member item appropriation, you might be circumventing the government agency to which you normally would be applying. That agency might not be too thrilled that your appropriation could lead to a reduction in its own funding.

Elimination of earmarks has become a political cause of the moment because of some conspicuous abuses by a few federal legislators, but don't feel you're doing something underhanded by requesting an earmark. The U.S. Constitution gives citizens the right to petition Congress, and that's exactly what requesting an earmark is all about. And remember—it's your tax money you're looking to get back!

The Least You Need to Know

- Grant opportunities exist at every level of government, but you might have to do some digging to find them all.
- Federal formula grants are given based on a statistical model, not necessarily the excellence of your charity or project.
- Federal project grants are highly competitive and are awarded on the quality of your charity and the specifics of your project.
- RFPs are requests to fulfill a government program, whereas a grant allows you to propose a program within general parameters.
- Government grants come with reporting and other requirements you might not expect.
- Federal grants, in particular, are usually made as reimbursements rather than outright payments.
- Earmarks are a fair and above-board means to reclaim some of your tax dollars and to do good in your community.

An Individual Donor Primer

In This Chapter

- Reasons people give to charity
- Why send a grant proposal to an individual donor?
- Pitching a proposal to a corporate executive
- Tax-deductibility and individual giving
- Sample proposals to individuals

A chapter on getting money from individuals might seem out of place in a book on grants. After all, in Chapter 2 I pretty much defined grants as coming from institutions. Although the checks might come from an institution's bank account, it's still an individual who reads your proposal and decides whether to make the grant or not. So it's good to understand the motivations behind an individual's decision to give away his or her own money, even if you intend only to send proposals to institutions.

Individuals make more charitable donations than any other sector. It might surprise you to know that according to the AAFRC Trust for Philanthropy's *Giving USA*, 75 percent of all donations in 2009 came from individuals—and that's not even counting the $23.8 billion individuals left as bequests that year. To ignore individuals in your fundraising would be a major mistake.

So where does the grant writer fit into this? Let's first look at why people give and then examine a few situations where a formal grant proposal to an individual makes sense.

Why People Give Away Their Money

Some very basic human needs and desires guide an individual's impulse to give to charity. Chief among these is pride of association. People like to be part of something positive that's larger than themselves. People join clubs and honorary societies for this very reason.

By making a contribution to your charity, the donor will be able to take pride in its accomplishments. If you do your job right, every contributor—large or small—will feel proud of your charity. For this reason, I remind you throughout this book of the importance of keeping donors—individual donors and all your contacts at the institutional funders—informed about your charity's accomplishments.

Fear of being alone, although perhaps a less noble feeling, also motivates individual giving. It's closely associated with pride of association: if donors feel like they're part of your charity's work, they're less likely to feel lonely. You might even have gatherings for donors, which could further dispel loneliness.

Compassion for people who have less than themselves motivates people like no other emotion. Whenever we show prospective donors, in words or pictures, those less fortunate and ask for their help, we call on their empathy and compassion.

Desire for continuity comes into play when asking for renewal of a past gift. Human nature prefers that things remain constant; change is disconcerting. After donors have given you a substantial gift, they very likely will continue giving so as not to waste the work done with their previous gifts.

PHILANTHROPY FACT

Individuals donated $227 billion in 2009, which was the same as the previous year—despite an ongoing economic recession.

By discussing these basic human emotions and desires, I'm not suggesting you write in a proposal, "If you make a contribution to my charity, you won't be lonely anymore." I am asking you to keep in mind that your charity has something to offer donors in exchange for their gifts, something that's completely tax-deductible and affectionately referred to in the fundraising biz as the "warm and fuzzies."

Propose to Me, and See What Happens

So when should you send a grant proposal instead of a simple letter to an individual donor? This applies in three situations:

- When you're asking for the big bucks

- When your prospect is a corporate big shot

- When your prospect is a family foundation trustee

Asking for the Big Bucks

If you plan to ask an individual for a major gift—and by that, I mean a gift the donor would consider major and is significant for your charity—a proposal that lays out all the aspects of your program might be necessary to help the donor decide to make a large gift.

You'll want to make proposals to individuals more succinct than those to institutions. A four- to six-page letter works best in most cases. If you need to give additional background or testimonials, use attachments. Most importantly, keep the tone personal, using *I* and *you* and avoiding *we* and *one*.

A very large individual gift can affect a donor's family by reducing current spendable income or decreasing what heirs will inherit. The donor will want to discuss the gift with her family and financial advisers. The proposal should give the donor details so she'll be able to easily answer any questions from family members.

Proposals to an individual should also include a project budget. The donor will want to understand how the amount you've asked for fits into the project's total budget and how her gift will relate to those from others. A well-prepared budget should inspire confidence that the gift will be well spent.

Because the donor's family will probably be involved in the decision, include any long-term benefits (a parking place near the auditorium entrance) or long-term recognition (the family name over the door) in the proposal. Take a look at the following example from a proposal for a major individual gift:

> To acknowledge your gift of $500,000 to the County Library, we would like to name the reference section "The Smith Family Reference Room." In this way, we can acknowledge you and your family's commitment to the library for generations to come. You spent so much time in the reference section

working on your last novel, we already think of it as your room. Of course, if you would prefer to remain anonymous, we will honor that request, but we hope to be able to honor you in this way, both to express our thanks and to inspire others to become major supporters.

WORDS TO THE WISE

Don't give away the store! A few donors will want to get as much recognition of their contribution as they can get. Be clear and specific about what you will offer and stick to it. Especially in a capital campaign, you don't want to undersell a prominent naming opportunity early in the campaign.

Note that I wrote "we would like to name the reference section," and not "we will name the reference section." Although you want to acknowledge the gift as publicly as the donor will allow, he might prefer anonymity, and you should allow for that preference from the beginning. Public acknowledgment of major gifts does inspire additional giving. (Just ask anyone at a charity that has a wall of honor or similar recognition method.) Also note that I've given a reason why the reference section was chosen. Tying the gift to donor interests is key in any proposal.

Here's another example, from another proposal:

> We would like to provide you with a reserved parking space near the entrance to the theater to recognize the importance of your $10,000 gift to the Hometown Theatre Company. We reserve these few spaces for those who have made the most significant gifts to the HTC. (Because the parking garage charges $10 for evening parking, IRS regulations require that we tell you that $1,000 of your gift will not be tax-deductible, based on your attending an average of ten performances a year for ten years.)

In this example, the wording is trickier because the entire gift is not deductible (see the discussion later in this chapter on tax-deductibility). Telling the donor about it certainly makes the whole paragraph sound less gracious, but you have to include this somewhere. I've also indicated that the free parking in this case will not last forever.

Now let's look at a full proposal seeking a major gift from a philanthropic couple for a new animal shelter. I've noted in the margins the important points.

Jane and Henry Bucks
456 Walnut Street
Anywhere, CA 90000

Dear Jane and Henry:

Your many contributions over the years have made a significant difference in how many orphaned dogs and cats the Community Animal Society has helped. Not only have we been able to place more pets in homes with loving families, but the neuter and spay program has been much more successful because of the advertisements we placed in neighborhood newspapers.

> I refer to their continued commitment.

I appreciated your speaking with Nancy Thomas and me last week about the Society and its future needs. It was great to learn that you have shared in our dream for a new home for some time, and I hope you will now help us make it a reality.

> Never ask for a major gift in a letter without first meeting with the donor. Reminding them of their friend who came to the meeting with you reinforces the personal connections they have to the organization.

Community Animal Society is at a critical turning point. The number of homeless animals brought to us far exceeds the capacity of our aging building to house and care for them. In examining the options open to us, the board of directors has given the go ahead to begin a capital campaign for a new building on the vacant lot adjacent to our current home.

The new building is necessary for a number of reasons:

- The present building dates to 1938, and its mechanical systems continually fail, making costly repairs necessary. In the last six months alone, $9,000 have been spent on various repairs, and $100,000 will be needed to replace the ailing heating and air conditioning system.

- The animal residence area is totally inadequate for today's needs. Our cages are almost all too small, as well as too few. As we have become better known, more animals have been brought to us.

- The medical facility does not meet the standards for modern animal surgery. The old materials are nearly impossible to clean. We collectively hold our breaths every time the health department makes an inspection.

> Clearly express the need for the gift with a sense of urgency. This could have been the place for some tragic or dramatic pet stories to work the emotions. I judged that was not necessary with these donors.

- The adoption area is small and uninviting. When people come in to adopt a pet, they have limited room to get to know the dog or cat before making their decision.

We estimate the cost for such a new facility at $2.5 million. At last night's board meeting, Nancy pledged $100,000 toward the new shelter, which provoked pledges from other board members of an additional $400,000. I hope you will consider matching the board's pledges with a $500,000 leadership gift.

> I mention their friend's gift first so they can judge their own gift accordingly and let them know the entire board backs the project.

I know a major gift from you will inspire others in the community to become part of the campaign for a new Community Animal Society building. If you can help us with such a generous gift, we would like to name the new building the Bucks Family Animal Center not only in honor of your gift to this campaign, but also in honor of the dedication you and your family have shown over the years. If, of course, you prefer to make your gift anonymously, we will honor that request, but we know that your name connected with the facility would bring increased support from many people in the community, now and in the future.

The new animal center will provide …

> Illustrate that a new building will provide solutions to all the problems in the present facility.

- A modern facility with state-of-the-art mechanical systems. Our engineer tells us we'll save $20,000 to $25,000 a year in utility bills as a result of more efficient mechanical systems in a better-insulated building.

- Five separate suites for housing our animals. Large and small dogs would have separate sections, and the cats and rabbits would be given their own room acoustically isolated from the noise made by the dogs. There would even be a small suite for the exotic pets (such as snakes and ferrets), whose numbers increase yearly. Additionally, animals with medical problems could be isolated from the healthy pets and from each other in a special ICU—the first of its kind in this part of the state.

- New surgery and examination rooms that will make it easier for our vets to treat the animals with the respect and care they deserve. It will also make it easier for us to attract young vets to work at the center by offering high-quality medical facilities.

- Six rooms of varying sizes adjacent to the waiting room in which prospective families could interact with the animal they are considering adopting. By having different size rooms, a family considering a German Shepherd could be given enough room for the dog to move around, but the family looking at a kitten could be in a more intimate space. Studies have shown that having better adoption rooms leads to more adoptions.

The prospect of having this new facility has energized the board and staff. You are the first ones outside the board we are asking to take part in the campaign. And by "take part," I do mean more than making an important donation. I know how committed you are to the care of our community's unwanted pets—and to making them wanted pets. Your active participation in inspiring others in the business community with your example (and possibly through your solicitations) surely will ensure the campaign's success.

> Emphasize how important their active participation is— you need *them*, not just their money.

If you have any questions about the plans for the new facility, please give me a call. Dr. Shepards will lead the committee that will work with the architects, and I know she would value your input.

Thank you for your kind consideration of this request. Together, I know we can create an animal shelter of which the entire community will be proud.

Sincerely yours,

Betty Lapsa

Betty Lapsa
President

> It can be dangerous to invite major donors to take part in the execution of the project. They might feel too much ownership and want to dictate the design. In this case, knowing these donors, there was minimal risk of that.

Your Prospect Is a Corporate Big Shot

When I have a meeting with a corporate funder—especially if he is on the corporate rather than the foundation side of the company—I put on my gray suit with a white shirt and power tie. By dressing in (what feels to me like) a disguise, I blend in and the corporate funder feels more comfortable with me than if I arrived in my typically casual nonprofit attire.

When you want to get a major gift from someone who is a corporate big shot, you want your written request to look as much as possible like something he or she sees on a daily basis. Familiarity breeds comfort. You want to craft your proposal to look something like a business plan, which is not so unlike a grant proposal when you see how the jargon translates, as I've shown in the following table.

Translation of a Business Plan into a Grant Proposal

Business Plan	Grant Proposal
Description of business	Project description
Marketing plan	Outreach plan
Competition	Others working on the same problem
Personnel	People who will work on the project
Financial data	Project and operating budgets
Metrics	Project evaluation

DEFINITION

Metrics is a term common in the corporate world that means the measurable outcomes of a project. Will the kids in your after-school program spend more time with their mentor? Will more seniors be able to attend free concerts? How many new books will you purchase for the library? How much will attendance increase if you print a new subscription brochure?

The Small Business Administration gives a sample business plan on its website (sba.gov/starting/indexbusplans.html) that you might find useful.

Now let's look at a proposal for that same animal shelter, this time addressed to a CEO. Note that the letter was sent the day after the meeting (and probably hand-delivered). CEOs will expect a quick follow-up. This letter would have been written before Betty and Nancy went to meet with Mrs. Banks and then quickly edited the next day to incorporate notes they took in the meeting.

I've made comments in the margins here only when they differ from those to the philanthropic couple. Please note: I would not offer naming of the facility to two people at the same time. Solicitations at this level must be done one by one.

Mrs. Marjorie Banks
President and CEO
Community Trust Company
123 Main Street
Anywhere, CA 90000

Dear Mrs. Banks:

Thank you for meeting with Nancy Thomas and me yesterday to discuss the need for a new facility for the Community Animal Society. We're writing to ask you to make a major financial commitment to this project.

> This letter comes to the point in the first paragraph, but the personal friend involved in the solicitation remains very important.

Your many contributions over the years have made a significant difference in how many orphaned dogs and cats we have helped. We have been able to place more pets in homes with loving families as a result of the new marketing campaign—200 in the last year. Two years ago, the neuter and spay program performed only 150 operations; thanks to the new marketing initiative funded by Community Trust Company, 477 operations were performed in the last twelve months.

> Note that results are quantified and "outreach" has become "marketing."

Due in part to the success of the recent marketing campaigns, Community Animal Society finds itself at a critical turning point: the number of homeless animals brought to us far exceeds the capacity of our aging building to house and care for them. In examining the options presented to us by architectural and fundraising consultants, the board of directors has given the go ahead to begin a capital campaign for a new building on the vacant lot adjacent to our current home.

The new building is necessary for a number of reasons:

> A just-the-facts approach usually works best. Depending on the CEO, an emotional pitch might work, but I've avoided it here.

- The present building dates to 1938, and its mechanical systems continually fail. In the last six months alone, $9,000 have been spent on various repairs, and $100,000 will be needed to replace the ailing heating and air conditioning system. We cannot afford to continue throwing good money at bad systems.

- The animal residence area is totally inadequate for today's needs. We operate at 110 percent capacity now and need at minimum 50 additional cages, which means at least an additional 1,750 square feet.

- The medical facility does not meet modern standards. So far, health department inspections have brought only warnings, but it is only a matter of time before we are fined due to the impossibility of maintaining antiquated facilities to present-day codes.

- The adoption area is small and uninviting. When people come in to adopt a pet, there is limited room for them to get to know the dog or cat before making their decision. As much as 5,000 square feet are needed for this area.

Reassure the CEO by sharing the marketing and fundraising plans.

We estimate the cost for a new facility at $2.5 million. At last night's board meeting, Nancy pledged $100,000 toward the new shelter, which provoked pledges from other board members of an additional $400,000. I hope you will consider matching the board's pledges with a $500,000 leadership gift. I've enclosed our preliminary plan for raising the remaining $1.5 million, prepared with the help of David Smarts, a respected capital campaign consultant.

A major gift from you will inspire others in the community to become part of the campaign for a new Community Animal Society building. If you can help us with such a generous gift, we would like to name the new building the Banks Animal Center in honor not only of your gift to this campaign, but also for the dedication you have shown over the years. If, of course, you prefer to make your gift anonymously, we will honor that request, but we know that your name connected with the facility would bring increased support from many people in the business community, both now and in the future.

The same solutions are listed, but descriptions are more focused on results of the new facility in terms of efficiency.

The new animal center would provide …

- A modern facility with state-of-the-art mechanical systems. Our engineer tells us we'll save $20,000 to $25,000 a year in utility bills as a result of more efficient mechanical systems in a better-insulated building.

- Improved living conditions for our animals. Separate housing suites will accommodate the different needs of dogs, cats, exotic animals, and those with medical problems (isolated in a special ICU—the first of its kind in this part of the state). Calmer animals are more likely to be adopted, thus decreasing our boarding costs in the long term.

- New surgery and examination rooms that will make it easier for our vets to treat the animals with the respect and care they deserve. It will also make it easier for us to attract young vets to work at the center by offering high-quality medical facilities.

- Six adoption rooms of varying sizes adjacent to the waiting room, in which prospective families could interact with the animal they are considering adopting. Studies have shown that having better adoption rooms leads to more adoptions.

The prospect of having this new facility has energized the board and staff. You are the first person outside the board we have asked to take part in the campaign for a new shelter. And by "take part," I do mean more than making an important donation. I know how committed you are to the care of our community's unwanted pets—and to making them wanted pets. Your active participation in inspiring others in the business community with your example, and possibly through your solicitations, will ensure the campaign's success.

If you have any questions about the plans for the new facility, please give me a call. Dr. Shepards is leading the committee and works with the architects, and I know she would value your input.

Thank you for your kind consideration of this request. Together, I know we can create an animal shelter of which the entire community will be proud.

Sincerely yours,

Betty Lapsa

Betty Lapsa
President

Note that I provide metrics throughout this proposal, as well as references to consultants involved with the project. I would attach a fundraising plan, as well as a budget.

Your Prospect Is a Family Foundation Trustee

As I discussed in Chapter 3, when your individual donor serves as a trustee of a family foundation, she might have the power to get your grant approved. Chances are, she will still ask you for a proposal. No matter how committed she is to your charity, she might have to get her siblings or other relatives to agree to do it.

These proposals should be big on bullet points that give your advocate good talking points. A strong executive summary might be all you need to prep your advocate, but give her a full proposal so she has additional information if needed.

The Cost of Giving

In the charity business, we make a big deal about contributions being tax-deductible, but does it matter? In surveys too numerous to count over the years, donors constantly say tax-deductibility is not their first concern when deciding to make a donation. Belief in the cause remains the top priority. So why make a big production about contributions being tax-deductible?

Well, first of all, the federal government requires us to state whether all or part of a contribution is tax-deductible. Secondly, people do like to know that they will get a little benefit from making their donation. And finally, donors need to know this information so they can stay on the right side of the IRS.

The IRS says that if donors receive anything that has more than a nominal fair market value, the amount of that benefit must be subtracted from the tax-deductible amount. For instance, if someone buys a $1,000 ticket to your benefit, she gets dinner, wine, and maybe even some entertainment when she attends. Those things would all have a value if the donor were to get them at a local restaurant. If a restaurant in your area would charge $80 per person for the same thing, then only $920 is tax-deductible ($1,000 – $80 = $920). But if you only give each person a baseball cap (which falls within the IRS guidelines of a nominal benefit), the gift is 100 percent deductible.

IRS regulations are fairly complex on what does and does not have more than a nominal value. If you feel so inclined, you can read the details for yourself on the IRS site at irs.gov/charities/article/0,,id=96102,00.html.

WORDS TO THE WISE

Save your charity money by letting donors decline benefits with value. When I worked for a museum, we spent more than $100,000 a year to send exhibition catalogs to members as part of their membership benefits. When we gave them the option to decline the catalogs and increase the tax-deductibility of their membership, our catalog costs went down $40,000.

When writing grant proposals to individuals, always state very carefully whether you plan to give a valuable benefit in return; if so, you should also offer them the opportunity to decline that benefit. If they want the goodie, they might send you two checks: one from their foundation for the tax-deductible amount and one from their personal checking account to pay for the dinner and dancing.

Tax-deductibility is not the prime motivator, but it is an important part of any request for money. Handle it carefully and with respect, and your donors will appreciate your thinking of their best interests.

It's seldom necessary to offer anything that affects tax-deductibility for a major gift. In general, major donors do not expect goodies, but they will want information and access when they make an important commitment to your charity. These things meet the IRS's definition of having a nominal value, and fortunately, they are just what major donors want.

Here are examples of things with a nominal value:

- A visit to your hospital to talk with doctors about how a new CT scan machine will benefit the community

- A backstage tour at your theater to see how the stage machinery works

- A visit to the studio of an artist who received a grant from your charity to see his work and hear him speak about it

- A donor newsletter that tells about research to develop a new vaccine

- A lecture for major donors to hear a field researcher tell of her findings

- Advance notice and reservations for popular public programs

And then there are also the warm and fuzzy things like having their pet's picture printed in the animal shelter's newsletter or putting the donor's name on your building.

The Least You Need to Know

- Pride of association, fear of being alone, compassion for others, or a desire for continuity motivate people to give.
- Provide major donors with all the information you would provide in a formal proposal, even if it's in letter form.
- Corporate CEO types will appreciate a proposal that shows respect for their business knowledge.
- Trustees of a family foundation might need a proposal from you for the record, even if your grant is a sure thing.
- Being meticulous about what is and isn't tax-deductible respects the donor and keeps everyone on the right side of the IRS.

Research, or Just How Nosy Are You?

You can't be a successful grant writer without a healthy, even overactive curiosity about funding institutions and the people who run them. Being nosy is definitely a virtue in this business.

Thanks to the Internet, the amount of information about grants available to you is staggering. Of course, it's knowing where to look and which sources to trust that brings success in grant writing, so I offer you my favorite websites and how to use them.

But offline research is still valuable. I show you where these valuable resources lie, sometimes as close as your mailbox and as convenient as your local library.

Because too much information is as useless as too little, this part also looks at how to whittle down your list to the best prospects and how to avoid false leads. I point out common mistakes to avoid and how to focus on the funder's interests.

You Can Find It Online

In This Chapter

- Discovering what foundations really fund
- Where to find clues to corporate giving
- Research tools already at your fingertips
- Uncovering people's contributions and affiliations

Your writing style might combine the sophistication of John Updike and the warmth and humor of Susan Isaacs, but if you haven't done your research, you might as well unplug the computer. Research is the most important thing a grant writer does. Really!

Funders find it insulting if you send them an inappropriate grant proposal. Wouldn't you? And raising money is just too hard to waste your time crafting a proposal only to have it fall flat because you didn't research the funder thoroughly.

Always be sure you have the most recent information. Several years ago, I had written off one foundation as a prospect because when I researched it, it had a small endowment and made only small grants to small arts organizations. But was I surprised when I recently visited its new website. One of its founders had died a year ago, leaving a major bequest to the foundation. Typical grants were now 10 times what they had been 8 years ago, and there were new program areas as well.

The Internet has revolutionized research for grants, just as it has everything else. Today, you really cannot do grant writing or any kind of fundraising well without utilizing the Internet. In this chapter, I'll introduce you to my favorite places to get the scoop on just about anyone and any funder. (The next chapter reviews the offline research tools you might also use, some of which duplicate online resources and others you'll find only in print.)

A word of warning: websites change every day. In the course of my research, I found that some sites I'd used recently no longer existed. Others were still there, but URLs of specific pages had changed. If you're unable to find a page I've given a specific address for (such as gpoaccess.gov/fr/index.html), try searching again by taking off the letters after one or more backslashes (for example, try gpoaccess.gov/fr or gpoaccess.gov) until you get the correct website. Then use the site's search tool or site map to locate the topic you need. Of course, you can also use any general search engine like Google or Yahoo! to find an organization if all else fails.

Foundations

Your research on foundations—private, public, corporate, and others—will usually start with an online directory, proceed to the foundations' websites, and then go on to look at their IRS informational return. Websites maintained by associations of grantmakers and others offer an alternative to directories, with the advantage of having already screened out foundations that, for example, don't fund your type of charity or don't make grants in your geographic area. Let's take a look at each resource.

Directories

Grant writers acknowledge the Foundation Center as one of the most important sources of information on foundations (private, public, and corporate) in the United States. You'll find the addresses of its five offices across the United States in Appendix B. There are also more than 400 reference sections in public and private libraries and at community foundations that make Foundation Center publications and other reference works available to the public. Addresses of these facilities can be found on the Center's website (foundationcenter.org).

WORDS TO THE WISE

To stay on top of the news about funders and the latest RFPs, sign up for a free e-mail subscription to *Philanthropy News Digest,* which is found on the Foundation Center website under "Newsletters." It also has a free weekly jobs listing.

The Foundation Center issues reports on different issues in philanthropy and provides access to a wide range of information on grantmaking. It offers a wide range of training and classes, including quick tutorials on writing grants, preparing budgets, and researching funders. It also offers classes on grant writing, some at its offices, many online, some free, and others for a fee.

Canadian fundraisers will find many of the same services at Imagine Canada (ccp.ca). These include a searchable database of funders and grants for a fee. Imagine Canada also researches issues in the nonprofit sector and acts to develop public policy favorable to nonprofits and donors.

The Foundation Center's home page is your first stop for many foundation research projects.

The Foundation Center publishes directories that are considered the standard in the business. Its signature publication is the *Foundation Directory*, which is available both in print and online.

The Foundation Directory Online

The Foundation Directory Online (or FDO; fconline.foundationcenter.org) puts at your fingertips all the critical information you'll need to research foundation funders, including corporate foundations and other corporate giving offices. You can search by the name of the funder as well as the name of the recipient. Look up which grants your closest peer nonprofits have received, and you have an instant prospect list! It offers many other search options, including what subjects are of interest to each funder, geographical locations and restrictions, and trustee names.

Once you've located a potential funder, you can search its grants using many criteria such as subject area, the year grants were made, or the amount. You can also use a handy map interface to quickly find grants made in your county. If you're more interested in grants made in your subject area, use the chart interface to break down the foundation's giving in that way.

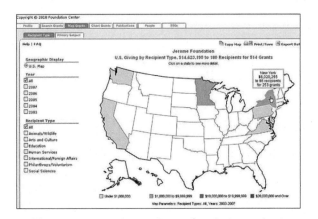

The map tool lets you see at a glance where a foundation makes it grants, and mousing over a state reveals the specifics on giving in that state.
(Map from Foundation Directory Online, Copyright © 2010 The Foundation Center. Used by permission.)

You can save searches and build a prospect list. You can even ask FDO to send you an e-mail each time a foundation you're interested in updates or changes its profile.

> **WORDS TO THE WISE**
>
> Although the premium Internet search tools are great, don't overlook what's available for free, including the Foundation Center's Foundation Finder, a wealth of information at GuideStar, and the links available on websites of community foundations and regional associations of grantmakers.

As you can see, FDO offers many tools for the grant seeker. One of FDO's most user-friendly aspects is the option to subscribe to it for as little as a month (ample time to do research for a particular project). A full year of the professional version with all the bells and whistles will cost you more than a thousand bucks, but if you're planning on getting into grant writing as a profession, you're going to need around-the-clock access to an online funder database.

The Foundation Center also offers a good deal of information on its website for free. The most important free resource for you is the Foundation Finder. This database contains the most up-to-date information you can find in one place on the Internet for foundation addresses and contact names. If a foundation has a website, there will be a link to it, and like GuideStar (discussed later in this chapter), the Foundation Center provides links to foundations' IRS returns. This is a great free resource.

The Foundation Center also is behind the website GrantSpace (grantspace.org), which brings together webcasts, podcasts, and other training opportunities. There are also sector-specific information areas for the arts, education, health, social services, and many other fields.

FoundationSearch

FoundationSearch (foundationsearch.com) provides the Foundation Center with some stiff competition. It offers pretty much the same search features, but it includes approximately five times as many grant listings. One reason for the discrepancy in the number of grants is the Foundation Center's policy of purging old grants when it adds new ones. Their point is that grants made more than five years ago might not reflect a foundation's current interests. There's a lot of truth in that, but for the most comprehensive list of grants, go to FoundationSearch. Another of FoundationSearch's distinguishing features is the inclusion of information on government grants.

Many grant seekers will find FoundationSearch's tools for building and managing a prospect list very helpful. Enter information about your organization and the kind of project you need to fund, and "My Prospect Generator" will return a list of potential prospects. You can then drill down and learn more about each of the prospects and save the best ones in a list for future reference. You can set up alerts to e-mail you when anything in a foundation's record changes and even get an e-mail to remind you of a foundation's upcoming deadlines.

A new feature for FoundationSearch in 2010 was Director Connections. This fun visual tool makes it possible to discover connections among foundation trustees and corporate directors. It's great for finding out who knows who. It's similar to a free tool you can find at muckety.com but is more focused for researching funders.

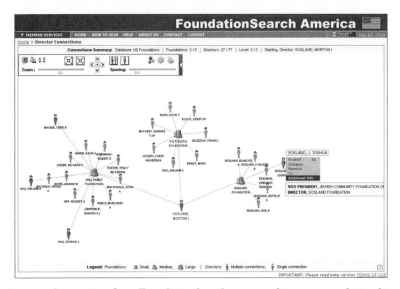

Director Connections from FoundationSearch can reveal important relationships among funders.

(Copyright © 2010 FoundationSearch. Used by permission.)

FoundationSearch has a minimum one-year subscription, which is quite pricey. You get big discounts for longer subscriptions, and with its most comprehensive subscription package, you also have access to classes that will help you qualify for the Association of Fundraising Professionals' CFRE certification.

FoundationSearch offers similar features and databases for foundations in Canada (where the company is located), the United Kingdom, and Australia.

GrantStation

Another good online resource is GrantStation (grantstation.com). Fewer funders are included in GrantStation's database (some 8,000+), but look at what it's left out:

- Foundations that do not accept unsolicited proposals

- Foundations that only fund one or two organizations

- Foundations that fund only scholarships

Most of the foundations left out are ones that wouldn't have been of use to you anyway (unless, of course, you're looking for scholarship funds). Foundations, corporate giving offices, and state and federal funding agencies are all included. GrantStation also provides information on about 1,000 international funders (half of which are in Canada).

WORDS TO THE WISE

You'll undoubtedly discover information on funders that doesn't fit with any grant you're working on now, but save it—it may just be what you need for a proposal you'll work on a year from now. Be sure to note where and when you found the information in case you need to consult that source for additional facts or check that the information remains correct.

GrantStation's approach is to provide you with detailed information on what the foundation will support, leaving information such as trustee names and extensive lists of grants for you to find on the foundations' websites—links to which are always provided. This practical approach can save you from becoming bogged down in information that's only of interest later in the grant-writing and research process.

This page from GrantStation.com shows a few of the search categories available. Also note the many other features listed in the left column.

GrantStation's "area of interest" database search provides, to me, more useful choices than other online directories (which offer general categories like "program support" or too specific such as "art therapy" while not providing a search on the more inclusive "art"). There are 160 different areas of interest to choose from, and each is clearly defined. Unlike the Foundation Center or GuideStar, GrantStation supplies integrated information on grants from all sources, including foundations, nonprofit organizations, corporations, and government agencies.

More than a database, GrantStation also provides the following:

- A free weekly funding update newsletter
- A very thorough grant-writing tutorial that includes many examples, how-tos, and worksheets
- Webinars
- Links to funders nationally
- Links to state government funding sources
- Listings of federal grants
- A grant deadlines listing

GrantStation also devotes considerable effort to keeping deadlines up-to-date so you won't miss an opportunity.

GrantStation's basic membership fee is about the same as the Foundation Center's mid-level service rate, making this a site definitely worth looking into.

GuideStar

GuideStar was the first website to make available the IRS 990 forms for every non-profit. As noted earlier, the Foundation Center also makes 990s available, but only for foundations and public charities that make grants. GuideStar includes *all* nonprofits that file these forms and allows you free access to the information if you take a minute for a simple registration.

WORDS TO THE WISE

Each nonprofit organization in the GuideStar database has the option to add a full report, including a list of its board of directors, goals for the year, accomplishments of last year, and even a newsletter. If your charity has not created a full report, do so. It's free marketing and, for an increasing number of individual funders, GuideStar serves as a charity marketplace. Do it today!

Funders' Websites

Funders' websites run the gamut from nonexistent; to a few static pages; to beautiful Flash presentations that elaborate on their funding philosophy, list all grantees with hyperlinks, and give you complete financial information. I would never prepare a grant without first checking a foundation's website.

Here are some really good foundation websites for you to explore:

Arthur M. Blank Foundation

blankfoundation.org

The visuals tell you a great deal—no matter what the focus area, the real focus is on kids. You'll find good explanations of programs and helpful grant lists here.

Joyce Foundation

joycefdn.org

Not only does it list its grants, but it also gives a short statement of what the grants were for—information every grant writer wants to know but seldom finds so easily.

W. K. Kellogg Foundation

wkkf.org

This is a real techie website. An interactive database gives you access to the details on grants going back more than 10 years. You can then use links to find grants to the same organization or to groups in the same city, and on and on. Additionally, it provides access to a number of studies and helpful publications for nonprofits. You also apply for a grant online.

The William Randolph Hearst Foundations

hearstfdn.org

The site gives the details on all their grants going back several years and links to each grantee's website. It also provides clear directions on how to apply and what kinds of projects it looks for.

Verizon

foundation.verizon.com

Verizon was the first company to accept grant applications online exclusively. The forms are easy to complete, and a quick online eligibility test prevents you from wasting time if you don't fit the guidelines.

Sector Websites

Grantmakers apparently never miss an opportunity to join an association of colleagues. There are associations of grantmakers by region, by state, by area of funding, by type (such as family foundations and a different one for small family foundations), by region and type …. Well, you get the idea.

Although intended for the grantmakers, grantmaker association websites offer information for the grant seeker as well. Many of the regional associations accept a standardized application form, which can save you some time. (But you will still customize each application, right?) Publications and notices of conventions—and they all have conventions—can give you clues to the hot topics with that group of funders and what jargon is currently popular.

Check out the following grantmaker association websites:

Canadian Environmental Grantmakers Network
cegn.org
This is a database of funders to environmental causes in Canada, with links to their websites. Membership in the CEGN gives you access to additional information.

The Council on Foundations
cof.org
Check out the links here to many foundations and other associations. Convention information is worth a quick scan for buzzwords and current interests.

Giving Forum
givingforum.org
This site provides links to the numerous regional associations and its standardized application forms.

Grantmakers Concerned with Immigrants and Refugees
gcir.org
This site includes links to foundations and tips on grant writing.

Grantmakers in the Arts
giarts.org
This site has all types of funders, from foundations to corporate giving programs and grantmaking public charities, in a listing with links.

Grantmakers in Health
gih.org
This site includes no links to foundations, but it has lots of links to studies that might provide backup for your proposal's assertions.

WORDS TO THE WISE

The sector sites narrow the playing field for you. Just don't let the funders on these sites be the only ones you investigate. Your organization is different in some way from every other organization performing the same services, and there are undoubtedly funders out there uniquely for you.

Corporations

You can find information on corporate funding with *The Foundation Directory Online*, FoundationSearch, GrantStation, and GuideStar. Everything I said previously about using these tools in researching private foundations applies equally to corporate foundations and corporate giving programs. (Note that you won't find information on corporate giving programs in GuideStar, which only includes nonprofit organizations.)

On one corporate site that seemed to have no obvious links to its foundation, typing "grants" in its site search box took me right to the foundation. With others, finding the corporate foundation requires knowledge of the latest euphemisms. *Social responsibility* appears to be the term du jour that allows corporations to combine all they do to be good corporate citizens in one place. Other popular names for corporate philanthropy are *community relations* and *community development*, but occasionally they will resort to *philanthropy*.

Be aware that some companies, especially those that sell merchandise on the web, keep their corporate information in a separate place. For example, TheGap.com is where you can find the nearest store, but you need to go to GapInc.com to find corporate information, including its foundation.

Because corporate foundations are connected to corporations, however, even more information exists on the Internet to help you determine how to get a grant from them. Knowledge is power, especially in the corporate world, so don't leave any stone unturned when seeking corporate funding. The more you know about the company and its principal officers, the better you can focus your proposal.

Today's News (and Yesterday's)

The business section of your local newspaper and business publications such as *The Wall Street Journal*, *Crain's*, *Forbes*, and *Fortune* are important sources of information on corporations (whose stock is up, whose is down) and corporate officers (who's in, who's out). You can find all these publications online and mostly free for at least some articles.

> **WORDS TO THE WISE**
>
> Can't stand the thought of reading business publications every day? Enlist a retired businessperson to volunteer to do this for you. She probably misses reading them and would welcome the excuse to read them again. Prep her with the names of the companies and people you want to know more about.

Most periodicals maintain an archive of past stories as well. Although many charge a modest fee for accessing the archived news, it's worth it if the story provides the key to your proposal.

EDGAR

You can gain access to all filings with the Securities and Exchange Commission through the EDGAR database (sec.gov/edgar/quickedgar.htm), although the information is probably more esoteric than you'll need. If your prospect is a top corporate CEO and you've heard that he or she has just received a major stock package, you can get the details from EDGAR and then decide how much to ask for.

Government Funders

Chapter 5 included a number of websites where you can find information on government funders. Here are a few more:

Environmental Protection Agency
epa.gov/seahome/grants.html
This section of the EPA site offers a free tutorial on how to write a grant for the EPA. It takes you through each part of the application, offering tips on what to include and how to say it along the way.

GovSpot
govspot.com
This site has an exhaustive set of links to state agencies plus subject listings for federal agencies.

Grants.gov
grants.gov
You can search here for information on more than $400 million in federal grants. You'll also find information on the multistep process required to apply online (which is your only option in many cases).

People

The more you know about the people at the grantmakers, the better you can write your proposal. In finding information about individuals, you'll use the same techniques as for institutions.

Google 'Em

To state the obvious, start your research by looking up the person in a general search engine. Google (google.com), Yahoo! (yahoo.com), and Bing (bing.com) give excellent results for researching individuals. In a small unscientific test I conducted, searching for information on several people (well known and fairly unknown) returned about 80 to 90 percent identical returns. Try using more than one search engine so you don't miss any important information. The differences usually show up in the first page.

> **WORDS TO THE WISE**
>
> Unless the subject of your research has an amazingly unique name, you'll find a lot of "imposters" along with your subject. To even the odds, always put the subject's name in quotation marks so you at least get only the Paul Simons, and not all the Pauls *plus* all the Simons.

Search.yippy.com clusters search results to help you sort through the hundreds of hits. Searching for "grants for teachers" groups the 257 hits into foundations (38), scholarships (20), technology (19), and other clusters. This will be especially helpful when you're looking for information on a person: results will be grouped for Paul Smith (doctor), Paul Smith (writer), etc.

Additional information is readily available for corporate leaders. Both Google (google.com/finance) and Yahoo! (finance.yahoo.com) offer special directories where you can find out a corporate officer's salary, stock holdings, and even what they do with those holdings—whether they cash them in or transfer them to someone or to a charity.

Civic or corporate leaders can also be researched through newspapers' and trade magazines' site searches to locate recent articles. Highbeam.com enables you to search on periodicals and corporate press releases (which will usually give you too many hits) or specific ones. This is a fee-based service, but Highbeam offers a free trial.

Need information on lawyers? Martindale (martindale.com) will give you their business address, area of practice, and the law school they graduated from. After you know what firm they work for, you might find that one of your board members knows someone in that firm, even if they don't know a particular lawyer. An introduction can be made, and you've got a contact with a funder.

Need information on a doctor? Use the search engine for member doctors on the American Medical Association's website (ama-assn.org).

Who's Who has a long history of compiling biographical data on (according to their website) millions of people worldwide. Marquis is the publisher of the most comprehensive Who's Who (marquiswhoswho.com). Use of their database is expensive, so this is another case where using the printed book at the library might be a better solution. If you're really lucky, your library will subscribe to the online version.

The Cadillac of Internet search engines (for people and businesses) is LexisNexis (lexisnexis.com). This is a very expensive tool, but it does give you access, for example, to a database with information on some 200 million households and 700 million phone numbers gathered from 45,000 sources. You might be able to gain free access at business or academic libraries.

Public Knowledge

Don't forget the telephone directory. Many years ago in one of my first jobs, I was given an intern's project to complete. The intern had spent the entire summer looking for home addresses for a large number of prominent people. She had found most of them, but a dozen or so remained elusive. I found half of them listed in the Manhattan telephone directory. Just because they're rich and famous doesn't mean they aren't listed.

WhitePages.com, Yahoo!, and other search engines offer free national online telephone directories. Search results will usually return a complete address as well as the phone number.

If an address is in the telephone book (online or offline), you should feel free to use it for your mailing list. This is public knowledge, after all. But you'll want to tread carefully; you don't want to end up alienating a prospect rather than cultivating one.

Other charities offer prospect information for you online in the form of donor acknowledgment lists. Occasionally, someone's name in a donor list will come up in a general search engine search. Check out the competition's websites for program and GOS funders. Comparing lists of two or more charities will reveal those funders supporting more than one—an excellent indication that they might support your charity, too.

Research Portals

Universities often maintain lists of research grants as a service to their students, but after the listings are on the web, they are there for you, too. You'll find references in Appendix C to the grant links lists on Michigan State University's website.

The TechFoundation (techfoundation.org) makes technology grants, as its name implies, but it also offers information on other funders and a newsletter about grants for technology.

The Internet makes so much information available that the challenge is to narrow the information down to just what you need to know. By using the websites I've recommended, you'll avoid information overload and be well on your way to a solid prospect list.

The Least You Need to Know

- The Foundation Center, FoundationSearch, GrantStation, and GuideStar are the top places to research funders online.
- The Foundation Center and GuideStar provide free links to funders' IRS returns.
- Be sure your information is current by cross-checking resources and noting when websites were last updated.
- Don't overlook obvious sources of information, including general search engines and online telephone directories.

You Can Find It Offline

In This Chapter

- Research without the Internet
- The best directories for institutional and individual donor research
- Tips for gathering information every day
- The research library in your mailbox

The Internet has transformed research of all kinds, including funder and donor research. But you can still do valuable research offline, and some resources you'll only find offline. There's also something to be said for using a printed directory of funders and letting your eyes scan listings adjacent to the one you looked up. Serendipity can play a role in research, just don't depend on it.

Of necessity, print directories can focus on only one approach to a subject at a time: who's giving money away (funder directories), who's receiving grants (grant guides), or what's the money being given away for (topic guides). You'll find trying to cross-reference this information quite interactive as you furiously flip pages in several books. Because most online directories owe their existence to printed directories, you'll find much the same information in both. The key difference will be the freshness of the data.

In this chapter, I look at some of the print equivalents of a few of the resources I discussed in Chapter 7, as well as some you can only find offline. (You can find complete bibliographical entries for all the books mentioned in this chapter in Appendix B.)

Directories

You'll want to make the Foundation Center your first stop offline as well as online when researching foundation and corporate funders. It started out publishing its funder directories in printed form, and it's continued to do so, although more and more it directs you to its online resources.

The Foundation Center operates offices in New York; San Francisco; Atlanta; Cleveland; and Washington, D.C. (Find the addresses in Appendix B.) Nearly 400 reference sections at public and private libraries and community foundations make Foundation Center publications and other reference works available for free. You can find these addresses in the front of directories published by the Foundation Center and on its website.

WORDS TO THE WISE

You can reliably assume that information in a printed directory is at least 18 months old, just allowing for the time to gather, print, and distribute a book. Always check addresses and grant guidelines with the funder before submitting a proposal.

The Foundation Center's *The Foundation Directory* contains several indexes that will make your research much easier and more fruitful:

Donor, officers, and trustees index. Has a trustee at one of your current funders been particularly supportive? Look here to see what other foundations he serves as a trustee.

Geographic restrictions index. Note here in particular any funders outside your state that fund your area. You might easily overlook these if you stick to the state-by-state listing. The foundations are numbered 1 to 10,000, so knowing that your state encompasses, for example, numbers 451 to 997 makes it possible to spot the out-of-state funders represented by numbers lower or higher.

Subject index. Quickly find out which funders make grants in your sector: children, health, culture, and so on. These categories are broad, so you'll still have to read all the listings carefully.

The Foundation Center's *Grants Guides* offer indexes of grants in 12 different sectors, including arts and culture, children, education, the environment, libraries, mental health, minorities, women and girls, and other topics. Here you look up grants and then find out the information on the funders. These are very helpful for finding out which funders support charities similar to yours. Note that the current editions of the *Grants Guides* are only available as downloads from its website.

The Foundation Center's *National Directory of Corporate Giving* contains information on more than 4,000 corporate grantmakers, including both foundations and company giving programs. The listings are particularly informative because they also give you information on the sponsoring company. This makes it possible for you to compare and contrast the funding interests of each, as well as noting all the names that might help you if you can find a contact within your charity.

WORDS TO THE WISE

When collecting research material, be sure to note where and when you found the information in case you need to consult that source for additional facts or for a citation in the proposal you're working on now or one you might work on a year from now.

Several publishers offer dozens of directories on funders based on subject (mental health, education, children services, performing arts, and so on). I've never found these directories very helpful. For example, one directory claims to be a directory of technology funders. On closer examination, the vast majority of the funders provide funding for the use of computers in schools K–12. That's not much help if you're raising money for a senior center or hospital. These books appear to be very specific, but to get to be book length, they end up being quite general.

Your Personal Assistant

If your organization has $995 to spare, you can get the staff at the Foundation Center to do some of your research for you. By joining its Associates Program, you receive the right to call or e-mail them as often as you like with research questions. If you have limited reference sources and very limited time, it might pay to have an expert help you. I've found this service to be very good at getting biographical information or answering a specific research question, but less so in developing a prospect list. Other grant writers might have had different experiences.

What if you don't have $995 to spare? Remember your local librarians are one of your greatest resources. If they aren't used to doing the kind of research you need, they'll probably welcome the challenge.

People Information

Never overlook the obvious sources for information. Case in point: the telephone book. People you'd think would have unlisted numbers can be found right there.

The Who's Who directories provide basic biographical information. Marquis is the publisher of the oldest and most comprehensive editions of Who's Who. It also publishes directories by profession and region. These might be of some use to you, too.

The social register might seem antiquated, but it, too, will give you addresses of potential major donors. It's particularly good for finding vacation home addresses and tracing family relationships. The membership lists of private clubs also offer addresses you'll find nowhere else. Although clubs won't give out information to nonmembers and restrict members from anything other than personal use, you might impose on a board member or volunteer to give you one or two hard-to-find addresses.

Periodicals

The *Chronicle of Philanthropy* is the nonprofit world's newspaper of record. Issued biweekly, it includes articles on trends in philanthropy. It also reports on recent grants by foundations and companies, which include *why* the grant was made. Skimming this listing is a great way to pick up some prospects for further research. Some of its content is available online (philanthropy.com), but some is reserved for subscribers to the paper edition.

The *NonProfit Times* offers articles for nonprofits beyond fundraising to include management issues; it's free if you're a full-time nonprofit executive. It also offers some of its content free online (nptimes.com).

The Stuff You Used to Throw Away

Believe it or not, a lot of information probably exists in your home and office right now that will assist your funder research. If you pay attention, everyday contacts with nonprofits will yield valuable information on their donors and board members.

Programs, Brochures, and Annual Reports

Being a fundraiser changes the way you experience the world. Attending a concert is great, but it's also an opportunity to obtain a list of the orchestra's donors, conveniently listed in the program. What restraint it takes not to read the donor list during the performance! Going to see the latest museum exhibition? Be sure to pick up the brochure to see who funded it (and don't forget to check the labels on the paintings to see who donated them).

PHILANTHROPY FACT

If someone has given to two charities similar to yours, the chances of their giving to your charity are excellent. Some people tend to be "joiners," who like to be associated with as many groups as possible. Membership officers at the three largest New York City art museums estimate that a third or more of their members overlap. Foundations behave similarly. Comparing the donor lists of three New York City nonprofit theatres, I quickly found seven foundations that supported all three.

It's not just arts organizations that offer this valuable information to the public. Brochures describing any type of service will likely credit the funders. But annual reports offer the greatest insight into who pays for what. Annual reports cost a lot to produce, so not every organization will have one, but even the simplest report will contain a list of the charity's most important donors.

How do you get hold of the competition's annual reports? Ask. Smart fundraisers know that a new grant to your charity will not result in a decrease in funding for their charity. After all, they hold the stronger position as a current grantee. I've had colleagues call to ask me what my experience has been with a particular foundation, and I've made those calls, too. Don't, however, ask a colleague for her donor list, a list containing addresses and other possibly confidential information. And if your colleagues aren't willing to share information, make a small contribution to get on their charities' mailing lists and then call as a donor to request a copy of the annual report.

After you've assembled a number of programs, brochures, and annual reports, it's time to cross-check names. You'll find that individual donors and foundations tend to support a limited number of causes. If the prospective funder appears in the listings of two organizations, definitely put them on your prospect list. If they turn up on three or more lists, put them at the top.

This can be somewhat tedious work, but it shows that some research still needs to be done offline.

Your Mailbox

Without even asking, you're probably receiving prospect information in your mailbox every day. Benefit invitations carry lists of donors. Plain old requests for donations might include board lists. As a grant writer, you don't have the luxury of throwing away unsolicited mail from any charity. Add these mailings to your offline research file for cross-checking and mining.

Although the most current information is usually found online only, directories, books, newsletters, and a wide variety of materials from nonprofits still appear in print. If you lack easy Internet access, you'll do well working with the print resources to get started, but you'll want to check the Internet for the latest information.

The Least You Need to Know

- Many online directories are available in print form with indexes that mimic online search capabilities.
- The Foundation Center publishes the best print directories of funders.
- Seemingly antiquated publications such as the *Social Register* can be useful in locating hard-to-find addresses of individuals.
- Concert programs, service program brochures, benefit invitations, and direct-mail appeals all contain useful funder information.
- Most fundraisers will share their publications that list their donors with you, but not their donor's addresses.

Narrowing Your Prospects

In This Chapter

- Determining funder interest through published materials and grant lists
- When a past gift is not an indication of foundation interest
- Addressing funder interests and avoiding common mistakes

Sending off a grant proposal without tying it to a funder's interests wastes everyone's time. Yet many grant writers make this mistake, even though they think that by reading the funder's mission statement, they've done their homework.

Just because a funder supports K–12 education does not mean it will necessarily support technology education for K–12 or an artist in the schools, for example. Support of libraries could include book purchases, technology upgrades, or programs for the public. Each funder will have its niche interest, and it's up to you to find it.

In this chapter, you learn how to avoid common pitfalls, find the information that will help you focus your proposals, and thoughtfully address the funder's interests.

Get the Details

Before you put fingers to keyboard on a grant proposal, you must carefully read the funder's mission statement, guidelines, lists of recent grants made, and program descriptions, which you can find online, in annual reports, or in other publications. Not all this information will be available for every foundation, but use as much as you can gather as your starting point.

Sometimes, the program guidelines a funder makes public are general and of limited use, but even if the funder provides detailed information, you'll want to go further by checking into recent grants it's made. Pay more attention to what it does than to what it says it does.

Many foundations' annual reports simply list the names of the grant recipients and the amount. In its 990-PF forms, this is almost always the case. Although that information will help you, it doesn't tell the whole story. For example, was the $10,000 grant to the after-school program for teacher training, operating support, or equipment? Unless you know, you're at a disadvantage when preparing your proposal.

Thankfully, a number of foundations do provide that kind of information. The ones I listed in Chapter 7 as having good websites all give you details about their grants online. Guides to funding in particular areas are worth checking out to see if they provide that level of detail. You can also look for funding credits and donor listings published by the grant recipients to discover the purpose of the grant.

> **WORDS TO THE WISE**
>
> A good prospect list for a program should have no more than 10 prospects—and even as few as 3—by the time you're ready to write the grant. I've seen grant writers with dozens of prospects. That's not a prospect list; that's a directory. Research potential funders thoroughly so you don't waste time preparing fruitless proposals.

There's enough to know about and do in preparing a successful grant proposal without following a false lead. By cross-checking funders' grant lists with reference books and recipients' listings, you'll narrow down your prospect list to the few foundations that will truly be good prospects for your charity.

Avoid False Leads

A popular European guidebook series refers to words that appear to be cognates but aren't (the Italian *caldo* looks like it would mean "cold," when it really means "hot") as "false friends." Funders make a lot of grants that are the grant writer's false friends. These sometimes come under the heading of discretionary grants in their annual report.

Discretionary grants enable trustees to support charities they care about but that lie outside the foundation's guidelines. It's sometimes seen as a perk for trustees. In family foundations, it can be a means of keeping the peace when family members' interests vary. Don't let them mislead you. They do not indicate an area of interest for the foundation. Unless you know which trustee made the discretionary grant and have a connection to him or her, this will be a dead end in your grant search.

False leads also show up in donor listings. I once noticed a familiar foundation in an opera company's donor list in the $25,000 category. But while checking out the foundation's grants listing, I saw that this was the only opera company the funder supported and it seldom made grants over $5,000. How can this be explained? Checking the trustee lists revealed a common person on both the foundation and opera boards. This was a discretionary grant, not a new direction for the foundation.

Well-intentioned volunteers and your board of trustees might feed you false leads. When periodicals from *Forbes* to the *Chronicle of Philanthropy* publish their lists of the richest or most generous people, people who are not professional fundraisers are apt to suggest you target some of them.

If your charity already has a relationship with one of the people on the list or one of them has a foundation that supports organizations like yours in your geographic location, he might well be a very good prospect—otherwise, pursuing him will be a waste of time. Wealth is not an indication of a good prospect, but involvement with your charity (or a similar one) is.

Funders Have Needs, Too

Now let's look at how to express your knowledge of a funder's interests and tie it to your program in a proposal. In a full proposal, each of the following examples would be the first or second paragraph in the cover letter or the proposal (or both).

These are examples of both how to tie your request to the funder's interests and how not to draw the wrong conclusion from a too-quick study of those interests. Although most of the examples are based on good and bad proposals I have seen, no foundation or charity names are real. Read each of them, make your own notes, and then compare with my comments that follow.

> **Example #1:** Knowing of your interest in education, we respectively submit this proposal for a $5,000 grant to provide new computers for the Community Children's Center.

> **Example #2:** The Rose Foundation's support of writers through its fellowship program has helped many novelists complete their works. At Fiction Writers' Center, we, too, provide fellowships to writers, and we request a $15,000 grant from the Rose Foundation to support this program.

WORDS TO THE WISE

Check to see if the funder issues RFPs. Even past ones will give you detailed information on the types of projects the funder prefers.

Example #3: Every year, 6,000 immigrants move to our city, but recent research shows that only a small number become citizens within 10 years. Like the Concord Family Foundation, those of us at New Americans strive to help immigrants become new Americans fully participating in our democratic society.

Example #4: The Downtown Foundation's dedication to all that is new in the performing arts has been well demonstrated through its support of The Basement, P. S. 111, and the All That's New festival. Our organization supports composers early in their careers so one day they will be presented by institutions such as these.

Example #5: We are writing to request a $10,000 grant from the Downstate Community Foundation to support education for inmates at the Big Prison upstate. The success of the program for inmates you supported through I&P Services locally is a model program we hope to emulate.

Example #6: Like the Hometown Community Foundation, our organization seeks to improve the lives of all the people of Hometown. We request a $20,000 grant to provide counseling services for at-risk youth, who are among the most disadvantaged of our citizens.

Example #7: We request a $5,000 grant to bring literary programming into community settings through readings by both authors and actors. The spoken word is a powerful force in involving people—particularly young people—in literature. When great writing is combined with a persuasive performance, magic can happen in people's lives.

Example #8: We would like to applaud the Leotard Company's support for performances of dance in all its forms in New York City. The field can easily become very fragmented, and your enlightened support offers one common element to tie the dance community together. At Dancers Plus Association, we also embrace a wide variety of dance forms, from tap to flamenco, ballet to modern. We hope you will become a supporter of Dancers Plus Association with a $20,000 grant as we strive to provide services to the same dancers you support in other ways.

WORDS TO THE WISE

GuideStar offers more than 990 forms. It also provides articles such as the excellent "What Grantmakers Want Applicants to Know." The 15 tips range from "Do your homework" to advice on what to send and not to send with your proposal. You can find it at guidestar.org/news/features/grantadvice.jsp.

The expression of the funder's interest in Example #1 is so vague, it's obvious the grant writer didn't read past the "interests" listing in the Foundation Center directory. (Has the foundation funded technology before? If so, that should have been mentioned.) This is the most common mistake made by beginner grant writers.

In Example #2, the right research was done but the wrong conclusion was reached. If a foundation makes grants directly to writers, it probably has a good idea of the kinds of writers it wants to support and would be unlikely to support a similar program over which it would have no control.

Example #3 gets it right with nearly an exact quote. This foundation's stated interest is "integrating new Americans into democratic society."

Example #4 shows by example other places that present contemporary music—all of which appear on the funder's list of past grant recipients. This one stands a very good chance of funding.

Remember geographic restrictions? Example #5 asks a local community foundation (that only makes grants in its service area) to fund a program many miles away. Even through they have shown an interest in this specific type of program, this proposal won't get very far.

Example #6 hits the nail on the head by asking for a project that meets the interests and geographic restrictions of the community foundation. "At-risk youth" is even one of the foundation's favorite buzzwords.

Example #7 doesn't directly compare the charity's program to the funder's, but the points it makes about the spoken word are exactly parallel to (but don't quote) the funder's stated interest "to develop an appreciation of spoken English." If you can make your point without an obvious "mine and yours" statement, do so.

HOW TO SAY IT

Never quote verbatim from a funder's mission statement or program guide in a grant proposal. It won't take you seriously unless you can express in your own words what your program will do and how it relates to its interests on more than a superficial level.

Example #8 begins by praising the funder for giving money to other people, and in doing so reveals they know who the funder supports and what form that support takes (in this case, for performances). The grant writer then ties his or her program directly to the funder's interest.

The good examples came about through careful research and cross-checking. Some of the negative examples contain mistakes that are obvious, some subtle, but all the mistakes would result in an immediate rejection.

In most of the examples, the grant writer has asked for an amount right up front. You don't have to do this, but it's good to get it out of the way. Another common mistake is to omit a request for a specific grant amount. You certainly don't want the funder to wonder about how much you're seeking.

The Least You Need to Know

- Detailed research will eliminate funders in your sector who have shown no interest in your specific kind of program.
- Avoid being misled by false leads by checking the grants list against foundation interests and trustee connections.
- Use common sense to eliminate funders with competing programs.
- When concentrating on funder subject and program interests, remember geographic restrictions.
- Express your charity's connection to the funder's interest without parroting the funder's own language.
- Whenever possible, show your knowledge of the funder's interests by referring to another grant it has made or a public position it has taken.

Strategies for Success

4

No grant proposal is an island. It exists in a busy world where funders are overwhelmed with proposals, nearly all of which deserve a grant. You can tip the odds in your favor by building bridges to funders before asking for their money. In Part 4, you learn how to do just that.

The funder courtship is as fraught with possibilities for false steps and detours as any personal relationship. This part examines how to introduce your charity to a funder through newsletters, formal letters of inquiry, and informal phone calls, all the while cultivating the beginnings of a relationship to move you toward success.

With all the information you've accumulated by this point, you'll be wondering what to do with it all. I help you organize your prospect files and put all the information you have gathered into a plan that makes sure that each funder will be approached in the best way and at the right time.

Chapter 10

Sow Before You Reap

In This Chapter

- Using newsletters to build knowledge of your charity
- Pros and cons of print and e-mail newsletters
- Elements of a good donor newsletter
- Creating a cultivation event that will appeal to funders

Looking back at the letter from Jack to his parents in Chapter 1, how successful do you think the identical letter would have been if his parents had received it from a total stranger? Right. So why would you send a proposal to a funder that has never heard of your charity?

By educating a foundation staff member (and hopefully one or more trustees) about your charity before submitting a grant proposal, you greatly increase your chances of success. Occasionally, a cold proposal will get funded, but by warming up funders, you definitely increase your success rate. In the fundraising biz, we call this *cultivation*.

Newsletters

Newsletters designed for those your charity serves can be an effective means of educating funders about your activities. These newsletters show firsthand exactly what services you provide, how you provide them, and how you interact with your clients. Consider putting the program officers of key funders on your newsletter mailing list in time for them to receive two or three issues before your proposal arrives. With political contacts, remember to send newsletters to their local as well as legislative offices when possible, and to include the top staff for each elected official.

WORDS TO THE WISE

If you don't have the name of someone at the funder, don't waste your stamps. After all, you know what happens to "Resident" mail that shows up in your mailbox. Check the funder's website, or call to find out who would be the best person to receive your mailings.

Newsletters written specifically for your donors can be very effective tools for cultivating institutional funder contacts. Your donor newsletter should give your spin on what you've done: reporting on program accomplishments, giving news of past clients who have gone on to great accomplishments, and reporting on your fundraising successes.

I like to put all my funder contacts on the mailing list for the donor newsletter and a smaller group who have a real interest in the field on the list for the client newsletter.

Just as you don't want your proposal to come out of the blue, your first newsletter shouldn't arrive out of context either. Always include a cover letter similar to the following one when you add a funder contact to a mailing list.

Dear Mr. White:

I have enclosed a copy of the Service Organization's recent newsletter, which contains information that might be of interest to you as the program officer for arts and culture. This issue has an article by Steven Critic on the Venice Biennale and a complementary article from Sara Painter on the artists who represented the United States in that exhibition.

This newsletter is published bimonthly and enjoys a readership of 50,000. You'll note that in the back we provide information on a wide variety of opportunities for artists, including many offered by other agencies.

We hope you will find our newsletter of interest. If, however, you would prefer not to receive future issues, please let me know by calling 212-555-1234 or by e-mailing smith@service.org.

Sincerely,

Sandra Smith

Sandra Smith
Director of Development

Note that the emphasis in the first paragraph is on the information Mr. White can use, not on the charity itself. Although this letter introduces a client newsletter, when sending a donor newsletter for the first time, you'll also want to point out an article that the funder might find useful for something other than learning about your charity.

If you mail out a couple dozen of these letters, you can expect to hear from one or two people who don't want to receive any future issues. This might be a good indication that your proposal will meet with the same reaction, or it could just be an overworked program officer. If an individual phones you to ask to be removed from your mailing list, try to find out which is the case by asking if anyone else at the foundation might be interested in receiving your newsletter.

Getting Your E-Mail Opened

If yours is an e-mail newsletter, it's just as important to send a "cover letter." I'd send a cover letter by e-mail a day or two before the first newsletter issue with language just like the sample snail-mail letter. Be sure to include something in the subject line that identifies your organization. Don't repeat words or use all uppercase (both typical of spam) in the subject line or in your message. And send these e-mails out one at a time so the recipient will think she is the only one you are approaching.

> **WORDS TO THE WISE**
>
> As long as you're preparing an introductory letter for your client newsletter, why not share it with whoever handles public relations at your charity? A similar approach works well at educating the press about what your charity does. (Your donor newsletter, however, will be of little interest to the press.)

Because we all receive so much spam every day, you might also send a printed letter by regular mail to introduce the forthcoming e-mail. Otherwise, the funder might automatically delete your introductory letter if he or she doesn't recognize your address or your organization's name. And remember that the best times to e-mail are Monday afternoon through Thursday.

Actually mailing a newsletter is becoming almost quaint in these days of increased electronic communications. A printed copy gives you complete control over how you present your story. But with nicely formatted HTML e-mails, you can distribute electronic newsletters that are just as attractive as printed ones. Plain text newsletters are quickly becoming obsolete. Long ones won't get read.

A number of vendors provide the means to both manage your e-mail lists and create impressive e-mail newsletters for as little as $50 a month. Most allow you to create fully designed (HTML) newsletters along with a plain text version for people using older e-mail software. It's well worth the cost to present your charity in the best possible light.

Hopefully, the program officers on your list will share your newsletters with others. This is really easy with e-mail newsletters, thanks to e-mail forwarding. But printed newsletters, especially if they're attractive and graphically interesting, will likely get circulated, too.

If your charity doesn't have a donor newsletter, seriously consider creating one using e-mail to keep down costs. As a grant writer, you're already familiar with your charity's current programs and those in the planning stages. Knocking out the text for a two-page newsletter should be easy.

Types of Articles to Include

Two medium-length articles are all you'll need to give your newsletter substance. You'll be surprised at how easy this is to do and what a positive response you'll get. Just keep everyone in your charity (including key board members) up-to-date on what you're doing.

Here are examples of content found in donor newsletters:

- Pictures of your staff helping clients. Pictures of people on the front page of the newsletter are particularly important to draw people in.

- News of accomplishments of current and past clients.

- Pictures of your supporters at benefits or cultivation events. People like to see other people.

- A report on a major grant recently received, including how it will be used and why the donor decided to make it to your charity.

- A report on successful programs, including comparison to past programs and prominent funder credits.

- Articles on giving that offer practical advice to donors, such as articles on bequests or charitable trusts that have benefited your charity.

WORDS TO THE WISE

E-mail newsletters (and printed newsletters) should also be posted on your website to give them a longer shelf life and increase readership. More and more, e-mail newsletters consist of short summaries of articles with hypertext links to the full articles on the website.

You'll find that some of the most successful articles in terms of donor response and appreciation are on resources outside your charity. The article could be on a crisis in your sector ("Funding for Libraries Slashed Statewide!") or about issues affecting your sector ("Early AIDS Vaccine Trials Offer New Hope"). You could also review a book on wise giving or profile the local community foundation. By including articles that lie outside your charity, you show a broader perspective that funders appreciate while offering information they'll find useful in several ways.

Events

Using benefits and other special events to cultivate funder contacts can be difficult. You'll find that program officers and trustees can be hesitant to accept complimentary tickets for events everyone else is paying for, especially if they're expensive. They rightly don't want to send the wrong message to you as a potential grantee by allowing you to think they owe you a favorable review of your proposal.

Instead of depending on fundraising events, or ticketed performances or exhibitions, to acquaint funders with your charity, develop events specifically to cultivate them. This isn't the place to ask for money. You want to cultivate them before you solicit them—and not all in the same night. Cultivation events should not cost you much money and should require a fraction of the time to produce that a benefit would.

Here are some cultivation events I think you'll find successful:

- A cocktail party at a trustee's home. People love to see how others live, and the trustee should foot the bill for the refreshments.

- A talk by a curator about an upcoming exhibition that promises to be controversial. Those who attend can "dine out" on the advance knowledge they receive for weeks. If you can hold it in someone's home, they'll have two reasons to attend.

- A preview of the work of regrant recipients, with some in attendance to speak about their work and others represented by slides or reports.

- A simple luncheon that mixes scholarship recipients with current and potential scholarship donors. There's nothing like a kid's firsthand testimonial to open those pockets.

- A more formal luncheon at which a prominent person speaks about issues confronting the charity's sector, but not necessarily about the charity itself. Although this might take your charity out of the spotlight, those who attend will remember that you were the one who provided the insights they gained from the talk.

Basically, any event that provides knowledge not readily available to the public will work. People love to know more than their friends and neighbors. And be sure to give them something to take home with them, whether it's just a brochure or a complete packet of information on your charity.

> **WORDS TO THE WISE**
>
> Developing and organizing cultivation events lies well outside your responsibilities as a grant writer, but you should encourage the fundraisers at your charity to plan them and be ready to give them names from your prospect list to invite.

Newsletters and events represent the cultivation you do before you apply for a grant. While the grant is under consideration, keep a respectful distance as far as cultivation is concerned and restrict yourself to answering the funder's questions. In Chapter 20, I discuss what needs to be done after you receive a grant to set the stage for a renewal grant.

The Least You Need to Know

- Client newsletters and donor newsletters provide different means of educating funders about your charity.
- Never put a funder on any newsletter list without first sending an introductory letter.
- Both e-mail and printed newsletters work well to cultivate funders.
- The best newsletters include information on more than your charity.
- Paid, ticketed events are not ideal for funder cultivation.
- Cultivation events that impart inside knowledge or provide contact with clients engage funders best.

Testing the Waters

In This Chapter

- Finding the best person to approach
- Why and how to write an inquiry letter
- When and how to make an inquiry call
- Handling a meeting with a funder
- Pulling strings without getting tangled up

You've done all your research, cross-checking and checking again. You've warmed up the program officers, at least to the point that they recognize the name of your charity. One additional step remains before you can start on the proposal: contacting the funder. Some fundraisers suggest that a preproposal personal contact with a funder can triple your chances of getting a grant. I'm not sure about that statistic, but it's definitely important to test the waters and, whenever possible, make a personal connection.

In this chapter, I take a look at the different ways of gathering information to further prepare the funder to receive your proposal in a positive light. I also discuss how and when to use board contacts.

Whom to Contact

Directing your inquiry at the right person is half the battle. With large foundations and government agencies, a program officer is likely listed as the contact. Corporations usually clearly indicate whom to contact, whether it's someone in the foundation or community affairs department.

One thing you should resist: do not "go senior," that is, approach someone higher up at the foundation or corporation. That would be going counter to the funder's instructions, which is always the best means to get your proposal rejected. Also, going over the program officer's head will surely alienate them, possibly weakening the presentation of your request to the trustees. And your senior-seeking inquiry probably won't be answered anyway. There's a reason the program officer was designated as the contact—the senior person has other things to do!

Inquiry Letters

An inquiry letter lies somewhere between a request for guidelines and a full proposal. In the inquiry letter, you want to describe your project well enough that the funder can give you the information you require, but you also want to avoid making it appear too much like a proposal. You may ask for a meeting in your inquiry letter, too. (I discuss meetings later in this chapter.)

WORDS TO THE WISE

If a year has passed since your last contact with a funder, you'll want to build the relationship almost as carefully as with a new funder. Follow the same steps, but accelerate the process. An inquiry letter might be better than a call if your contact no longer works there or if more than two years have passed since the last grant was made.

Peer-to-peer contact usually works best. You should, when possible, address inquiry letters to a program officer, not the head of the foundation. At smaller funders, there may be no program officer, so you'll have to start at the top.

If the letter is to a program officer, you or your director of development should sign it. If the letter is to go to the head of the foundation, your director of development or executive director should sign it.

An inquiry letter should include …

- A reference to the newsletters and other materials you've been sending.

- A clear request for information about *their* programs.

- A general description of your project that shows a connection to and your understanding of the funder's interests (see Chapter 9).

- Easy ways to contact you, especially an e-mail address.

- A list of your board, only if one or more names might be recognizable by the funder. (Having the board list as part of your letterhead design works better than an attachment.)

- A request for a meeting to discuss the project (optional).

- A copy of your organization's general brochure if you believe your previous cultivation might not have sufficiently paved the way (optional).

- If available, one (and only one) short press clipping to show the prominence your charity has achieved.

WORDS TO THE WISE

Never send an inquiry letter or proposal to more than one person at the same funder. If you can't decide to whom to send it, you haven't completed your research. The only exception would be when you have a connection to one of the funder's trustees, in which case you would CC the trustee when sending the letter or proposal to the usual contact person.

An inquiry letter usually should *not* include …

- A direct request for money.

- A budget.

- Supporting materials, such as your tax-exempt letter.

- Annual reports or other bulky items.

Many foundations require an inquiry letter, in which case they typically will specify what information they want in it. Always follow funder instructions exactly.

The purpose of any letter of inquiry is to get the funder to request a complete proposal or to meet with you. To accomplish this, you have to give the basics about both your nonprofit and the project for which you seek funding, including what size grant you would like and what other funding you can draw on. It might look something like the following example.

Ms. Sara Brown
Program Officer, Health and Human Services
Jones Family Foundation
456 Broadway
Anytown, IL 60000

Dear Ms. Brown:

I hope you have found the clinicians' newsletter from the Counseling Center of Broome County (CCBC) informative about the need for psychiatric counseling to the disadvantaged citizens of Broome County. The CCBC has provided these services for more than twenty years.

The CCBC has made great strides in reaching more people through its mobile facility, reaching clients in even the most remote areas of the county. As you probably know, state funding has been drastically reduced for next year, and we must replace that $25,000 in the next six months to continue this service. We already have pledges for $13,000, and we hope to raise the remainder from one or two foundations, including the Jones Family Foundation.

The speech given by Dr. Phelps, who I understand is your health adviser, at the Illinois Association of Psychiatry on just-in-time services certainly spoke to the types of situations we at the CCBC deal with daily, and that the mobile facility helps so much in meeting.

If you could possibly meet with us to discuss our current programs, we would greatly appreciate it, but I understand the limitations you have on your time. I'll call you next week to see if we can arrange a meeting, or failing that, perhaps we can speak then about how we might develop a proposal to the Jones Foundation. In the meantime, you can reach me at 312-555-1222 or ssmith@ccbcounty.org. I look forward to speaking with you.

Sincerely,

Susan Smith

Susan Smith
Director of Development

Procedures differ slightly for a current or past funder:

- For a renewal grant for the same program from a current funder, you would probably just send in the renewal proposal (after making the necessary reports). An inquiry letter would serve no purpose because you know the funder likes your charity and its programs.

- For a grant for a new program from a current funder, you would probably phone your contact at the funder to discuss the new program rather than write an inquiry letter, which might seem too formal given the current relationship.

- If the funder has not given you a grant in more than a year, you might skip the inquiry letter and instead phone before sending the proposal, even if the grant would be for the program they supported previously.

An inquiry letter might be answered with a letter telling you to look elsewhere. In these cases, it's unlikely that a full proposal would have done any better, but when this happens, you can't help but wonder what would have happened if you'd been able to state your case directly. For this reason, many grant writers prefer to take the bull by the horns and make an inquiry call.

Inquiry Calls

The peer-to-peer principle applies equally, if not more so, when making an inquiry phone call. It's unlikely that the grant writer will be able to get through to the head of a large foundation. Also, it might be interpreted as a breach of protocol for the grant writer, rather than an executive director, to call a foundation head about a proposal.

WORDS TO THE WISE

Be strategic about when you place an inquiry call. The day applications are due or the day before a board meeting will probably be particularly hectic for the program officer. If possible, determine when these events occur and avoid them. If you must leave a voice mail message, state your name clearly, explain the reason you're calling, and repeat your phone number. Make it as easy as possible for them to pay attention to you.

Before you call, line up all your facts and put them down as a series of bullet points you can easily refer to. Go over what you plan to say with a colleague, asking her to try to anticipate what questions the program officer might ask. If someone else will make the call, give that person your bullet points and review them together to be sure any questions that might come up can be quickly answered.

You don't, of course, have to have the answers to every question—you can always say you'll get back to them with that information—but you should be prepared to respond to the obvious ones, such as who will run the program or what's the total budget.

When you have the program officer on the phone, be professional at all times. Don't try for a breezy or too informal manner, and don't address the program officer by first name unless you actually know her. Keep in mind the things that should and should not appear in an inquiry letter, and try to stick to those topics in your call. Take notes on everything discussed. It will all come in handy at some point.

If your main purpose in calling is to arrange a meeting, be clear about that before you get into describing your project. The program officer might prefer to hear about it over the phone rather than in person, but give her that option.

If you've been sending your newsletter to the funder, I'd start by asking if she has received it and, if so, if she found it informative. If your inquiry call is following up an introductory letter (that accompanied a newsletter, for example) or an inquiry letter, state that right away to make a connection between you and what she should have seen or known about your charity.

Work to keep the conversation positive and general. You want to pique their interest in your proposal in hopes of gaining insight into how best to pitch it to the funder's specific interests. If you're told that the funder wouldn't consider your project, ask if you can continue to send your newsletter and if you can call again when a different project requires funding. Try to get some positive action out of the call.

Informational Meetings

With the huge number of applicants knocking at their doors, funders will rarely agree to an *informational meeting*. Many funders include in their guidelines a request that you not ask for a meeting before submitting an application, after which they will determine if a meeting is warranted. If the funder you plan to approach says this, don't ask for a meeting.

> **DEFINITION**
>
> **Informational meetings** with funders are no different from those advised by many books for job seekers. In both cases, you're asking someone to meet with you to gather information, when in reality you're hoping they'll be so impressed they'll give you money (either as a paycheck or a grant). In both cases, the pretense fools no one, but it allows each party to learn about the other.

On the other hand, if your charity and the project you want funding for fall clearly within the funder's interests (and their guidelines don't preclude meetings beforehand), they might be willing to meet with you. A meeting with a funder offers you your very best chance to make a good impression: you establish a personal connection, you get instant feedback on your projects, and you learn about the funder's current priorities.

If you're fortunate enough to get a meeting, remember these points:

- You are there to listen as much as to talk.

- Be precise and stay on point. Don't give a complete blow-by-blow history of your charity's last 20 years in response to the what's-new-at-your-charity question.

- If you've had a grant previously from this funder, report on how that project went (or continues to go), stressing its accomplishments. Talk about its challenges only if you're there for funding for the same project.

- Don't give the funder any materials at the beginning of the meeting. It will only distract her, and you want to maintain eye contact. If you have materials for her, present them as you're saying your good-byes—and be sure all materials are directly to the point of your program *and* that your name and contact information appear on everything.

- It's much better not to refer to notes, but if it's absolutely necessary, have your list of bullet points to remind you of the topics you need to cover and the questions you need to ask.

- Do take notes when the funder speaks (on the pad you brought with you), even if you know you'll remember every word. Taking notes shows interest.

- Don't doodle instead of (or in addition to) taking notes.

- Ask questions about the funder's interests that show you've done your research.

- If the funder has been in the news recently, comment on it to show your interest.

- If you feel like your project pitch is getting nowhere, have a fall-back project to offer. You're not going to get a second meeting anytime soon, so make the most of this one.

- Call or e-mail the day after your meeting—not two days later—thanking the funder for meeting with you and highlighting points from the meeting needing amplification or emphasis, or making a point you forgot to make in the meeting.

> **WORDS TO THE WISE**
>
> Using a PowerPoint presentation might be tempting when visiting a funder, but only do this if you know you'll be speaking to a number of people. Eye contact will serve you better than a slick presentation if you're meeting with one or two people. Let the funder know if you plan to make a formal presentation, and keep it short, making sure you have time to get to know the funder's representatives before you turn down the lights.

You want to be sure the funder understands not only the details of your program, but also your charity's passion for it. If possible, a program person directly involved in the program should go along with your executive director or development director. Although you'll want to be there, too, don't send so many people that you outnumber the funder's staff attending the meeting.

Only occasionally have I had meetings with funders that did not result in a grant. If they take that kind of time with you, they're probably serious about funding you. Program officers can be very helpful in coaching you in the forms and buzzwords their board looks for, so it pays to take notes and follow them to the letter.

When to Pull Strings

So you've had a really positive meeting with the program officer, and you know just how to pitch your proposal. Now you discover that one of your board members went to college with one of the funder's trustees. So you call your board member and ask her to phone her old school chum to recommend your charity.

That's all well and good, but you've skipped an important step. The program officer who you've worked so hard to cultivate might feel blindsided if word comes from above to take special care of you. Instead, upon discovering your connection, phone the program officer and tell him or her of your discovery and ask for the program officer's advice on using this knowledge. Or at the very least, let the program officer know you're planning to use your connection.

If, of course, you'd discovered the board connection earlier, an inquiry letter might not have been necessary. If one of the funder's trustees has invited you to apply, you'd state that in the very first sentence of the proposal's cover letter. Knowing someone on the inside with the authority to ensure that your proposal will receive serious consideration separates yours from the masses of proposals the funder receives every day. Just be up front with your contact at the foundation about what strings you plan to pull.

When you've discovered a personal contact between your charity and a funder (usually through one of your board members), ask that board member if he or she will contact the foundation on your behalf. In the case of foundations that do not accept unsolicited proposals, this will be the only way you can get your proposal read. In other instances, it can make your proposal stand out from the other proposals.

WORDS TO THE WISE

Circulate a list to your board at least twice a year giving the names of trustees at the foundations on your prospect lists, asking that they note anyone they know, and how well, and return it to you. Keep these contacts in mind when you begin preparing the various proposals.

Your board member's contact with the funder could take several forms, listed here in the order of decreasing effectiveness:

- A phone call to the foundation trustee.
- A letter followed by a phone call to the trustee.
- A letter sent well ahead of your proposal to the trustee.
- A letter you can use as your cover letter or include as a support letter with your proposal.

Use whatever method your board member is most comfortable with, but you can certainly encourage the phone call.

Chances are that if a letter is involved, you'll be asked to write it. If this is the case, be sure to use a different tone and don't repeat phrases from your cover letter or the proposal. Indent the paragraphs of the board member's letter to make it look more personal, and be sure to use the correct salutation (first name, nickname, whatever). Letters from a board member ideally will be on their personal or business stationary, not that of your charity.

Managing Your Contacts

After all your hard work developing contacts at funders through cultivation activities, mailings, phone calls, and meetings, you'll want to keep track of everything relating to your new relationship. Some donor software or calendar programs include a "contact manager" that enables you to note every piece of mail sent and phone call made. By tracking this information, you'll avoid contacting funders too often or not often enough. More importantly, you can set up reminders for yourself to follow through on mailings and phone calls.

How often is too often to contact a funder? During the courtship/cultivation phase, once a month is probably the most you'll want to do. After you've had the first date/informational meeting, the all-important follow-up note should set the stage for the proposal.

HOW TO SAY IT

As time goes by, you'll probably become very friendly, if not actually friends, with program officers at funders. Remember, however, that this is an unequal relationship because you'll be the one asking for something 98 percent of the time. Remaining somewhat circumspect in talking about your charity—even off the record—will serve you well.

Basically, your instincts on how the program officer responds to you are more important than any guidelines I can give you. Don't be a pest, but don't wait so long between contacts that they forget who you are.

The Least You Need to Know

- Inquiry letters and phone calls are essential parts of the grant process.
- Don't "go senior." Direct your inquiry to the person designated by the funder, not someone higher up.
- Use the inquiry process to gather information about the funder's specific interests, and avoid anything that appears to be "an ask" when making an inquiry.
- Prepare carefully for both inquiry calls and meetings.
- Make the most of any meeting, including having an alternate project to discuss if necessary.
- Use trustee connections in a way that will not alienate or undermine program officers.

Planning for Success, Now and Tomorrow

In This Chapter

- Why you should create a grant-writing plan
- The elements in a plan
- Meeting deadlines
- Using a schedule to create success

You're not quite halfway through this book, and already I've given you a lot to remember. There's a lot to know, but with planning and scheduling (and good record keeping), you can make it work. This chapter's title refers to "Now and Tomorrow" because no grant exists in a vacuum:

- Research for one program turns up leads for a different one.

- Your contacts at funders come and go.

- Sometimes you discover the perfect funder the day after the grant application deadline.

- Good grant proposals are based on knowledge of a program's long-term plans.

This chapter shows you how to manage all the information you gather through research, organize input from program staff, and chart your way through the grant-writing process.

Developing a Grant-Writing Plan

What could possibly sound more boring than developing a grant-writing plan? Plenty! (How about writing a summary of the American Institute of CPAs' changes in accounting rules?) You'll be surprised at how helpful it will be to assimilate all the information you've gathered into a plan. Your ideas about a proposal will coalesce, and any omissions in research, program descriptions, or budgets will become obvious.

Forming a plan also provides a mechanism for working with the program staff. They'll appreciate knowing what's expected of them and when. A grant-writing plan also involves working with finance and executive staff and possibly board members. You are the glue that holds all this together.

Articulating the Program

Before you can do anything else, you must know what you need to raise the money for, and this means working with program staff. Schedule time with the senior people involved with a program to discuss what they have in mind. Come prepared with a list of questions you'll have to address in any proposal. Ask about items such as …

- The program's mission (or purpose) and goals.

- Your charity's history with similar programs and how it fits with your charity's mission.

- Why the program is needed.

- Whom the program will serve.

- How the program will be run.

- Who will run it.

- How the program will be evaluated.

- How you will measure the program's success.

WORDS TO THE WISE

Most program people won't understand how you work, what you do, or what a grant proposal represents. It's a fact of nonprofit life, and if development and program staff are working at odds, the charity will suffer. Do your best to educate them, but be prepared for misunderstandings. Although you certainly want your proposals to be an accurate depiction of what the program will finally be, details will undoubtedly change and funders understand this. Be sure program staff also understand there's some flexibility with any funding request.

When seeking answers for these questions, don't be content with hearing about what will happen over the next year. Get the program staff to lay it out for you for three years. Even though they probably won't be able to give you very specific information about subsequent years, by forcing them to think in longer terms, you'll get a clearer idea about how the program will function in the short term. And besides, the next step in this process is …

Developing a Three-Year Funding Plan

Funders commonly ask you to address how you'll pay for the program after their funding ends. If you don't know what will happen programmatically in the second and third years, you can't know how much it will cost, and therefore cannot know how it will be funded. Asking for a three-year budget might throw program staff for a loop, but if they've given you a clear direction, you might be able to construct a rough budget with help from the finance staff. Just be sure the program staff have a chance to review what you end up with if you intend to use it in a proposal. (I discuss budgets in detail in Chapter 15, including multiyear budgets.)

A discussion of future funding plans presents a good opportunity to get information from program staff for any outstanding reports. If activities included in the original grant proposals weren't completed, be certain to find out why and what, if anything, was done instead. You don't want to reiterate something in a new proposal that didn't work the first time.

Following is an outline to use as you develop your funding plan, creating a separate page for each program. The plan will contain broad strokes as to the program and budget, but funding sources and deadlines will be detailed. (A plan created by the program staff would contain information in reverse proportions.) The funding plan isn't intended to be the outline for your proposal, just the facts on which you'll later base the proposal. If the program is expected to grow in subsequent years, note that here for future reference.

The most important costs to note in a funding plan are the total project costs. Creating a budget is part of the proposal process. You don't have to come up with one at this point. If, however, one or two activities or items make up the majority of the expenses for this program, include those details in your plan because they'll influence which funders you can approach. For example, if the main program expense will be making *regrants*, your funder list should consist of those that allow regranting.

DEFINITION

Regrants are grants made by a charity with funds it has raised for that purpose. When seeking a grant to support regrants, be sure the funder allows this—many don't, including many federally funded grants.

Finally, include important deadlines for all activities associated with the program, beginning with grant deadlines, but also including dates for reports, cultivation activities, and any related public programming. When you've completed a funding plan for each program, the deadlines from the funding plan sheets will feed into your grant schedule.

Sample Funding Plan for Evergreen Conservation Society

Program #1

Forest land acquisition

Program staff contact: Henry

Purpose

To preserve native forests through acquisition of extensive first- and second-growth tracts, focusing on land adjacent to the nearby national forest. Benefits to the community include preserved watershed and recreation. Additional benefits include wildlife habitat preservation. Goal is to acquire at least 1,000 acres each year for ten years.

Relationship to past programs

In the early 1990s, Evergreen purchased 2,500 acres south of the city, establishing it as a nature reserve for teaching and passive recreation. That land remains largely in its natural state through Evergreen's management. Funders from that project will be approached for the new one.

Cost

$100,000 to $500,000 each year, depending on the land that is acquired, in direct costs plus $15,000 to $22,000 in personnel and indirect costs each year.

Funders for the first year

$20,000	John Bunyan Foundation (renewal)
$100,000	EPA (requires 2 to 1 match)

$50,000	Wildfowl Society
$ unknown	Major individual donors, including direct land donations (coordinate with major gifts officer)

Funders for subsequent years

Renewals from Bunyan and Wildfowl

Need to find five additional prospects by end of September. Look for capital funders as well as other environmental funders.

Important deadlines and other dates

9/5	Boilerplate proposal completed
9/24	John Bunyan Foundation
10/16	EPA application
11/1	Report to Baumlieber Trust on last year's grant for a feasibility study and legal research

Program #2

Environmental education on the secondary level county wide

Program staff contact: Mary

Purpose

To provide instructors to work with teachers in public and private secondary schools to integrate environmental awareness and knowledge into secondary school curricula. A model curriculum will be made available and the instructors will assist teachers in adapting it for use in various courses. Instructors will also be available to give special lectures during or after school hours.

Relationship to past programs

Evergreen has offered evening classes in environmental studies to an adult lay audience for more than 15 years. Nature talks have been offered at Evergreen's nature preserve to groups of mixed ages since 1998. Last year, a grant from the

Smith Family Foundation made possible the creation of a curriculum for secondary schools, which will serve as the basis for this program.

Cost

$65,000 for instructor fees, coordination by Evergreen's education department, and printing of curriculum materials.

Funders for the first year

$50,000	Community Foundation
$25,000	Frances P. Jones Charitable Trust
$5,000	Local fuel oil distributor
$10,000	Commercial Bank and Trust
$ unknown	Other banks

Funders for subsequent years

Smith Family Foundation: $25,000. Although they paid for the curriculum development, they made it clear they wanted to see other funders make a commitment to the program and would not make another grant this year.

State Department of Education: $50,000 over two years. We just missed this year's deadline due to a delay in completing the curriculum. (They have an 18-month time lag from application to start of grant period.)

Renewals from some first-year funders.

Important deadlines and other dates

9/15	Boilerplate proposal completed.
9/8 and 9/15	Presentations of curriculum at Board of Education program—good education/cultivation opportunity for all potential funders to attend.
9/15	Report to Smith Family Foundation.
9/20	Community Foundation. They have no set deadline, but their next board meeting is in late October, after which they don't meet again until February.
10/1	Meet with fuel oil distributor. Follow up immediately with grant request.
10/3	Frances P. Jones Charitable Trust.

You might not have all the prospects you need for a program (especially for the second and third years) when developing your plan. That's fine, but note the number of funding sources you need to approach and a date when you expect to complete the research to find them. The amounts you request from your prospects should add up to much more than the program cost—not all your proposals will be successful, no matter how good a job you do.

Also note which funders have supported each program or another program at your charity in the past. Remember to include funders for every sector: foundation, corporate, government, and individual major gifts.

For each funder on your schedule, you'll want to compile a prospect worksheet, which summarizes your plan to approach the funder, relevant grants it has made to other organizations, your current and past relationship with the funder, and contact information.

You can download the Funding Plan Worksheet, Grant Schedule Worksheet, and Prospect Worksheet templates at idiotsguides.com under "Book Extras."

Prospect Worksheet

Prospect	
Programs best suited for this funder	
Application Deadline(s)	
Stated interests	

Recent relevant grants	Amount	Organization & purpose of grant

Our funding history with funder	Amount	Program funded

Key contacts @ funder	
Our contacts	

First contact	Date	Method (mail, phone, etc.)	Result

Next contact	Date	Method (mail, phone, etc.)	Result

Notes	

A prospect worksheet helps you keep track of the details on each funder.

Live by Your Schedule

Deadlines are one means by which funders separate serious proposals from those prepared by amateurs. Serious grant writers will be acutely aware of any deadlines and submit their proposals on time—and early whenever possible.

> **WORDS TO THE WISE**
>
> If your proposal will be delivered at the last minute and the funder has strict deadlines (and especially if the funder receives hundreds of proposals), ask for a receipt when the proposal is delivered. They won't mind giving you one, and it will protect you against a misplaced application.

All too often, grant writers create a schedule that targets proposal completion to the funders' deadlines, getting the proposal in just in the nick of time. Doing this makes it impossible for the program officer to give you any feedback and invite you to revise your proposal. Also, if you have to use an expensive messenger service or next-day mail delivery, the funder might see that as a waste of money. At best, it can look amateurish.

Many program officers at all kinds of funders (even government agencies) will look at a draft proposal and offer suggestions. They can't do this if you send it to them when they're the busiest—the week applications are due. Ideally, you should time your applications to arrive one to two months before the deadline, possibly even earlier. This allows plenty of time for review. If you miss a deadline, your proposal is dead. Don't call and ask that an exception be made if you can help it.

A lot of funders have a rolling deadline, which means they accept an application at any time. What this really means is they have no *published* deadlines. These funders, too, have board meetings at which proposals are considered. Try to find out when the program officer would ideally like to receive your proposal so as to present it at the earliest possible board meeting.

It's equally important that grant reports be submitted on time. If your reports to a funder are late, that can put your next proposal in jeopardy. If it looks as if the program staff will need additional time to complete the project, request an extension of the grant period. This requires a progress report, including a budget showing how the funder's grant has been spent so far and what remains to be spent. Request extensions at least two months before the end of the original grant period. (I go over reports in detail in Chapter 21.)

If you're a full-time grant writer, you have dozens of deadlines for proposals and reports to meet during the course of a year. A schedule committed to a calendar can be a lifesaver. The following table presents an example of just such a schedule. Your grant schedule should include all important dates and basic program information organized by kind of activity. (Note that foundations listed here, amounts, and programs they give to are for illustration only and are not meant to reflect any real funding interests.)

The September calendar includes dates in October and even November. Keeping your eye on what's next helps you manage your time, prepare for each activity, and anticipate conflicts.

Grants Schedule for Evergreen Conservation Society: September

Proposal Due Date	Foundation	Purpose	Grant Amount	Staff
9/15	Geese Unlimited	Wetland preservation	$25K	Polly
9/24	John Bunyan Foundation	Land acquisition	$20K	Henry
9/27	F. P. Jones Charit. Trust	Environ. education	$5K	Mary
9/30	Community Foundation	Environ. education	$10K	Mary
10/5	EPA	Land acquisition	$100K	Henry
	(real deadline is 10/16; get all info from Henry by 10/5)			
10/12	Thomas Family Foundation	Gen. operating support (GOS)	$8K	N/A
Looking Ahead:				
11/1	Ford Foundation	Wetland preservation	$100K	Polly
Reports Due:				
9/15	Smith Family Foundation	Environ. education	$35K	Mary
10/1	Baumlieber Trust	Land acquisition	$50K	N/A
Research:				
Five new prospects for EPA matching requirement				
Two new GOS prospects				
New education funder (talk to program officer at Smith Family Foundation for suggestions)				
Review periodicals for current environmental issues to use as background in various proposals				
Cultivation:				
9/8 and 9/15	Presentations of curriculum at Board of Education program			
9/9	Funder tour of forest land under consideration (RSVPs by 9/3); Henry			
9/16	Exec. Director to lunch with Thomas Family Foundation chairman			
10/1	Fall donor newsletter (check with major gifts office on actual availability)			

To Win Friends and Manipulate People

Program people are usually caught up in managing their programs, giving little thought to when new funding proposals need to be submitted and when reports are due. By adhering to your schedule and helping others do so, too, you'll be more likely to keep the money flowing in, which should make everyone happy.

To Save Your Sanity

A grant proposal is not a term paper—there should never be a need for an all-nighter to complete a proposal if you have a clear and accurate schedule. Keeping to your schedule helps you avoid ever having to tell your boss you missed a deadline. Insisting that everyone involved in the grant development and review process stick to the schedule garners respect and makes them appreciate you as a professional. A complete schedule also brings peace of mind, knowing you have everything under control.

> **WORDS TO THE WISE**
>
> If your program people tend to be slow in responding to requests for information, you might want to create artificial deadlines for them well in advance of the real ones. Having a cushion of time saves you all a lot of panic. Be sure to include a second cushion to allow for internal review before you mail the proposal.

The Least You Need to Know

- A funding plan lays out goals, budget, funding prospects, and significant dates for each program.
- Developing a funding plan requires collaboration between development and program staff.
- A grant schedule includes, in calendar form, proposal and report deadlines as well as research and cultivation activities.
- Strive to submit proposals well in advance of the deadline. Early proposals invite helpful comments from a funder's program officers that can result in a revised and stronger proposal.
- Sharing the grant schedule with program staff enhances cooperation and information-sharing.
- If necessary, create artificially early deadlines for program staff to ensure you have information in time to create a successful proposal or grant report.

Writing the Proposal

It's been a long journey, but you're finally ready to write an actual grant proposal. In this part, I go through each element of the proposal—cover letter, executive summary, proposal narrative, budget, and attachments—showing you how to make each part reinforce the others to create a persuasive case for supporting your project.

Do "goals" and "objectives" sound like the same thing to you? They won't after you learn how funders use these terms to evaluate how you will carry out a project. You'll also learn different ways to structure your proposal using my "process" and "outcomes" methods to show it in the best light.

Budgets are the part that most often puzzle people. I show you how to be as eloquent and convincing with numbers as with words. Included are ways to show the valuable contributions volunteers make to your project and how to cover your everyday costs like rent and utilities in every project budget.

The Parts of a Grant Proposal

In This Chapter

- Making a convincing argument for support
- What goes into a program description
- Addressing your proposal to the right audience

When you use the word *proposal*, the program (or project) description is probably what comes to mind. It's the heart and soul of your proposal—the place where you go into all the details about the program's execution as well as its underlying philosophy. Although the pitch you make in the cover letter (see Chapter 16) might more obviously be written to sell your program, don't forget that the program description must reinforce everything you put in the cover letter, continuing to sell the funder on the program and your charity's ability to perform it.

To write a program description that sells, you have to keep in mind what the funder wants to support and balance that against what your charity plans to do. You have to preserve both perspectives through the numerous stages in editing. I show you how to do that, as well as explain the many elements that go into a proposal, in this chapter.

Making the Case for Support

If you want a funder to support your project or organization with a grant, you have to present a convincing argument to bring them to that conclusion. This is known as making the *case for support*. Each element that makes up the project description helps make the case for support.

DEFINITION

The **case for support** is the essential part of any funding request. It engages the reader, explains why the project or organization needs and is worthy of support, and demonstrates the urgency with which funding is needed.

A good case for support immediately captures the reader's imagination, usually with a bold statement of purpose or a surprising fact the reader might not know. It goes on to describe the problem you plan to solve and how your charity will work to solve it. It must also convey a feeling of urgency to make the reader want to give you the grant *right now*.

Good cases for support bear a strong relationship to other types of persuasive writing. In their book *Made to Stick: Why Some Ideas Survive and Others Die*, Chip and Dan Heath sum up their guide to successful writing with the mnemonic "SUCCES," which stands for "simple, unexpected, concrete, credible, emotional, and stories." That's the best summary of how to create good fundraising copy I've ever seen. As you read on, think about how each part of the case for support fulfills one or more aspects of their principle.

Here are the essential parts of the proposal (or case for support):

Purpose of the program. Stated simply, what will the project accomplish?

Why you are doing this project. Why is the program needed? Does any other organization have a similar program? If so, how does what you will do differ? How does your program fit with your charity's mission?

How you will make it happen. What resources (personnel, technical, facility, financial) are needed to carry out the program? What are the steps you'll take to prepare for and to execute the program?

Who will do what. Who will run the program? What staff will be involved, and how much time will each person devote to this project? Will you use consultants? A combination of staff and consultants? What will the roles of each be?

Who will benefit. How many people will the program serve, and who are they? Why is it important to serve these people? Can you illustrate the effects of your program with a story about one of your clients or constituents?

How you will know you've done well. What results do you expect from the program? What are its *goals* and *objectives*? How will you evaluate the program?

DEFINITION

Goals and **objectives** are often spoken about as if they are the same thing, but they're actually quite different. Goals represent what you want to have achieved at the end of a program. Objectives are the measurable steps you need to take to get there. Goals are about the outcome; objectives are about the process.

Summing it all up. Can you sum up the proposal in two or three sentences to leave the funder with a simple picture they can really remember? People tend to skip to the end of documents. Can you use a surprising example here to stick in the reader's memory?

The ability to weave together the answers to these questions into a seamless, readable narrative represents the grant writer's primary skill. In large organizations, different people conduct research, and still others prepare the budgets, but writing the project description remains the province of the grant writer.

The order you present the necessary information can vary, especially if a funder specifies some other order. Always follow the funder's instructions to the letter.

You can use this list of elements as a questionnaire to gather information from the people running the program. You'll probably go back to them several times in the process for more information or clarifications. Be sure to let someone directly involved in carrying out the program read your proposal before you submit it to be sure nothing got lost in the translation.

Now let's look at each part to delve more deeply into what makes a successful grant proposal.

Purpose of the Program

So what is the purpose of your program? You might be able to answer that question in two or three words: alleviate hunger; purchase library books; vaccinate children; find a cure; make a film. Unfortunately, you can't stop there. The funder knows that any number of organizations have programs that work toward the same purpose, so you must show why *your* charity should receive a grant to pursue this goal.

NEWARK PUBLIC LIBRARY
121 HIGH ST.
NEWARK, NY 14513

A strong, even bold, statement of purpose at the beginning of a proposal can grab the reader's attention and set an ambitious tone for the rest of the proposal. For example:

> Community Food Bank will provide two meals daily to 100 homeless people, none of whom are now reached by any other agency.

> Nonprofit managers attending the Managing Your Board workshops will come away with the knowledge and skills to transform their relationships with their boards, resulting in more productive nonprofits throughout the city.

> The music workshops we propose will give the forgotten children in the city's homeless shelters a new sense of identity.

Note that in each of these examples, I used the helper verb *will* instead of *would*. *Will* makes a more positive statement, implying that the project will go forward no matter what. *Would* is weaker, implying that the project is not only conditional on this grant coming through but perhaps on other factors as well.

HOW TO SAY IT

Beginning grant writers often hesitate to make bold, sweeping statements, having been taught in English classes to avoid generalizations and not to make any unsubstantiated statements. Sweeping statements are a means of getting the reader's attention, and although you need to support your assertions somewhere in the proposal, the substantiation doesn't necessarily have to immediately follow your bold declaration.

You should always create a one-sentence summary that describes the project's essence in a way that makes a strong case for funding. And it should be a *really* good sentence! If you can't do that, you don't understand the project well enough to write the proposal. Review your notes and talk again with people involved in the program until you can write one dynamite sentence.

A good accompaniment for your bold statement (and possibly preceding it) is a dramatic and surprising statistic related to your project, such as:

> 2,800 adults and 1,200 children in our city go to sleep hungry every night.

> 98 percent of nonprofit executives identify working productively with their boards as one of their top three issues.

> The 400 children living in our city's largest homeless shelter have no access to after-school activities.

Why You Are Doing This Project

One of the critical points you have to make concerns the *need* for your program. The funder wants to know you have a thorough knowledge of the issue you seek to address and how what you propose to do fits in with what others are doing or have done. Is your approach different or complementary? Why is it needed? In what way will the program aid the program's clients? What would they do if your program didn't exist?

DEFINITION

Need is one of those nonprofit words that gets bandied about in many guises. Every project must fulfill some need, but every grant award is not "need based." Need-based grants use the need of the applicant as the primary or sole criteria in deciding on the award. Disaster relief grants are an example. Your proposals will mostly be for merit-based awards. You'll not only have to demonstrate your clients' needs, but also why your charity merits the award.

The need for the program should resonate with your charity's mission. Just because you're a good organization and the community has a need doesn't mean your charity is the best one to address that need. Explain how this program fits in with everything else you do.

Proposals that are too inward looking—that is, concentrated too much on what your charity needs—are doomed to failure in most cases. Proposals that focus on clients' needs—the people you will help—stand a much better chance of success. Remember: funders make grants to solve a problem other than helping you make your budget goal.

Never trash the competition in your proposal. Today's competitor is tomorrow's panelist deciding the fate of your grant proposal. It's also not polite or necessary. That's not to say you shouldn't contrast your approach to that of other organizations, but you should do so in a way that offends no one. For example, you'll say …

> The Community Food Bank will provide meals to 100 people daily who are now being missed by other social service providers.

Or:

> The Community Food Bank will provide meals to 100 people daily who are unable to get transportation to food services offered by other social service providers.

Either version is much more positive than "The Community Food Bank will provide meals to 100 people daily who Food for People does not reach because of its unwillingness to look outside its immediate neighborhood."

You can make your need statement stronger by including in your proposal statements from neutral third parties that express or reinforce the need you seek to address. These could be stories in the press or studies groups other than your charity have done, including studies commissioned by funders. This not only gives greater credence to your cause, it also shows that your charity sees itself as part of the larger issue and that it keeps abreast of the latest thought on a subject. Here are a couple of examples:

> *The Daily Times* reported that Mayor Thomas stated in his speech to the Rotary Club last week that "hunger remains one of the city's most pressing problems, especially among the transient population that lives on the fringes of the industrial area." Community Food Bank agrees, which is why we approach the distribution of meals through a mobile facility rather than depending on our main office to handle all clients.

> Social Think Tank, Inc., in its report issued last month, drew attention to the difficulty that traditional place-based food banks have in reaching the most needy populations, which tend to exist outside central urban areas where most of these agencies are located. Community Food Bank agrees, which is why ….

Testimonials to your charity's ability to carry out a project will also strengthen your case for support. We look at how to do that in detail in Chapter 17.

How You Will Make It Happen

You have to give the funder a concrete description of how the program will work. Be as specific as possible without putting too many limitations on your program staff. Will you meet with each client five times? How many hot lunches will you distribute? What are the steps your literacy program follows to involve adults and children? Let's look at a couple of short examples:

> The Managing Your Board workshop series will consist of four weekly sessions, each lasting two hours. Workshops will begin with a lecture by an expert in board and executive director issues followed by a question-and-answer period. During the final half hour of each session, participants will

break down into groups of 10 or fewer to discuss what they have learned in practical terms that relate to their organizations. The themes of the workshops will be Avoiding Micromanagement, Helping a Board Fundraise, Making the Executive Director's Performance Review Work for You, and Building the Board You Need.

The Music for Kids program will provide musical instruction to young people living in the city's largest homeless shelter. Transportation will be provided to our partner's recreational facility after school two days each week. The emphasis will be on rhythm and simple songs, rather than trying to teach them how to read music. This remains a transient population requiring short-term goals each of the young people can meet. Most of the 90-minute sessions will be devoted to working all together, but there will be time each day for more personalized attention from the teaching assistants.

HOW TO SAY IT

Never underestimate the power of negative writing. Any negativity in your proposal about a past failure to meet a goal or frequent personnel transitions at your nonprofit will cast enough doubt to sink your proposal. Be honest by all means, but keep it positive.

Note that both paragraphs briefly describe the format of the sessions, give information on the content, and give the time participants will be involved in the programs. A real proposal would go into additional detail. You might also want to include a month-by-month time line to show how the different steps in a program will come together.

When deciding how technical you can be in your proposal, take into consideration who will be reading it. You want to give details and examples the reader will understand. In general, proposals reviewed by peer panels can include more technical language than ones that will be seen only by foundation trustees who may or may not possess technical knowledge related to your proposal.

Also take into consideration other grantees of the funder and any other nonprofit connections the funder's trustees might have and how your proposal might affect them. An online service for which I was raising funds, on face value, might have appeared to compete with services offered by other grantees of a particular funder.

I was careful in the cover letter and the proposal to describe in detail how our new service would drive people to the websites of the other grantees rather than taking clients away from them.

Do not mention anyone or any organization as participating in your program without clearing it with them first. This is especially true if a peer panel will evaluate your proposal. When writing your proposal, keep in mind whom those people might be. If your proposal calls for working with other organizations (or even just using their mailing lists), give examples that include some of the potential panelists if possible. Be especially sure you don't criticize any other organization.

HOW TO SAY IT

Don't let too many details take away the flexibility the program staff will need to run the program. Don't say "We will hire John Jones as our management consultant." Instead say, "We will hire a management consultant such as John Jones, Mary Chin, or Thomas Brown."

Who Will Do What?

The funder will also want to know who will carry out the program. Will your staff do everything, or will you use outside consultants? It's critical that the staffing described in this section exactly matches the staffing detailed in your program budget. You needn't get too specific, but give them an idea of where the responsibilities will lie.

You want to build in the reasoning for participation by staff members at various levels. Will the executive director be involved in program development or execution in any way? If so, you can allocate a small part of his salary to this project. (After you've done that for enough programs, you've gotten your boss's salary paid for through restricted grants!)

The staffing sections of the two programs described previously might read like this:

> The director of programs will select the consultants who will lead the workshops in consultation with other members of the program staff and from referrals from colleagues at other service organizations. Program staff will manage the enrollment of the workshop sessions and be present at each workshop to assist with the breakout groups. One consultant will lead each of the first three workshops, with two consultants jointly leading the final session.

Our education staff will provide the musical instruction throughout the program. They will be supervised by the director of programming and the director of education; both will assist in creating the lesson plans and review progress with the instructors weekly. We will be paying a fee to our partner organization for the use of their bus and bus driver. We will also pay the custodial staff at the partner facility from program funds.

> **WORDS TO THE WISE**
>
> Use the names of staff or consultants when they're well known or are included in a "key staff" attachment. Otherwise, you're just as well off using more general descriptions like "program staff" or "clinicians" to allow greater flexibility in the program's execution and still make it clear to the reader who is doing what.

Who Will Benefit

Who will benefit from the program is, of course, *the* important part of a program description. Foundations and other funders seek to solve some social problem, whether it's hunger, literacy, access to the arts, or helping nonprofits work better. In submitting a proposal, you are volunteering to help them solve one of their problems. Focusing on the needs of the ultimate beneficiaries of the program (rather than on your charity) will resonate more strongly with the funder's "problems."

Emotional stories about the people your project serves enrich this section. Even a short anecdote gives your proposal a human dimension the reader can respond to compassionately.

This section must also include some cold, hard facts about how many people you will serve and how well you will serve them. To corporate and some other funders, the numbers make a huge difference in judging the worthiness of your proposal. Giving exact numbers before the program even begins is impossible, but you can give ranges.

You might feel you need to inflate the number of people who will be served to make the funder feel like it will be getting its money's worth. Don't! Those numbers will come back to haunt you when it's time to report on your results. But don't give numbers that are too low, either, or funders might think the program isn't cost-effective.

Funders realize that different kinds of projects are more efficient than others and that efficiency is not the sole judge of worthiness. A website might cost $50,000 to make and reach 250,000 people or 20 cents per person, whereas a workshop series might cost $50,000 and serve 100 people or $500 per person, but in a much more direct and personal way. The value of the program is not just in the math—it's in the ability of your charity to deliver a program that accomplishes its goals and serves a worthy purpose.

How You Will Know You've Done Well

Program evaluation should be an integral part of everything your charity does. How else will you be able to show others that you have done the job well, if people benefit enough to justify the expense, and if the program should continue? A lot of charities coast along with only anecdotal evidence of program success. These charities eventually get an unwelcome surprise when a funder starts asking hard questions.

Lack of a current outside evaluation has prevented me more than once from approaching several foundations that insist on a third-party analysis of a program. One of these foundations seldom makes grants less than $50,000, so it's easy to see how a $20,000 professional evaluation would pay for itself in short order.

Don't let your charity be one of those getting caught short. Talk to program staff about evaluating their programs at various stages. Evaluations can be as simple as a survey given to each participant or as complicated as a multi-month study by an outside evaluator. Find the appropriate solution that best suits your program (and fundraising) needs.

HOW TO SAY IT

Funders won't judge your program solely on the numbers—the ability of your charity to deliver a program that accomplishes its goals and serves a worthy purpose is much more important. But do supply whatever *realistic* numbers you can to provide an idea of the scope of your program.

Just as your program evaluation needs to be carefully considered, so does the way you describe it in the proposal. Don't say you'll use an outside evaluator (which is usually expensive) unless you know your charity will do it.

Don't try to hide the lack of evaluative procedures by giving some vague statement of your charity's belief in evaluation like "Our charity follows a rigorous evaluative process to assess the efficacy of all programs through surveys, interviews with participants, focus groups, and independent evaluators." That's all well and good, but how will you evaluate *this* program? A sound evaluation provides excellent material for all future proposals.

Nothing in the project description should deviate from the sole purpose of generating interest and enthusiasm for the project. Don't get sidetracked recounting your charity's history or describing other programs.

For the workshop series on How to Manage Your Board described earlier in this chapter, an evaluation plan might read like this:

> Short surveys will be provided to participants at the end of each session in which they will be asked to grade the speaker, the content, and the overall workshop on a five-point scale. They will also be asked for information about themselves and the organizations for which they work so that *cross-tab* reports can be prepared to assess the program from many angles. We will also interview workshop leaders to gain insights from their point of view. Subsequent workshop series will be modified should the analysis of this data indicate a need for a different approach or different instructors. The cross-tab reports will also help focus the marketing and outreach for future programs.

DEFINITION

Cross-tabs are tabulations of one set of data in terms of another set of data. In the example here, that might mean counting the number of people from large charities rating the workshop excellent and comparing it to the number from small charities giving it an excellent rating to see which group was better served by the workshops. You should familiarize yourself with some of the jargon of the evaluation world before getting too deeply involved in describing evaluations in your proposals. The Management Assistance Program for Nonprofits offers a free guide to program evaluation and more at mapnp.org.

Given the ages of the participants in the music workshops for homeless children (also described in this chapter), surveys would not be as effective a method of evaluation. In this case, an evaluation from the charity's director of education might be best, especially if you can show that she has a background that allows her to do this objectively.

Summing It All Up

At the end of your proposal, clearly sum it all up for the reader. The summary should usually be no more than one or two paragraphs and should include …

- A moving argument for funding your proposal stated differently from elsewhere in the proposal (which includes both needs and the results).

- A restatement of the amount of the grant you're requesting.

- A thank you for considering your proposal.

This is where you want the reader to hear the violins soar and see the cowboy ride off into the sunset. *This is your big ending.* Make it a good one. Here's an example:

> Life in a shelter for homeless families is especially hard on the children. Going to school provides some respite, but often the school day simply exchanges one institutional environment for another. Music for Kids will ensure that for at least three hours each week, as many as 60 kids living in these shelters will be taken out of the institutional environment and out of themselves through music.
>
> Individual and small group instruction will provide much-needed personal attention, and group singing will encourage community and cooperation. Such simple activities have an enormous potential to assist these young people, as has been shown in the recent study by Urban Educators Conference. Thank you for considering our $20,000 grant request. It will make all this possible for these lost citizens of our city.

A common question is "how long should the proposal be?" Without being facetious, the answer is "as long as it needs to be." Some funders impose limits on length (as little as 3 pages), but I've written 15-page proposals that (at least to me) didn't seem long. The important thing is to stay focused on the project and avoid any tangents. If the proposal will be more than five pages, you might want to include a table of contents, and you'll definitely want section headers to help the funder's staff skim through to find particular information.

The Least You Need to Know

- If you can't sum up a project in one persuasive sentence, you don't understand it well enough to write a proposal.

- Making a clear case for supporting your charity includes information on what problems you seek to solve, how you will solve them, who will work on the project, and most importantly, who will benefit from it.

- Proposals that focus on your clients' or constituents' needs are stronger than those that stress the needs of your nonprofit.

- Take into consideration who will be reading your proposal when deciding how technical you can be in describing how you will carry it out.

- Use concrete methods for evaluating a program you know you will be able to include in your report to the funder.

- Use a moving closing section to reinforce the key points in the proposal and repeat "the ask."

Selling Your Project

In This Chapter

- Identifying your project with funders' interests
- Writing a jargon-free proposal
- Different ways to structure a proposal
- The special case of the operating support proposal

In Chapter 9, I touched on customizing your proposal to match a funder's interests. In this chapter, I provide in-depth examples, and I show you how to move beyond parroting back the funder's language to make a more convincing case.

Having taken you through the different parts of a proposal in the preceding chapter, here I show you how to use one of two different methods to give a focus to the proposal while incorporating all those parts. One method concentrates on the process used to carry out a program, and the other stresses the results. I also help you decide which method is right for your proposal.

The preceding chapter and most of this chapter's material help you write program proposals, but what about proposals for general operating support (GOS)? GOS proposals need a different approach, so I've included a special section on them in this chapter. The other special case I present for your consideration is the use of jargon, which can take the life right out of an otherwise excellent proposal.

Making a Persuasive Argument for Each Funder

Making the proposal fit the funder is where you really turn a project description into a grant proposal. Starting with the description you and the program staff have agreed on, you'll use all you learned during your research to create a new description that expresses the project in a way that will get it funded.

You'll modify your base description for each funder to appeal to its specific interests. You'll also include references to any past funding of similar projects and anything else that will build recognition on the part of each reader.

> **WORDS TO THE WISE**
>
> Don't sink your proposal with a word-processing error. There's no excuse for sending out a proposal to one funder with a different funder's name in the project description. Keep a clean, unmodified version of your project description—free of any funder's name or specific interests—to use as the starting point for all proposals.

Before going any further, make a checklist of all the elements each funder requires, both in the proposal and as attachments. As you develop each proposal, refer to these lists and use the checklists again for your final sign-off.

Let's look at a few examples of customization based on the slightly differing interests of three funders. (You might also want to review the examples in Chapter 9 as illustrations of how to tie your proposal to grantmakers' interests.)

First, take a look at the main section from a proposal for a literacy program that everyone concerned with the project at the charity has reviewed and which is ready to go.

> The Ralph Goodson Literacy Project works with young people and their families in the inner city to promote literacy and the pursuit of knowledge. We do this through three initiatives.
>
> (1) To develop a love of reading in the early years, we sponsor story times at daycare centers. Volunteers read to the 2- to 5-year-olds twice a week. Art projects based on the stories extend the children's interests. Older children can take home copies of the stories they have heard to share with their families.

(2) We also work with children in grades K–3 to develop reading skills to further learning in all subjects. After-school tutoring ensures that each child will reach or exceed his grade-appropriate reading level. Students are encouraged to complete writing exercises about what they have read to further develop skills and learn to express themselves in writing.

(3) Studies have found that reading skills must be cultivated at home to become engrained. Too often, parents lack good reading skills themselves. Volunteer tutors work with entire families on reading skills in one of our four centers or, in some cases, make house calls for the more difficult-to-reach families.

We have found that this holistic approach provides the best environment over a sustained period to develop advanced reading skills in children from any background.

The following excerpts are from the guidelines of three real foundations, after which you'll find the preceding program description modified to match those interests. I've italicized passages that have been changed and used ellipses (…) to indicate that the remainder of a paragraph would be repeated unchanged from the basic description.

Foundation 1. "Helping children and youth develop the skills and experiences they need to reach their full potential."

The Ralph Goodson Literacy Project works with young people and their families in the inner city to promote literacy and the pursuit of knowledge. We do this through three initiatives.

(1) *For each child to have the opportunity to develop into the best person and citizen he or she can be, a love of reading must be established in the earliest years. The Literacy Project sponsors* story times at day-care centers *to achieve this.* Volunteers read to the 2- to 5-year-olds twice a week. …

(2) We also work with children in grades K–3 to develop reading skills to further learning in all subjects *and ensure continued development.* …

(3) …

We have found that this holistic approach provides the best environment over a sustained period to develop advanced reading skills in children from any background. *After being equipped with the marvelous skill to read anything put before them, the students participating in this program have unlimited opportunities available to them, no matter what their field of endeavor.*

Foundation 2. "Development of a broader knowledge base ... so students make the transition from learning to read to reading to learn."

The Ralph Goodson Literacy Project works with young people and their families in the inner city to promote literacy and the pursuit of knowledge. We do this through three initiatives.

(1) To develop a love of reading in the early years, we sponsor story times at day-care centers. Volunteers read to the 2- to 5-year-olds twice a week. [The remainder of this paragraph was omitted for this funder.]

(2) We also work with children in grades K–3 to develop reading skills to *help them move from simply learning to read to applying their reading skills to every subject they study.* After-school tutoring ensures that each child will reach or exceed his grade-appropriate reading level, *working with them to read and comprehend texts in many subject areas. ...*

(3) ...

We have found that this holistic approach provides the best environment over a sustained period to develop advanced reading skills in children from any background. *After being equipped with the marvelous skill to read anything put before them, the students participating in this program have unlimited opportunities available to them, no matter what their field of endeavor.*

Foundation 3. "Stimulate personal development and encourage commitment to social equity ... through writing, literacy, and the promotion of the voices of youth."

The Ralph Goodson Literacy Project works with young people and their families in the inner city to promote literacy and the pursuit of knowledge. We do this through three initiatives.

(1) To develop a love of reading in the early years, we sponsor story times at day-care centers. Volunteers read to the 2- to 5-year-olds twice a week. Art projects based on the stories extend the children's interests *and encourage them to tell their own stories.* Older children can take home copies of the stories they have heard to share with their families.

(2) We also work with children in grades K–3 to develop reading skills to further learning in all subjects. After-school tutoring ensures that each child will reach or exceed his grade-appropriate reading level. Students are encouraged to complete writing exercises about what they have read to further develop skills and learn to express themselves *creatively* in writing.

(3) Studies have found that reading skills must be cultivated at home to become engrained. Too often, parents lack good reading skills themselves. Volunteer tutors work with entire families on reading skills in one of our four centers or, in some cases, make house calls for the more difficult-to-reach families. *By working to improve the reading skills of the entire family, the program makes it possible for the adults to participate more equitably in society and ensures that their children will have opportunities to do so as well.*

We have found that this holistic approach provides the best environment over a sustained period to develop advanced reading skills in children from any background *and to bring more children and families into the mainstream of American society.*

Each version speaks to the funder's interests without parroting back the same language. Some points get expanded for one funder, while other points get condensed for another. The actual program, however, remains the same.

Buzz, Buzz, Buzzwords

I couldn't write this chapter without addressing the scourge of grant writing—jargon. A few years ago, consultant Tony Proscio wrote a much-discussed booklet, *In Other Words*, about the use of jargon in the foundation world. He took particular exception to terms such as *at-risk* for its vagueness (at risk of what?); *capacity* for its overuse, especially when not referring to something measurable; *proactive* when *preparatory* or *preemptive* would be more precise; and many other buzzwords.

PHILANTHROPY FACT

You can download Tony Proscio's book-length essay *In Other Words,* and its sequels, *Bad Words for Good* and *When Words Fail,* at the Communication Network's website (comnetwork.org/node/620). You'll find they breathe fresh air into your writing.

Proscio's booklet points out how using buzzwords reduces clarity. Describing your project in your own words is always best. Some people advise throwing the funder's jargon back at them in your proposal. I think this just shows a lack of imagination and a superficial understanding at best. The more you can get beyond buzzwords and to the heart of what the funder wants to support, the more successful you'll be.

If a funder's guidelines state that their interests lie in "pedagogical initiatives designed to stimulate systemic change" it's fine for you to write that your project "seeks to develop new teaching methods that will transform the way teachers relate to their students." The funder will see that you understood their jargon-filled interest statement but have a mind of your own.

Even though you'll want to avoid funder buzzwords whenever possible, it's even more important to avoid your charity's internal jargon. Nonprofits become mired in program names and acronyms along with technical language peculiar to each of them. Don't use any of this in your proposals. I know you'll probably be stuck with whatever name your charity calls a program, but after first stating that name, you can thereafter refer to it in simpler terms.

Acronyms can be off-putting to someone trying to understand your organization. Even if your charity uses acronyms, try to stay away from them in your grant proposals. If you need a shorthand term for a long program title, use one or two words from the title rather than the acronym, and the reader will understand what you mean. For example, "Ecology Education for Tomorrow's Leaders" could easily be referred to as "Ecology Education" and is more understandable than "EETL." Never sacrifice clarity for insiders' lingo.

> **WORDS TO THE WISE**
>
> Chances are, your charity loves using acronyms for program names, but acronyms are the worst form of jargon. They attempt to give those in the know a special feeling of inclusion, but they also give those not in the know a feeling of exclusion.

Your teacher-training course might be known within your charity as Training Talented Teachers to Teach Better or T4B (ugh), but you don't have to use the cute acronym, and you could also refer to it simply as "our teacher training program."

Process Versus Outcomes

Chances are, the first draft of the proposal was all about the *process*, that is, how the program will be carried out. The *outcomes* method, in contrast, focuses on the results anticipated at the end of the program. I usually prefer to use the outcomes method because I can grab the reader's attention with the anticipated results and express my enthusiasm for the project right up front. When I later describe the steps leading to the glorious outcome, the reader has a reference point for each step in the process.

> **DEFINITION**
>
> **Process** and **outcomes** are the macro versions of goals and objectives, mentioned in Chapter 13. To decide which method to use to organize your proposal, ask yourself what will be more interesting to the reader: the process by which you will carry out the program or the results (outcomes) you expect to achieve.

Outcome-focused proposals are particularly effective when you're seeking a grant to continue an existing program. You can use all the program's accomplishments thus far to bolster your case for the grant. Preparing a proposal this way is similar to the general operating support proposal described later in this chapter.

In some cases the process method is best, especially if you're developing a new method of performing a service or one where the outcomes might not be dramatic. For example, a project description for a program that works with severely disabled children might concentrate on the process. The outcomes might not be dramatic in themselves, but the ways the clinicians work with the kids day after day to effect incremental changes over a very long period might well make a moving story.

A process-focused proposal can also be effective with a relatively new program for which measurable outcomes are not yet available. Here's an abbreviated program description for just such a program using the process method.

Program Description Using the Process Method

The Curatorial Internship program seeks to increase opportunities for minority art historians to become curators with major museums. Art museums have long been perceived as bastions of WASP culture and the preserve of the wealthy. The old saying goes that the first qualification to becoming a curator is an independent income. At City Art Museum, we believe this represents outmoded thinking that is out of step, not only with the times but also with the art we collect.

City Art Museum will recruit candidates for this program through outreach to universities with large minority student bodies and through referrals from a wide variety of galleries and alternative art spaces. Interns will work closely with a number of departments within the museum to gain practical experience in the range of activities in which professional curators must be proficient.

Learning by Observation

Interns will assist museum curators in mounting at least one major exhibition each year. The interns will be part of the entire process, from assembling the exhibition checklist to hanging the art works. In addition, they will be involved in the research that goes into planning exhibitions for future years. The research will encompass working with the development department to craft grant proposals, visiting private collections, and providing detailed research working with the museum's registrar and librarian.

Learning by Teaching

Today's curator must also be an educator. The modern museum expects curators to be able to communicate with a variety of audiences to engage them with the art on view. The interns will actively participate in the museum's education program for young people and adults under the supervision of the curator for education. We believe the interns will be particularly effective in working with the preteens who form a large part of our arts-in-the-schools programming. Being nearer in age to the students than typical docents and in many cases more closely matching the ethnic makeup of the schools, the interns will have a unique opportunity to engage the students with the mostly Western art we collect. Interns will also lead some special tours for museum members.

Learning by Doing

All the preparation in the world will not build an intern's resumé as much as credit for curating an exhibition. Using our new alternative space for twenty-first-century art, each intern will curate an exhibition at the end of his or her second year using works from the museum's permanent collection along with contemporary works the intern has selected from artists in our studio program.

By thoroughly immersing the interns in the workings of the museum, we will help them build a resumé that will get the notice of any museum director to whom they apply for work. The curators for whom the interns work will serve as their mentors for at least two years after they leave our program to help them in their career development, offering advice and making personal connections when possible.

The actual proposal covering the previous material would be about four pages, which would be filled out with background on past programs and on the curatorial process, specific examples of work that would be done, and quotes from past participants and curators. The proposal gives the reader a feeling for how the interns would work, but the specific outcomes of each section are left pretty much to the imagination.

This is very similar to a proposal I once wrote that received a major grant, so the approach works. But now let's look at a condensed proposal for the same program using the outcomes method.

Program Description Using the Outcomes Method

The Curatorial Internship program seeks to increase opportunities for minority art historians to become curators with major museums. Art museums have long been perceived as bastions of WASP culture and the preserve of the wealthy. The old saying goes that the first qualification to becoming a curator is an independent income. At City Art Museum, we believe this represents outmoded thinking that is out of step, not only with our times but also with the art we collect.

City Art Museum will recruit candidates for this program through outreach to universities with large minority student bodies and through referrals from a wide variety of galleries and alternative art spaces. We will choose three interns each year to work closely with a number of departments within the museum to gain practical experience in the range of activities in which professional curators must be proficient.

Interns will sharpen the research, communication, organization, and diplomacy skills needed to be a modern curator. Coming up with the concept for an exhibition can be the easy part. Curators must also be prepared to articulate the exhibition for use in grant proposals and press releases. The laborious process of piecing together works of art from many public and private sources requires in-depth knowledge of how to conduct scholarly research into the location of the works and their provenance. Curators also must exhibit diplomatic skills in working with the owners of the art works. Interns will make contacts through this process that will benefit them throughout their careers. Interns will assist curators as they go about these tasks and others in the mounting of one exhibition each year.

Interns will curate an exhibition at the museum's alternative space for twenty-first-century art in their second year, gaining a major resumé credit and putting to use all they have learned by assisting. Until one has actually received credit for curating an exhibition, the only positions open will be those of assistants. When curating exhibitions, interns will have the full resources of the museum behind them, as well as their curator mentors to turn to for advice and assistance. The curators will, in fact, continue to mentor the interns for at least two years after they leave the program, providing advice and exposure in a wide variety of museum and gallery opportunities. The effect of this program will only be evident after a period of years. For this reason, we will maintain contact with the interns for at least five years to assess their professional success.

Interns will gain advanced skills in imparting their knowledge to a variety of audiences. Modern curators must be willing and able to engage a number of different audiences with the art they love. Interns will visit classes in the schools and guide the preteen students through exhibitions. Just as a curator must be prepared to cajole a reluctant art owner to part with a painting for an exhibition, a curator must also be skilled in speaking to groups of art collectors and museum donors. By giving exhibition tours to membership groups, interns will gain these skills as well.

Interns who complete this two-year program will gain significant experience that will make them more employable, as well as connections with curators and art collectors that will benefit them for years to come.

Whichever approach you determine is best for your proposal, you still need to cover all the parts of a proposal described in Chapter 13.

Operating Support Proposals

The project description for a proposal seeking GOS would technically include everything your agency does. If your charity does only one or two things, you may be able to use the process method to describe each of them in a GOS proposal. Otherwise, the outcomes method is your only practical choice. The project description for a GOS proposal will frequently read much like a report on the previous year's activities. You can use a list of notable accomplishments from the previous year as a starting point for briefly describing how you will achieve similar outcomes in the current year. Here are some examples:

Information Services provided assistance to some 380,000 artists in all disciplines last year through publications, Internet resources, and a toll-free hotline. In the coming year, we expect the number of artists served to increase significantly through the introduction of a new database of opportunities for artists that we will promote nationally through announcements on public radio stations.

Public school students had the opportunity to work with artists in their classrooms through the Arts in Education program last year. Some 3,000 students were served through 20 residencies in 18 cities. We have modified this program for next year to allow the residencies to expand beyond the schools to involve members of the local community. By creating interactions among the students, community residents, and the artists, we seek to effect a more long-lasting change on how art and artists are perceived by members of the public.

WORDS TO THE WISE

Don't neglect a bold opening statement for your GOS proposal. Don't be shy. State clearly and succinctly what good your charity does at the beginning of the proposal (and in the cover letter) to get their attention and provide a focus for your GOS proposal.

Create a paragraph such as one of the preceding for each of your programs, add a strong introduction and closing, and you've got yourself a GOS proposal. This approach is a lot more interesting than operating support proposals I've seen that consist of an organization's history with a few recent statistics sprinkled in. Don't confuse your charity's history with a GOS proposal. A GOS proposal is about the present and future, *not* the past.

Even if the GOS proposal seeks support for everything you do, you don't have to describe every single program and activity with the same level of detail. Keep the proposal focused on what will be of interest to the funder. And just because it's a GOS proposal doesn't mean you won't customize it for each funder. If the funder makes a lot of education grants and one of your programs involves education, move that section to the top. In some cases, you might expand on some sections to suit the funder's primary area of interest or add statistics that correspond with the funder's geographic target area.

> **WORDS TO THE WISE**
>
> Using boilerplate text is more common for GOS proposals, but you'll better serve your charity if you customize each one. This might just involve changing the order so the program of greatest interest to each specific funder comes first.

One GOS funder I deal with has a three-county area as its primary service area, even though it provides funding much more widely. They ask for, and I give them, the numbers of people in their primary service area we've assisted at the end of each program's description in the GOS proposal.

Last Call

By this point, program and executive staff have edited the basic proposal. Before putting it into the mail, it's a very good idea to have someone read over it one last time. If someone at your charity has not yet read the proposal but understands the program you're seeking funding for, that person would be ideal to give it a look now. A fresh pair of eyes can catch jargon and those fatal word-processing errors that allow language and names from past proposals to creep into new ones.

The Least You Need to Know

- Customize every proposal for every funder.
- Avoid buzzwords—both those of the funder and of your charity—and acronyms that might confuse the reader.
- Organize proposals using the outcomes method whenever possible to stress the effect the project will have.
- Organize proposals using the process method when the outcomes might be small in comparison with the process needed to achieve them.
- General operating support (GOS) proposals can use a list of recent accomplishments as starting points for present and future program descriptions.
- Give everyone involved in the program (including executive staff) a chance to review the final draft of your first completed proposal on a project.

Chapter 15

Dollars and Cents

In This Chapter

- What to include in a budget
- Telling your story in numbers
- How administrative personnel costs fit into a program budget
- Dealing with indirect expenses
- Explaining the big numbers

A budget is an integral part of a grant proposal. Many funders go right from the cover letter to the budget to see how it fits with what you propose to do. Program officers and others working for funders might see hundreds of budgets for programs similar to yours. Usually they can quickly spot an inconsistency, so don't take the budget casually.

The most important thing to remember about budgets is that they should answer the funder's questions—not provoke questions. This chapter is devoted to helping you answer questions through a clear presentation of the important numbers related to your grant proposal.

Budget Basics

The way you present a budget is just as important as what you put in it. Jargon is as out of place here as it is anywhere else in your proposal. You'll want to label each expense as clearly as possible. Large amounts listed as "miscellaneous" or "other costs" will send up red flags, so don't use these terms.

Grouping together similar expenses and subtotaling them makes it easier for the funder to evaluate the relationship between aspects of the budget. At minimum, use subtotals for personnel, direct expenses, and indirect expenses. Depending on the nature of the program, you might further group expenses to show mailing and distribution costs (if your program involves a publication, a marketing campaign, or some similar project) or different types of consultant fees (if you will use a number of different kinds of consultants).

Your budget deserves careful consideration, because it will be an integral part of the contract that results from a successful grant proposal. You'll eventually report on the finances as well as what happened programmatically.

A really well-prepared budget tells a story as clearly as a narrative description. You were probably taught that "Who, What, When, Where, Why, and How" all should be explained in a good newspaper story. I like to use those same headings to help remember what goes into a good project budget. (Except for "Why," which I've not yet found a way to explain with numbers, but I'm working on it!)

Who

Funders want to know who will be involved in carrying out a project, so this is an important part of every budget. Staff, consultants, and volunteers all have a place in this part of your budget. In thinking about staff, don't forget support staff and supervisory staff. They may spend only a fraction of their time on a project, but some portion of their salaries should be included.

And think about what you'd have to pay people to do the work of your volunteers. If you include volunteers in your staffing, list them on a separate line and put a corresponding line for the same amount in the Income section of the budget as donated services.

PHILANTHROPY FACT

Salaries at nonprofits became headline news several years ago when the exorbitant salaries of a very few executives were made public. Since then, the public perception has seemed to be guilty until proven innocent. There's a much greater expectation today that charities will make this information readily available, however uncomfortable it might make nonprofit executives.

I'll Take 75 Percent of a Program Officer and ...

Seldom will you actually use an employee's full salary in a program budget. It's a fact of nonprofit life that most of us have a variety of duties that cross a number of program areas. More typically, you'll have a listing such as the following:

Executive director (10 percent)	$12,000
Program director (30 percent)	$29,000
Program officer (75 percent)	$32,000

The percentages reflect the amount of each employee's time spent on the program. Always include them to help the funder understand how the program will be staffed. You'll need to consult with the person in charge of the program to get an idea of what percentages to use. If he has trouble coming up with a percentage, ask him how many days a week he'll spend on the program. You can use that to determine the percentage (1 day a week = 20 percent).

If you're including volunteers in your budget, value their time for what you would have had to pay someone to do the job.

Fringe Benefits

The bane of nonprofit budgets these days is fringe benefits. Insurance rates of all types seem to go up and up, so it's only fair that a funder who's paying part of someone's salary cover a proportionate amount of her fringe benefits. Your charity probably has an average number to use for fringe benefits (possibly 20 percent or even more). Get this from your finance staff, and use it consistently in all applications. (You don't need to worry about who signed up for the dental plan and who didn't; an average rate will do.)

The Full Personnel Budget

Your proposal will need a detailed personnel budget, showing how the program will be staffed, including all consultants.

Personnel Budget	
Executive director (10 percent)	$12,000
Program director (30 percent)	$29,000
Program officer (75 percent)	$35,000
Program assistants (2 @ 50 percent)	$40,000
Subtotal	$116,000
Fringe (@ 20 percent)	<u>$24,200</u>
Total salaried personnel	**$140,200**
Part-time instructors (3)	$60,000
Evaluator	<u>$45,000</u>
Total consultants	**$105,000**
TOTAL PERSONNEL	**$245,200**

This presentation clearly shows how much time the charity's staff will spend on the program and what parts of the program they'll entrust to outside contractors (consultants).

Typically, only small portions of higher-level staff members' salaries will be attributed to a single program. Obviously, these are the people with the widest responsibilities. For example, attributing 30 percent of the executive director's time to a program would raise eyebrows at the funder unless yours is a very small agency with few programs and where the executive director actively participates in programs on a daily basis. Including small parts of high-level employees, however, is good budgeting that contributes to your charity's bottom line.

WORDS TO THE WISE

Personnel expenses are one of the fuzzier items (or fungible numbers) in a budget. That your executive director has something to do with most programs is obvious; the exact amount of time she spends on each program is less clear. The ability to find ways to include operating expenses (such as administrative salaries) in a program budget creatively is a talent highly valued by every executive director.

Unfortunately, you can never include any of your time or that of any other development staff in program budgets. The only exceptions are capital campaign budgets because raising money is one of the major activities of the campaign. If, of course, fundraising staff perform other functions (such as marketing), you can include their time, but refer to the position according to its function (marketing, for example) rather than fundraising.

Many nonprofit employees don't realize that the salaries of the five most highly paid employees making $100,000 or more are listed in their charity's 990 IRS information form. (On forms prior to 2009, charities had to list salaries of $50,000 or more.) What your top people make is part of the public record (and available for all to see on the Internet at sites such as GuideStar), but people remain naturally sensitive about having their salaries revealed. For small nonprofits that don't file a 990 form, executive salaries remain private, but some funders will ask you to include them as part of your proposal.

As a grant writer, you're privy to information on salaries and other costs; maintaining the confidentiality of this information is your responsibility. If you need to circulate the budget for review by program staff, black out the salary details, leaving only the total personnel amount visible. You might also put a blacked-out version in your files as part of the final proposal.

What—Direct Expenses

The expenses you will itemize are those that relate directly to the program. If you weren't doing the program, you wouldn't have any of these expenses. Typical direct expenses include the following:

- Art, laboratory, or other consumable supplies that program participants will use

- Supplies your staff will use beyond what they'd need without this project, including increased use of letterhead, pens, notebooks, tape, and so on

- A new computer workstation and even a new desk, if needed, for a new staff position related to a program

- Travel expenses (including a *per diem*) to get staff, consultants, or participants to where the program will take place

- Duplicating and printing costs, including fees paid to designers for creating the printed materials

- Postage, freight delivery, and mailing house costs

- Long-distance telephone related to the program

- Website maintenance (If you will be posting anything about the program on your website, someone will have to do it. Even if it's a staff member, it's still a direct program expense.)

- A small amount (around $200 to $500 or 1 percent of the total direct expenses) for "contingency," which sounds better than "miscellaneous"

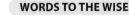

WORDS TO THE WISE

Be prepared not only to justify expenses if asked, but also to spend them. Many funders will ask that when reporting to them you compare actual costs line by line with your budget and explain any discrepancies of as little as 10 percent. Everyone at your charity involved with the program should understand that not spending one budget line does not give him more money to spend in another one.

If a company will be donating supplies or free travel, you should include these items in your expense budget. (It would look odd if they were missing.) You might want to separate out these in-kind expenses so the funder can easily compare them with the corresponding amount you include in the income section of your budget.

What—Indirect Expenses

I've not yet touched on what are among your charity's major expenses: rent, utilities, and fundraising and administrative personnel. You can help cover the costs of these overhead expenses by including a portion of them as indirect expenses in every program grant proposal. If you work for a large charity, you can just ask your finance officer to give you the indirect rate. If you have to figure the rate yourself, read on.

To get started, add up all the expenses that can be considered indirect—that is, everything not specifically related to your programs, including the following:

- Rent

- Utilities

- Security

- Insurance

- Equipment rental and maintenance

- Facilities maintenance and cleaning

- Telephone use

- Internet connection

- Website hosting and maintenance

- Supplies

- Administrative salaries (including fundraising, finance, marketing, and executive staff)

WORDS TO THE WISE

There's no indirect rate for a general operating support (GOS) proposal because you'll use the total organization's budget and everything is already included.

For each of these items, exclude the cost of anything used solely for a particular program. So if the gym is used only for the physical fitness program, or the art supplies are only used by the after-school program, or your executive director spends half of his time teaching an after-school class, do not include those costs as part of your indirect costs.

Divide the amount of all indirect costs by your total budget to come up with your overall indirect rate. It'll likely be at least 20 percent of your total budget. If it's more than 30 percent, reexamine your expenses to see which can be attributed to a program. Few funders will accept indirect costs as more than 30 percent.

Now multiply the total direct costs for your program by your indirect rate. This is the amount you should include in your program budget. Obviously, the amount will be different for each program because each program's direct costs will be different. Here's an example:

Let's assume the total of all the indirect expense items listed earlier is $120,000. However, your executive director spends 20 percent of her time teaching a literacy class. She makes $80,000, so that's $16,000 you can't count with your other indirects (20 percent of 80,000 = 16,000). Therefore, your true indirect expenses are $120,000 − 16,000, or $104,000.

The organization's total budget is $640,000, so, 104,000 ÷ 640,000 = 0.1875 or rounded up, 19 percent, which is your indirect rate.

Your direct project costs add up to $95,000, so multiply $95,000 by 19 percent, which equals $18,050, which is the amount of indirect expenses to include in your project budget. Remember: the indirect expenses include all your occupancy costs, so you can't use any of those items as a direct cost.

Having figured all that out, I have to warn you there are two exceptions. The first has to do with indirect rates on government grants and contracts, which I discussed in Chapter 5. These official indirect rates must be negotiated *before* you apply (many months before, to allow for the negotiating and processing). If you don't have a negotiated indirect rate, you can still include an allocation of your rent, utilities, etc. in a government grant budget by itemizing them as direct expenses.

The second exception is with foundation and corporate funders who have a maximum indirect rate they'll accept in a budget. I've dealt with funders who allowed as much as 20 percent or as little as 9 percent. There's no way to know how much they'll accept without asking the foundation's program officer. It's unfortunate that you can't always cover all your indirect costs in a project budget, but hopefully, your general operating grants will cover any gaps.

Don't try to double-dip on your basic expenses. If you're using an indirect rate, you cannot also include any of the expenses that go into that indirect rate as direct program expenses.

When

You want to be clear in your grant budget when the grant money will be spent. Typically, grants are made for a one-year period, but that year may not correspond to the period in which your program will take place. If that's true for your program, you can make it clear when the grant will be spent by including an additional column that pulls out the funder's grant amount.

This would look similar to the example given in the following "Budget Narrative" section. Although there, the second column is used to show *how* the funder's money will be spent, you'd use a similar process to show *when* it would be spent simply by labeling each column with the appropriate dates.

Where

If you must rent additional space for a program, be sure to include the rental cost and any associated costs such as additional utilities, security, or insurance. In many cases, you'll operate your program from your current facility, and those costs will be included in your indirect expenses.

How

How will you pay for the project? That's the million-dollar question, so to speak. Many funders don't like to be the only ones contributing to a program, so it's important to show other sources of income. You might not know where all the money is coming from when you apply for a grant. That's okay, but you will need to indicate the possible sources, such as in the following example.

Income	
Requested from the Smith Foundation	$10,000
Continental Airlines (in-kind, committed)	$2,500
Jones Family Foundation (received)	$10,000
Community Foundation (pending)	$15,000
Participant fees	$5,000
Total	**$47,500**

Always list the request from the funder first, and label it "request." (You don't want them to think you've counted their money before you even applied.) You might have three other applications pending, but only list enough funders to make the budget balance. If all the other money is pending, you might give a footnote to explain that you're also submitting applications to additional funders at the same time, whether you name them or not. Also note if any of the pending funders have supported your program in the past.

WORDS TO THE WISE

The total income should always equal the total expenses, exactly. In the real world, this will never happen, but this presentation should show that your goal is a balanced program budget. You might have to adjust a couple of expense lines slightly up or down to get a perfectly balanced budget.

Notice that participant fees are included in the income projection in the previous table. If your program will generate several types of earned fees, you might want to subtotal earned versus contributed income. Funders love to see earned income, so make the most of it.

And just as you included indirect costs in your proposal, you might want to list indirect income—that is, income used to support your project but not coming in as a direct result of your project. You may well need to include a portion of your operating funds or income from a refreshment stand to make your budget balance. Unlike with indirect expenses, you're free to include whatever indirect income you like. Just be prepared to explain where it comes from if asked.

If you're requesting a funder to make a challenge grant, you'd need to devote a substantial part of the program or budget narrative to how you'll raise the additional funds and why this funder's making the grant as a challenge would help you raise the balance of the funds.

If you're asking a funder to help you meet another funder's challenge grant, mention the matching grant in your proposal narrative and cover letter, and list it separately, as in the following example.

Contributed Income	
Smith Family Foundation (requested)	$10,000
Community Trust challenge grant (pledged)	$50,000
Widget Corp. of America (received)	$10,000
Jones and Jones Trust (received)	$5,000
Benefit dinner income (projected)	$25,000
Total Contributed Income	**$100,000**

Always think strategically about which other funders you list, keeping in mind that funders know other funders and some even have overlapping trustees. Also, don't use *miscellaneous* or *unknown* or *new funders* in the income section. You should have at least some idea of where all income might come from or else you need to do more research before submitting any proposals.

Budget Narrative

Even when you have demonstrated the who, what, when, where, and how of your budget, additional explanation may be necessary. That brings us to the budget narrative.

Occasionally, a funder will request a budget narrative. This entails a brief paragraph of how the expenses relate to the project, explaining in particular the major expenses. Budget narratives are especially important when you're asked for budgets covering more than one year. Multiyear budgets will inevitably have variations from year to year. The narrative gives you the opportunity to explain them.

Even if you're not asked for a budget narrative, you might want to include footnotes at the bottom of the budget page to explain major costs and point out ties to the program narrative. Remember: in the budget, you want to *answer* any questions the funder might have before she asks them.

Take a quick look at the program budget in Chapter 21. Scan the Program Expenses to see if anything stands out to you in Year 2. Your eye probably went right to the $40,000 for exhibition expenses. That one line is 84 percent of the program expenses, yet it's not broken down. This is what I call a "big sore thumb," because it calls attention to itself.

That $40,000 consists of a number of expenses, including building materials, painting, sign silk screening, lighting, and labor. You could add all those categories to your budget, or itemize the larger ones in a budget note.

Putting It All Together

Here's a sample budget that includes all I've discussed so far. (You can find additional budget examples including a multiyear budget in the appendixes.) This budget is for a program that trains educators to teach literacy skills to adults learning English as a second language.

Literacy Teachers' Training Program

	Budget September 2011–July 2012	Requested from Bank Foundation
Expenses		
Director of Programs (10 percent)	$8,000	$0
Program Officer (50 percent)	$23,000	$0
Program Assistant (20 percent)	$6,000	$0
Fringe Benefits @ 18 percent	$6,660	$0
Subtotal: Full-Time Staff	**$43,660**	**$0**
Stipends to Participants (20 @ $250)	$5,000	$5,000
Program Consultant	$8,000	$0
Evaluator[1]	$20,000	$0
Subtotal: Consultants	**$33,000**	**$5,000**
Total: Personnel	**$76,660**	**$5,000**
Participant Travel	$2,200	$2,200
Printing[2]	$4,500	$4,500
Postage and Mail Preparation	$1,200	$1,200
Supplies	$260	$0
Advertising	$1,500	$1,500
Website	$500	$0
Delivery/Freight	$260	$0
Hospitality[3]	$1,100	$600
Subtotal: Nonpersonnel	**$11,520**	**$10,000**
Indirect Costs @ 20 percent[4]	$17,620	$0
Total Expenses	**$105,800**	**$15,000**
Income		
Bank Foundation (requested)	$15,000	$15,000
Smith Family Foundation (received)	$50,000	$0
Mayor's Office for Adult Literacy (rec.)	$25,000	
Community Foundation (pending)	$10,000	
Other Pending Proposals[5]	$5,000	$0

	Budget September 2011–July 2012	Requested from Bank Foundation
Subtotal: Contributed Income	**$105,000**	**$10,000**
Application Fees	<u>$800</u>	<u>$0</u>
Subtotal: Earned Income	**<u>$800</u>**	**<u>$0</u>**
Total Income	**$105,800**	**$10,000**
Surplus/(Deficit)	$0	$0

1 An outside evaluator will be hired to review the program and prepare a written report, which we will make available to all program funders.

2 Includes printing of application forms and a teacher's guide.

3 Lunch will be provided for participants each day.

4 Includes occupancy allocation. All sessions take place in our facility.

5 Five additional proposals have been submitted, all but one to new funders. Several board members are also expected to contribute through their family foundations toward this total.

From this budget presentation, you can see at a glance all the elements of a good budget:

Who: Three staff members and one consultant will run the program. An outside evaluator also will be hired. In addition, the teachers taking part in the program will receive a small stipend.

What: The largest expense is for printing, which the footnote tells us will be for application materials and a teacher's guide. Participants' travel will be subsidized.

When: The column header gives the dates of the project.

Where: No direct costs are specified for rent, but footnote 4 tells us that space is covered in the indirect costs.

How: The amount requested from this funder is listed first. Grants that have been received appear next, followed by grant proposals that are outstanding. You'll note that a small amount ($5,000) does not have a specified source, but the footnote explains where we expect to raise that money.

This budget presentation contains a second column showing exactly how the Bank Foundation's grant will be used. This foundation specifies that it will not pay for the applicant's personnel costs or any indirect costs. From the remaining expenses, I chose to show their money going to the participants and for most of the other direct program expenses. I could have also put their money toward the consultants, but I thought this funder would like to see more of their money going to the participants. Such an allocation of a funder's grant is not that common, but I've encountered more than one who asked that it be done.

WORDS TO THE WISE

When you isolate the exact expenses a grant will pay for, you make reporting more difficult because you will report on smaller sums, which are more likely to vary. Only do this if required by the funder.

This two-column presentation is also effective when you're asking a funder for a grant for a particular activity that's part of a larger program. Showing the larger program gives a fuller picture of what your charity is doing to address a problem, but separating out a particular activity allows funders to get a better picture of what they will be paying for. For example, if this teacher training program included a summer camp for kids learning English and you had a funder interested in that part of the program, you might pull out the camp expenses in a second column so the funder could see what it would be supporting and what other funders were helping to support the camp.

If, instead of footnotes, you wanted to (or were asked to) include a budget narrative, it might read like the following:

> Agency staff will conduct the teacher training, assisted by a consultant. The program evaluator will follow the program and write a report on its effectiveness, which we will share with funders. Participants will receive a small stipend, travel subsidy, and lunches each day of training. Printing a teacher's guide is the single largest nonpersonnel expense.

> Five additional grant proposals have been submitted, all but one to new funders. Several board members are also expected to contribute through their family foundations toward this total. We are confident we will raise the remaining funds. Should the funds raised fall somewhat short of the goal, we can reduce or postpone the role of the evaluator to the following year.

The income section shows that nearly two thirds of the total cost has already been received. This funder, the Community Foundation, and a number of unnamed other outstanding requests will be expected to make up the balance to cover administrative costs. Had there been solid prospects for the additional costs at the time you submitted this application, you would have given the names of those prospects. If too large a proportion of the income appears in "other funders," the funder might doubt your ability to fund the program completely.

PHILANTHROPY FACT

Although I've repeatedly pointed out that you should not include fundraising costs in program budgets, some funders will make grants specifically to pay for additional fundraising consultants or staff, usually under the heading of "capacity building."

In some cases, your project and organizational budget may be the same. For example, if you're raising funds for the Friends of the Hometown Library, you might devote virtually your entire budget to raising money for the library. Fundraising expenses can appear in this budget because that's pretty much all the Friends group does. You won't, however, be asking for a grant to cover fundraising costs but rather to support the library in some specific way. If the Friends organization has its own nonprofit status, its budget might look something like this one.

Expenses	
Fundraising consultant	$2,500
Building staff overtime[1]	$1,200
Printing[2]	$2,000
Postage	$500
Volunteer reimbursable	$300
Total direct expenses	**$6,500**
New Book Fund donation	$15,000
Total Expenses	**$21,500**

Income	
Thomas Family Foundation (requested)	$5,000
Community Foundation (received)[3]	$6,000
Membership dues	$6,000
Bake sales and other activities	$4,500
Total Income	**$21,500**

1 The Friends must pay overtime for the library's janitor when holding events at the library.

2 Printing of flyers advertising the various fundraising events.

3 The Community Foundation matched one to one the funds raised in membership dues.

If the Friends organization were not tax-exempt, you would need to apply to the foundation using the library's status, and therefore would use the library's total budget with your proposal. In this case, you'd separate out (and subtotal) the Friends' expenses. You would also highlight the Friends' donations to the library from its various fundraising activities in the income section.

Multiyear Budgets

Many programs take place over a number of years (such as the curatorial internship program, which I used as an example in Chapter 14). In cases such as this, most of the grants you'll apply for will be for the entire time period of the project. Many foundations make such grants, but they usually make the grant payable as "$10,000 a year for two years" rather than giving you $20,000 up front. This way, they delay payment until they've received a report from you letting them know you're continuing the program. It's not necessary for each year of a multiyear budget to balance, but by the end of the program, everything should come out neatly to a $0 balance.

The budget for the two-year curatorial intern program appears in Chapter 21 (where I give it as an example in reporting on grants). Many of the expenses I've simply allocated equally to each of the two years. Other expenses obviously belong to one year or the other. For example, the exhibition the interns will present takes place only in the second year, and the outreach efforts to find qualified interns takes place only in the first year.

Organizational Budget

Proposals will also require an *organizational budget*, which includes all your charity's expenses for every program as well as general operating expenses. An organizational budget follows the same general format as the program budget, but you use a condensed personnel budget rather than list the salaries of every single person who works for your charity.

 DEFINITION

Organizational budgets represent your charity's total operations, including all personnel (fundraising staff, too) and expenses and all sources of income. If you're writing a proposal for general operating support, the *program budget* and your *organizational budget* are one and the same.

The personnel section could look like one of the following examples.

Example 1	
Personnel	$350,486
Fringe @ 20 percent	$70,922
Total salaried personnel	**$421,408**
Consultants	$100,000
Total Personnel	**$521,408**

Example 2	
Administrative staff	$156,200
Program staff	$194,286
Fringe @ 20 percent	$70,922
Total salaried personnel	**$421,408**
Management consultant	$40,000
Clinical freelance staff	$60,000
Total nonsalaried personnel	**$100,000**
Total Personnel	**$521,408**

The second example makes clear the relationship between administrative and program personnel costs—in this case, administrative salaries are only around 10 percent less than those for program staff. If accompanying a program proposal, this might look like too little (relatively speaking) was being spent on programs, so you might not want this breakdown. For a GOS proposal, however, the relationship might present a good argument for increased support of general operations.

Your financial officer should prepare the organizational budget for you, but you'll probably want to do some additional formatting. Just as you did with the program budget, you'll want to group similar activities (such as making regrants or running a clinic) and subtotal them so they tell the story you need to reinforce the message in your narrative.

Income in an organizational budget is usually broken down by type of funder rather than specifying individual ones. For large organizations, you might break down the types into subgroups to make a point about where your funding comes from. Here are two examples to illustrate what I mean.

Example 1	
Contributed Income	
Government	$400,000
Foundations	$190,000
Corporations	$140,000
Individuals	$30,000
Subtotal Contributed Income	**$760,000**
Earned Income	
Clinic fees	$25,000
Interest and investments	$85,000
Subtotal Earned Income	**$110,000**
Total Income	**$870,000**

Example 2

Contributed Income

Government

Federal grants	$370,000
State grants	<u>$30,000</u>
Subtotal Government Grants	**$400,000**
Foundations	$190,000
Corporations	$140,000
Individuals	<u>$30,000</u>
Subtotal Private Support	**<u>$360,000</u>**
Total Contributed Income	**$760,000**
Earned Income	
Clinic fees	$25,000
Interest and investments	<u>$85,000</u>
Total Earned Income	**$110,000**
Total Income	**$870,000**

Whether income is contributed or earned is pretty clear except, perhaps, with corporate contributions. Most charities list corporate grants under contributed income. Corporate sponsorships, however, are usually listed as earned income.

HOW TO SAY IT

One of my pet peeves is the use of the term *unearned income* to categorize donations. What's unearned about it? We fundraisers work very hard to earn it, as does the program staff to create and run programs worthy of donations. A more accurate description is *contributed income.*

By breaking down the sources of the government support, the charity's significant dependence on federal support becomes clearer, illustrating the need for greater support from other sectors. To dramatize a need for general operating support, the budget narrative might contrast the amount of support received for programs versus operating expenses.

Of necessity, budgets are frequently the last part of a grant proposal you will prepare. Don't let your rush to get the proposal in cause you to present a budget that's not in sync with the proposal narrative, or one that does not reinforce the narrative's most important points. Get help when you need it from program and finance staff. You'll find more budget examples in Chapter 21, where I cover grant reports.

And last but certainly not least, check your formulas! No matter if you or someone in your finance department prepared a budget, check and double-check the formulas in your spreadsheet. A mistake in the budget can call into question the veracity of your entire proposal.

You will find a Budget Builder workbook for a project grant at idiotsguides.com under "Book Extras." It includes a personnel worksheet and a calculator for indirect expenses that feed into the main budget worksheet.

The Least You Need to Know

- Your budget should describe in numbers the activities included in your narrative.
- Include part of the salary of everyone who will work on a program and state the percentage of their time next to their title.
- Include numbers for the expenses for who, what, when, where your program will need as well as how you will pay for them.
- Figure your indirect costs by adding up everything that's not directly related to a program and then dividing that number by your total budget.
- If permitted by the funder, always include indirect expenses, using your indirect rate multiplied by your total direct expenses.
- Use footnotes or a budget narrative when your numbers require context and explanations to be effective, or when the funder requests an explanation in some form. Explaining the largest numbers in your budget in a footnote or narrative is also a good idea.

The Cover Letter and Executive Summary

In This Chapter

- Grabbing your reader's attention
- Playing to your audience
- Cover letters for new versus renewal grants
- Differences between a cover letter and an executive summary

The cover letter is the most important part of your proposal. It is, after all, what funders see first. If you can capture their attention—or even better, their imagination—with the cover letter, you'll immediately separate your proposal from all the others.

Many grant writers create the cover letter last, which makes sense, because it needs to include information from all the other parts of the proposal. Coming last in your writing, however, shouldn't mean you write it in haste on the day before the proposal deadline. The cover letter is just too important to rush. I like to work on the cover letter while others at my charity review the proposal narrative.

A cover letter should …

- State the purpose of the proposal in one sentence, including the grant amount requested.
- Connect personally to the reader whenever possible.
- Relate the proposed program to the funder's stated interests.
- Provide a context for the request, either in the form of background on your charity or a brief report on a previous grant.
- Present clearly the three key arguments why you should receive the grant.

- Include contact information for additional questions (not relying on the phone number on the letterhead but giving a direct line or extension and an e-mail address).

- Thank the funder for considering your request.

In this chapter, I show you how to create some of these parts, as well as address tone, personality, and style.

Know Your Audience

People, not institutions, make grants, and the cover letter gives you an opportunity to show you understand this. And grants are made to people, not institutions, so your cover letter needs also to reflect the personality and style of the person who signs the letter. If possible, your cover letter should connect with the reader on a personal as well as a professional level.

Address the letter to whomever the funder gives as the contact person, unless your contact at the funder told you to send it to her instead.

If one of your board members knows someone at the foundation other than the contact, you can go one of two ways: send the original letter to the person with the personal connection and CC the official contact person, or send the original to the official contact person and send a CC with a handwritten note from your board member to his or her contact.

With either approach, you cover all the bases and ensure that your proposal will be processed through the usual channels even if your special contact drops the ball. The second method has the advantage of respecting the chain of command at the funder and giving a more personal touch to the personal contact.

It's About the Reader

If your research revealed that the contact person has a background in education and pedagogy and your proposal addresses the training of teachers, you can discuss the subject using terminology appropriate to addressing another expert in the field. If you know the contact has young children, you can address his or her interests as a parent in improved teacher training. If the contact is a young program officer fresh out of college, you might connect your discussion of teacher training with the reader's own recent educational experiences.

Whoever the reader is, you want to make that person your advocate when the funder's board meets. You therefore want to include the strongest parts of your rationale for funding in the cover letter and present them in such a way as to make it easy for the reader to remember them when discussing your proposal with others. Bullet points help the reader find your key points. Good writing helps him remember them.

It's About the Writer

The person who reads the cover letter is, of course, only half of the equation. The letter must also be appropriate for the person who signs it. In larger organizations, this rarely will be you. More likely it will be your charity's executive director, development director, or board president. For simplicity's sake, I refer to the writer as the executive director.

If possible, read any letters or speeches the executive director has written (or approved) to get an idea of the degree of formality she uses in different situations. Through trial and error, you'll eventually get a good handle on the executive director's personal style. The better you can do this, the more effective the letter will be.

HOW TO SAY IT

The simple word *draft* at the top of any document you present to others for review makes a world of difference. By signaling that you acknowledge the document is incomplete without their input, you'll make your job easier. Always put a date on each draft to avoid confusion.

Negotiating the tone of the letter with the executive director is part of the process, but too often overediting can dilute the letter's message. It's your job to be sure this doesn't happen. Executive directors and others I've worked for have usually listened when I objected to one of their edits because it changed the meaning or weakened the argument. Usually we compromised on a third version of the text.

When to push for your language and when to accept the executive director's edits must depend on what will best serve the proposal, taking into account your experience with the particular funder versus the executive director's experience. This applies to the entire proposal, not just the cover letter. With the cover letter in particular, the signer has every right to have the letter reflect her style—it is, after all, her signature at the bottom of the page. Just don't water down the message in the interest of personal style.

One executive director I worked for drove me crazy with repeated changes to a government proposal. (I had started to label the versions of the proposal with the day, hour, and minute to make my not-so-subtle point about all the revisions.) As annoyed as I was, I knew he had more than twice the experience with this particular funder than I had. Trying to keep the language to my prose in this situation would have been foolish and detrimental to the proposal's chances for success. In the end, I learned a lot from his edits that has helped me write proposals for all kinds of funders.

Above all else, make the letter's salutation appropriate for the executive director. If your executive director is on a first-name basis with the reader, using a formal salutation will be a real turnoff, but overfamiliarity will have the same effect.

Personal Versus Personality

You want your cover letter to be personal and have a personality, by which I mean a distinctive point of view. Don't be afraid to be dramatic:

> The Community Food Bank prevents a thousand of the community's least fortunate members from going hungry every day.

HOW TO SAY IT

We've all received those magazine sweepstakes mailings that repeat our names every few lines in boldface type. That kind of personalization is out of place in grant writing. Avoid overusing the funder's name in the letter and proposal other than when thanking them, referring to past or anticipated support, or possibly referring to something in their guidelines or one of their publications.

And don't be afraid to praise your charity's work:

> The Community Food Bank does more than any other agency in the city to prevent hunger.

But avoid blatant overstatements, claims that you could never quantify, and exclamation points.

> The Community Food Bank has transformed the lives of thousands, making them better, more productive citizens!

The cover letter must have a style and a personality that makes it human. Never forget that this is a personal communication.

If the executive director knows the recipient well, she might want to add a personal note about a recent social occasion or inquire about a spouse or child. I think these comments are best done in a handwritten note accompanying the proposal rather than making them part of the formal cover letter that a number of other people will read.

Handwritten notes on the cover letter itself, however, provide an important personal touch. A note such as "Thanks again for inviting this proposal," or "It was good seeing you at the mayor's awards ceremony last week" warms up the letter without making it overly personal.

For Current and Recent Funders

You can assume the reader has a degree of familiarity with your organization if you're applying for a *renewal grant* or for a new grant from a funder who supported your charity in the recent past. You might therefore be able to leave out (or move to an attachment) background information such as the year you were founded, your mission, and a list of programs. But remember to follow the funder's instructions, and include background in the cover letter if it is asked for.

 DEFINITION

Renewal grant can be a loaded phrase. On the one hand, it signifies a continuing relationship with your charity, which is a good thing to remind funders about. On the other, it might imply to a funder that you expect them to continue supporting your charity or maybe even take their continued support for granted. Learn all you can about a funder's attitude toward continuing support before referring to your grant request as a renewal.

With a current or recent funder, you'll stress how its previous grant helped your charity accomplish the program's goals and where that program stands now (even if you're now applying for a different program). Don't waste this opportunity to reinforce the importance of past funding and to thank the funder once more.

With rare exceptions, funders will not accept a new proposal if you haven't reported on their past funding. If the timing of a program makes it necessary to apply before reporting, call the funder before you send anything to see if they will make an exception.

Here's an example of a cover letter to a funder that already supports this charity.

Ms. Sara Silver
Trustee
Silver Foundation
98 Oak Street
Anytown, TX 77000

Dear Ms. Silver:

I want to express my sincere thanks for the Silver Foundation's past support of Countywide Literary Project's services to the community. Your last grant was instrumental in allowing us to maintain all our classes for young people and adults during a perilous economic period. With this letter, I have enclosed a report on Countywide's activities during the past year and also a request for a renewal grant in the increased amount of $40,000.

The past year has been a difficult time for everyone in Butler County, as the recession has reached every corner of the community. Demands on the Literacy Project's services have been higher than any time in memory. Significantly more adults have come to us when they realized that basic English literacy was key to making them more employable.

We have devised a plan for serving the increased demand on our services that calls for decentralizing the teaching facilities and offering classes in English as a second language. The former part of the plan will allow more people to take classes before and after work by holding the classes nearer to where they live. The latter scheme recognizes the large number of non-English speaking immigrants in our community and their need for instruction separate from illiterate English speakers. Specifics on these plans for the coming fiscal year are enclosed.

Expanding services while the community remains in a recession will be particularly challenging. For this reason, we are asking all of our funders to consider a significant increase in support. As you know, few funders are taking on new charities, so we must rely on our old friends to see us—and our clients—through this period.

If you have any questions about the report or the proposal for a renewal grant, I can be reached at (414) 555-1234 or exec@litprod.org. Thank you again for your continued support.

Sincerely,

Kay Lang

Kay Lang
Executive Director

For New Funders

New funders need to have some background information on your charity in the cover letter (even if you include it in the proposal or an attachment and even if you've been cultivating them for months). You need to position the program you're seeking funding for in the context of what your charity is all about.

The following letter to a new funder makes a point of the charity's background as well as its recent accomplishments. This theoretical foundation's primary interest is helping nonprofits develop sources of earned income. They've also been supportive of many arts groups serving African Americans.

Mr. Matt Sterling
Chairman
James and Mary Brush Foundation
1 City Plaza
Anytown, FL 33000

Dear Mr. Sterling,

Sheila Burns recommended that I write to introduce you to the African American Literary Council and ask for your support through a $10,000 grant from the James and Mary Brush Foundation. Your grant would be used to support increased marketing of *Black American Voices*, our quarterly journal of fiction and literary criticism. Local writers such as Sheila and Joshua Jefferson were first published in our journal years before their popular and critical successes. Both have been loyal to the journal, allowing us to continue to publish their new works alongside stories by new African American writers. No other African American journal offers this combination of accomplished and emerging talents.

The council also takes an active role in the local community, providing literary opportunities for adults and students alike. We have concentrated our after-school program on middle school students for the last two years after a study by the state university revealed students at this age were at particular risk of dropping out of school.

By providing creative writing workshops, we encourage the students to express themselves by telling their stories in a supportive environment, which has resulted in greater retention and less truancy.

To continue our tradition of success, we must broaden our base of support. As you might know, the Butler County Community Trust has provided a substantial part of our funding for the last six years. They have informed us that their support must end next year because of their limit on consecutive-year funding, and we are writing in hopes that you will help us fill the gap left by their departure.

I've enclosed a copy of the most recent journal along with a proposal outlining the goals and objectives we have set for it in the coming two years. The journal's editor and I would welcome the opportunity to meet with you to answer any questions you might have and to discuss how the council and the James and Mary Brush Foundation might work together. You can reach me at president@ aalitcouncil.org or (904) 555-1234. Your kind consideration of this request is greatly appreciated.

Sincerely,

Mary Adams

Mary Adams
President of the Board

Note in this letter that Sheila Burns, a writer published by this journal, obviously knows Mr. Sterling and allowed the council to use her name when applying for a grant. Putting the familiar name right up front helped ensure the letter (and the proposal) would get considered.

Cover Letter Checklist

Here are questions to ask yourself when writing a cover letter:

- ❒ What do I know about the person who will receive the letter? Could anything I know about her personally relate to my proposal?

- ❒ Does the person signing the letter know the contact at the funder? If so, should she be addressed by first name or a nickname?

- ❒ How can I address the funder's interests and relate them to my program?

- ❒ What key points are my best arguments for funding?

- ❒ How do I lay these out so the reader can easily find them?

- ❒ If the letter is to a current or recent funder, did I thank them for their previous gift and report something about that project?

- ❒ If the letter is to a new funder, did I include enough background and information on recent accomplishments to place the program in context and give my proposal legitimacy?

- ❒ Have I slipped into jargon of my charity's or the funder's invention? (If so, return to Chapter 14 and read up on buzzwords.)

- ❒ Did I include contact information prominently for the letter's signer and possibly an additional person at my charity for questions?

- ❒ Does the letter have the current date and has it been signed?

- ❒ Is the letter two pages or less? (If it's longer, it becomes too much like the proposal.)

- ❒ Did I ask for money?

An Executive Summary Is Not Another Cover Letter

You might think an excellent cover letter perfectly summarizes your program, and therefore is also an executive summary, but that's not the case. These two related parts of a proposal have some key differences.

Whereas your goal was to make the cover letter personal by connecting with the individual and with the institution, in the executive summary, you should present your proposal in a more formal manner. This isn't the place to mention that your kids are on the same soccer team.

In the cover letter you highlighted the key reasons they should fund your program. In the executive summary, you should include *all* the reasons for funding. If something doesn't fit into the summary, you probably don't need it in the proposal. Keep the summary to one page, and make it a terrific page. Often the executive summary and the budget are the only parts copied for everyone evaluating your proposal to see.

HOW TO SAY IT

Save the personality for the cover letter. Make the executive summary business-like and straightforward. It should still, however, convey to the reader your passion for the program and its importance for your constituents.

Here's a sample executive summary for the same grant as the cover letter from the African American Literary Council given earlier.

The African American Literary Council requests a $10,000 grant from the James and Mary Brush Foundation to support the publication of *Black American Voices*, a quarterly magazine of fiction and literary criticism focusing on African American writers in northern Florida.

Begun in 1990 as a 16-page unbound photocopied book and circulated largely as a free publication in regional bookstores, *Black American Voices* has since grown into a respected literary journal with 6,600 subscribers, including 220 university libraries throughout the United States. Issues now typically consist of 64 pages, which are saddle-stitched and printed in two colors.

Short stories originally published in *Voices* have won O. Henry and other respected awards. Major publishers, such as Penguin Putnam, have published writers we introduced. Essays in *Voices* have similarly been honored by the African American Journalists Association and others.

Black American Voices has now reached a turning point in its development. The subscription base, although steady, has not grown significantly in the last two years. The grant requested would, in part, make possible additional marketing through a 100,000-piece direct-mail campaign, which will result in 900 to 1,100 new subscribers. A larger subscription base increases earned income, which will help sustain publication in future years. We must expand the subscription base now, when the Butler County Community Foundation's long-standing support is ending because of their limit on consecutive-year funding. The Community

Foundation has agreed to make a $15,000 one-time grant specifically to support the subscription campaign. Your funding would complete the funding needed to enable us to take this important step forward.

Our editor, Tanya Mills, oversees the journal's content and works closely with our marketing consultant to make the journal more visually appealing. A consultant, Mark Jacobs, has developed the marketing plan, including the proposed direct-mail campaign.

Your grant will allow us to achieve two important goals simultaneously:

1. It will allow us to bring the writers in *Black American Voices* to the wider audience they deserve.

2. It will increase earned income that will help support the publication for years to come.

Sheila Burns, O. Henry Award winner and one of the first short story writers we published, has written us that *"Black American Voices* believed in me when I wasn't sure if I believed in myself. Seeing my first published story changed everything for me. All I have accomplished since can be traced back to the success of that one story."

Help us introduce more writers like Sheila Burns to the literary community. Help *Black American Voices* grow.

Note that the executive summary concentrates on the program for which funding is sought. The other programs the charity offers are not mentioned. (You can cover them in an organizational history, which would be one of the attachments.) The executive summary gets more specific about the program, including how you will use the grant.

Executive Summary Checklist

An executive summary should summarize your entire proposal, including …

❐ A one-sentence statement about the program for which you are applying and the grant amount you seek.

❐ Mention of any grant history with this funder.

❐ A highly condensed context paragraph pointing out your charity's qualifications for carrying out this program.

❐ A one-paragraph description of the program, including the program's main activities, goals, who will run the program, and anticipated beginning and end dates.

❐ A reference to the budget, noting areas of greatest expense to be covered by the grant and if any other funder has already committed to the program.

❐ A moving closing paragraph stating the difference the grant will make to your constituents and to the community (where applicable).

There will of necessity be some redundancy among the cover letter, executive summary, and proposal. Occasionally you may even repeat some language exactly, but try not to do this. To make an effective proposal, however, each part must reinforce the others and remain consistent in conveying your message. Stay on point, and no matter what order the funder reads your material, she will understand why your proposal must be funded.

The Least You Need to Know

- Customize every cover letter to reflect what you know about the addressee and the person at your charity who will sign it.
- Grab the reader's attention with your cover letter, and point out the key reasons why you should receive the grant.
- Use clear language and formatting to make it easy for the reader to find and remember the points in your cover letter to advocate for your proposal.
- Use the cover letter to current or past funders to briefly report on their last grant and thank them one more time.
- Use the cover letter to new funders to place your program in context within your charity's mission and goals.
- Make the executive summary a true summary, touching on all aspects of the proposal, including the budget.

Repute and Tribute

Before the funder decides to make the grant, they want to know more about your charity than the one program you have described. In the background section, you get to tell your charity's history in your own way and throw in tributes from grateful clients and others to reinforce your claims.

So far in the proposal, you've been the one saying how great and deserving your charity is. You can gain greater credence with the use of quotes or entire letters testifying to your charity's ability to carry out the project. And testimonials from members of the press can carry additional weight. Here's how to put it all together into a package that will help your proposal, rather than just fill pages.

You've Got History with This Issue

Most organizations have a standard history their grant writers have used so many times they can recite it from memory. (Even a new charity has some history behind it: the background of the founders can show your history with the issues.) You can just drop that old history into your proposal and call it a day, or you can take the time to give it a special spin that relates to the rest of the proposal.

For example, your charity is probably known for more than one activity. Rather than treating each equally, condense the areas that don't relate to your proposal and beef up the ones that do. It's a little extra work, but if you do it well, it will reinforce your proposal rather than drag it down.

> **WORDS TO THE WISE**
>
> Your charity might want to post the history you craft on its website. Keep in mind that once it's on the Internet, anyone can access it and use it to write about you, so keep it current and reflective of your organization's mission and present goals.

For example, a service organization that's best known for making grants to individual artists usually begins its history with a description of that program:

> The Gotham Arts Association provides more fellowship support for artists than any other private organization in the United States. Since 1985, more than $10 million has been awarded to artists in the performing, visual, and literary arts.

Gotham also provides a wide range of information services, which reach a huge audience through the Internet. For grant proposals to support these programs, a better spin on its history would begin with the following:

> The Gotham Arts Association today provides information to some one million artists annually through Internet, telephone, and print resources. Its history with technology extends back to the founding of its e-mail newsletter in 1995. It has continued to innovate, most recently by introducing an integrated opportunities in the arts national database in 2005 along with a toll-free telephone inquiry service.

If your history goes for more than a page, use boldface headings to draw the eye to important sections. Use bullet points to give prominence to listings of accomplishments.

Although a history implies a chronological narrative, you'll be better able to make your points about the importance of your program if you organize it according to your principal accomplishments instead. Follow a rough chronology only if detailing how your charity has met challenges over time makes a better story.

You can also use the process and outcomes methods I discussed in Chapter 14 to organize histories; only in this case, process almost always involves a chronology. Process, unfortunately, is mainly interesting to historians and management consultants, not funders. Focus instead on accomplishments when you can. Notice the contrast in the following two examples.

Outcomes-Focused History

The Friends of the New Town Public Library make it possible for the library to offer services far beyond what public funding alone provides.

Since 1988, the Friends have annually purchased 20 to 100 new books—1,200 books so far. These have included multiple copies of best-sellers, replacements of popular children's books, and new reference works. The Friends' book fund thus touches a wide variety of library users.

Literary readings sponsored by the Friends bring talented but lesser-known writers to the attention of the community. Four hundred people now annually attend these events, begun in 1995, with an average of 45 people attending each event.

The Friends raise the funds for these activities through book sales (of unneeded copies of books and books donated by the community), bake sales, and grants from foundation and corporate sources. Membership dues (now ranging from $25 for individuals to $500 for patrons) paid by the Friends, however, now constitute the major source of funding. The Friends are an entirely volunteer-run organization made up of 700 citizens who contributed $58,000 this year to New Town Public Library.

Process-Focused History

The Friends of the New Town Public Library make it possible for the library to offer services far beyond what public funding provides.

Founded in 1988 to supplement the library's book acquisition fund when city budget cuts were greatest, the activities now identified with the Friends began with a fall bake sale that raised $398. Librarians identified the major areas of book acquisitions needing support as multiple copies of best-sellers, replacements of popular children's books, and new reference works.

The response from the community to the 1988 sale and the number of people who asked to get involved led to the founding of a formal Friends group that was incorporated the following year. Membership dues were established at $25 for individuals and $40 for families.

An annual book sale was begun in 1990 using donated books and unneeded copies from the library. The book sale, bake sale, and dues from the Friends amounted to $2,200 that year, representing a significant growth in only two years of existence.

Success bred success, and in 1995 the Friends were able to provide support for a series of literary readings as well. This program was begun with the first grant the Friends received, from the New Town Community Trust for $6,000.

The literary events not only introduced lesser-known writers to the community, they also brought the Friends to greater attention, so much so that today membership in the Friends stands at 700. This year, the all-volunteer Friends raised a total of $58,000.

Both versions of the history convey the same information, but the outcomes-focused history gives a better picture of the impact the Friends group has on the library, whereas the process-focused history better conveys how the organization grew dramatically in a short time. I believe the former would make a greater impression on the funder, but either is acceptable.

Testimonials

There's nothing quite like including a quote from a satisfied client to strengthen and personalize your proposal. Your charity probably receives letters like this from time to time. Be sure executive and program staffs know to give you copies of any that come in.

WORDS TO THE WISE

Always get permission from the person who praised you before printing a quote attributed to them. Otherwise, you could use the quote without attribution, but it won't seem as genuine.

It's great if you can quote exactly what someone said, but frequently he will use incorrect grammar or include something personal in the middle of his praise for you. Don't use awkward devices common in academic writing such as "[sic]" for misspelled words or bad grammar, ellipses to show that you omitted some words, or "[T]oday" to show that a word did not originally begin the sentence.

Improve the grammar and make the quote shorter. No one, including the person who gave you the quote, will ever notice the difference. But *never* make any changes in the meaning of the quote. Retain as much of the original language as you can to maintain the tone of the original.

Several times in my career, I've wished I had a quote from a famous person whom my charity helped in her early days. Chances are, your famous former client would be happy to give you a quote but just doesn't have the time to put one together. On several occasions, I've included in a letter or e-mail a prewritten quote to be edited or ignored. One famous author changed all the adjectives but otherwise stuck with my quote.

Other Endorsements

If your charity is collaborating on a program with another charity or business, include with your proposal a letter of understanding between your charity and the collaborator stating the roles you will each play in the program, or at least obtain a letter of support stating that the other charity endorses your applying for the grant.

If your charity has been (favorably) in the news, by all means include quotes from articles or in some cases the entire article, as additional confirmation that yours is a legitimate charity worthy of support. When your charity appears in the news is a great time to submit proposals because the funder might already be thinking about you.

Staff and Consultant Bios

Many funders ask for biographies of key personnel. For general operating proposals, that means your top three to five staff members and possibly your board president as well. For program proposals, key personnel are those who have some control over the execution of the program, either as supervisors or through doing the actual work involved.

HOW TO SAY IT

Write bios in the third person (not first), and begin by giving the person's relationship to the program and to your charity. The experience detailed should mostly relate to the program. This isn't like a resumé for a job where every year in someone's career must be accounted for.

Keep each bio short—no more than a half page at the most. Never send full resumés unless requested because they take too much time to read. By converting a resumé into a 125- to 150-word paragraph, you save the program officer a lot of time, which she will appreciate. Needless to say, mention experience in bios that directly applies to the program for which you seek funding.

Are You Legal?

As I discussed in Chapter 2, you must be a recognized nonprofit organization to receive most grants. Enclose proof of nonprofit status with every grant proposal, including renewal proposals. If you have a fiscal sponsor, include proof of the sponsor's tax-exempt status. The only exceptions to this rule are government agencies (such as public libraries and schools) and religious organizations.

Federal recognition as a 501(c)(3) organization trumps every other kind of nonprofit status. If you have it, you don't need to include proof of state exemption.

Everything Else

Most funders ask for a list of your charity's board of directors with their professional affiliations, such as "General Manager, Community Bank" or simply as "Philanthropist." If someone is retired, give the former occupation and note "retired" after the job title. The board list should be on a separate page, and don't give personal addresses or phone numbers. Some funders might want to know how long each board member has served on your board.

Funders also like to know who else supports your charity. Funders seem to be able to come up with an amazing number of ways to ask for your donor list, but mostly they want to know the institutional funders (not individuals) in the last year that have given you $1,000 or more. Occasionally, you'll also be asked to include funders to which you have applications outstanding. Mark these "pending," and give the amount you expect to receive.

You'll be tempted to include other items to support your proposal, yet too much material can hurt rather than help your application. Usually, send only those attachments the funder specifically requests. You might, however, also consider including the following materials *if they are germane to the proposal:*

- A general organizational brochure will supplement the background information you've given as part of the proposal. These are particularly helpful to new funders.

- Two or three press articles (not press releases) that pertain directly to your project (or for general operating support, anything about your charity) will reinforce your charity's reputation.

- Documents that support your claim to have done similar programs in the past, such as a lesson plan, teacher's guide, disease prevention pamphlet, concert program, publication, or flyers announcing your programs, are also of interest. Keep these to a minimum unless the funder specifically requests them.

- Annual reports are good for new funders. Current funders should have already received them. Of course, it would be even better if the new funder had received your most recent report as part of your cultivating them.

HOW TO SAY IT

A list of attachments helps the funder by identifying the content and order of the attachments, and it also helps you by serving as a checklist of what you intend to include. You can give the list of attachments at the end of the cover letter (in which case you'd also list all the parts of the proposal), in a table of contents (ditto), or at the end of the proposal narrative (before the budget).

Never include DVDs, videotapes, audiotapes, or books unless requested to do so by the funder. With all the materials the funder must already process, these will simply add an awkward bulkiness to your proposal. They won't be seen, heard, or read.

The Least You Need to Know

- Don't rely on the same statement of your history to convey the important points relevant to your proposal. Customize it.
- Consider applying the outcomes method of proposal construction to your history to provide a clear picture of your charity's impact.
- Use testimonials from clients and those in your field to reinforce your message.
- Use press reports to increase your credibility.
- Always include proof of nonprofit status, even with renewal grants.
- Keep staff and consultant bios brief.
- Don't include bulky items such as DVDs or books unless requested.

Chapter 18

Putting It All Together

In This Chapter

- Making the best first impression with your proposal
- Presenting your proposal
- Formatting the proposal to win friends
- Making special presentations
- Delivering your proposal to best effect

After you've completed what might be months of work on a proposal, you want to be sure it leaves your charity with the blessing of all involved. You also want to ensure it makes the best impression on the funder. The smallest details can make a difference, and no matter how trivial some details might seem, your proposal deserves to be received and seen in the best possible light.

When I prepare a proposal for submission, I look at the package as a little drama that will unfold as the funder opens and first looks at it. I carefully place the parts in the order I want them to be read, and I also take time to decide where page breaks occur (especially in the cover letter) and which paper it's printed on. Yes, I do get a little crazy about this, but it makes a difference.

In this chapter, I give you tips on how to make a good impression—and how to avoid making a bad one.

Final Internal Review

Chances are, the proposal has changed a lot since the program officer (or clinic director, librarian, coach, and so on) last saw it. It's usually a good idea to give her one last chance to review the entire proposal, complete with attachments. (Remember to cover or exclude any confidential salary information when sharing the proposal with anyone who doesn't already have access to this information.)

Be sure to remind the program officer that you have to present the program in terms that will appeal to the funder. Just because her language has been largely left behind doesn't mean the program has changed. Offer to translate the proposal back into the original terms if necessary. If you think bringing program staff back into the process at this late stage will delay submission, you might skip this step with your executive director's consent.

Make notes for your own use that explain how you arrived at each budget line. You'll be asked to review this with the finance or program staff after the grant comes in, and believe me, in six months you'll have forgotten how the printing line got to $6,000.

When I discussed customizing the proposal for each funder in Chapter 14, I asked you to create a checklist of the required parts of the proposal and attachments. Use that checklist now to be sure you've prepared all the parts. You might even ask a colleague to review the checklist with you. After the proposal has been completely assembled and all concerned have had a chance for a final review, it's time to prepare your package for the mail.

You Can Be Too Pretty

Print the cover letter on your charity's letterhead. If it takes more than a page, use blank pages of similar color and quality for subsequent pages. Use regular photocopy paper for everything else. Using heavier paper looks wasteful. If you're fundraising for an environmental organization, always use recycled paper. Recycled paper makes a good impression on other socially conscious funders, too, and you'll be doing the environment a favor at the same time.

HOW TO SAY IT

I like to make the cover letter stand out as the personal communication it's meant to be. Not only should it be on different paper (namely the charity's letterhead), but you might also indent the paragraphs to distinguish it. Changing the font, however, might make it look too unlike the proposal.

Twelve-point type is optimum for proposals and cover letters, and never use a font smaller than eleven points. Budgets and charts with numbers might use a font as small as 10 points if the spacing makes it easily legible. You might laugh at these guidelines, but the trustees who will read your proposal are mostly, like me, over 40 with eyesight that isn't what it once was. They'll appreciate receiving documents they can read easily. In print, fonts with serifs (such as Times Roman) are easier to read than sans serif fonts (such as Arial). You'll also find you can get more words to a page using Times New Roman as opposed to using Arial.

Margins of at least 1 inch all around also make a document easier to read. Using a discrete header or footer that identifies your charity and gives page numbers can come in handy for the funder if pages get scrambled in the funder's photocopying process. Avoid putting the funder's name in a header or footer. It's too easy to forget to change these when revising the proposal for a new funder, and failing to do so will make you look incompetent.

Standard proposal formatting calls for paragraphs not to be indented. In addition, I like to have paragraphs formatted flush left with a ragged right margin. Justified text might make pretty blocks on the page, but because justification compromises the spacing between letters and words, it ends up making the text harder to read.

Save your beautiful glossy folders for press packets and sponsorship proposals. Spending a lot on presentation materials can put off funders.

To staple or to paperclip, that is the question—one with an easy answer. Paperclip, always. Chances are the funder will need to make additional copies of your proposal. Stapling makes this more difficult. I clip together each section separately (cover letter, executive summary/proposal, and each attachment) and then use a large clip for the entire package so it comes out of the envelope in one piece. A thick annual report or other publication might not fit into the clip, but all the unbound sheets should.

Use an envelope that looks professional but not flashy. I think white envelopes are always best. The brown craft ones look too plain. Colored ones might make the proposal stand out in a stack of mail, but I don't think it does so in a positive way.

Label your envelope clearly as a proposal, letter of inquiry, or report. This makes it easier for the funder to sort their mail, and they will appreciate it. You also avoid your time-sensitive proposal getting lost in a pile of reports from other charities.

Playing to Your Audience

Arts organizations, especially large ones, are expected to present themselves in a more dramatic manner. But even arts groups should consider the impression that very elaborate materials will make on the funder because of the expense involved in printing and mailing them.

Social service agencies, even large ones, usually have more simply produced materials. I once quit making contributions for several years to a social service agency that sent me an elaborate annual report, complete with vellum overlays and embossing. I suspected that the printing and design had been donated, but it was really off-putting to receive such an expensive report, considering their mission.

There are, of course, exceptions to every rule. When going to the sponsorship office of a major company, you might want to gloss-up your presentation a notch or two. In this situation, the people reviewing your proposal are more likely to believe that it takes money to make money and that a successful organization won't be shy about looking successful.

The sophistication of word-processing programs makes it tempting to format proposals using all the bells and whistles available. Don't do it. Rather than impressing the funder with your sophistication, you might give the impression that you spent too much time on the appearance of the proposal—time that could have better been spent creating and submitting additional proposals.

This isn't to say you should never include an illustration in a proposal. Charts and graphs created by a spreadsheet program can make a point better than dozens of words, and a photograph illustrating your program description can also be effective. But never add any kind of illustration just to break up the page or because it's a nice picture related to your organization. *Everything* in the proposal—words and images—exists to tell *one story only*. Don't confuse the funder with extraneous materials of any kind.

Chances are that at some point you'll want to raise money for an Internet project. Submitting samples of your work on the Internet can be tricky. Will the people reviewing your work be savvy enough using the Internet to understand what you want them to see? This is another place where redundancy can serve you well.

For a sample of work on the Internet, I include instructions on how to find the pages I want them to see (with URL and a sequence of items to click), but I also include pictures of those pages, frequently with commentary in the margins. That way, they can view it online or on paper—whichever works for them. (Hint: use the *Print Screen* key on your computer and then paste the screen capture in the Paint program [found under *Accessories*] to save a picture of any Internet page.)

Getting the Package Delivered

Unless the funder has specified some other method of delivery (such as electronic), send your proposal by U.S. mail whenever possible. Express delivery companies offer highly reliable service, but the funder will note the additional cost. This might send the wrong message about how your charity spends its money.

> **WORDS TO THE WISE**
>
> Ironically, some federal government agencies advise you to use any service other than the U.S. mail for your proposal because of security requirements for mail going to government offices, which slows service and can destroy some types of enclosures. A quick phone call to the agency can help you make the right delivery choice.

If you've planned ahead, you shouldn't need to send the proposal express anyway. If you're running late, however, by all means use the express delivery rather than miss a deadline. If the funder has a firm deadline *and* you're running late, use a service (such as certified express mail) that will give you proof-of-mail date and delivery. If you've submitted your proposal well in advance, the proof of delivery will be unnecessary because you can call and check on the receipt.

Many deadlines will be a postmark deadline, which means the post office must post-mark your proposal by that date. The date on your metered postage machine doesn't count. Get a stamped receipt from the post office when you mail your proposal, because frequently the return receipt you pay extra for will never be returned or returned unsigned.

So let's talk stamps. Yes, even the stamp is important, especially when sending a proposal to an individual. The larger the funder, the less important the stamp because at a large foundation, the person opening the mail will have no part in evaluating the proposal. Metered postage works fine in these cases.

Stamps have a hand-prepared look that sends a subtle message that a real person prepared this proposal just for them. When sending a proposal to an individual, use large commemorative stamps rather than the standard flag stamps or the small ones that look too much like third-class mail postage.

One last reminder: follow the funder's instructions to the letter as to order of materials and delivery, just as you did for content.

> **WORDS TO THE WISE**
>
> Mail even a short proposal flat. If you fold it and the funder needs to make an additional copy, it will be that much harder for them.

First impressions are always important. A perfectly written proposal can be sunk if it arrives out of order or is hard to read. By making it easy for the funder to process your proposal, you're starting out with points in your favor. Formatting and presentation are simple things to do right, and they can make a real difference in how funders perceive your charity.

The Least You Need to Know

- Give those most involved with a program a final chance to review the grant proposal before you send it.
- Use a serif font in 12-point type on inexpensive plain white (or recycled) paper and similar paper for your envelope.
- Keep document formatting simple with flush left paragraphs, varying it only to make an important point.
- Paper clips win out over staples every time.
- Avoid expensive express delivery of proposals unless it's the only way to make a deadline.
- Use the same care in assembling proposals sent by e-mail, and clearly identify all files.
- Follow the funder's directions for putting the parts of the proposal together and for mailing.

Other Types of Applications

In This Chapter

- Condensing your entire proposal into a letter
- Making foundation forms work for you
- Electronic proposal submissions

Fifty percent or more of the proposals you submit, you will prepare just as I've described in the preceding chapters, but you do need to be familiar with some exceptions. With a full proposal, you have the most control over how you present the case for your program to the funder, making some parts longer and others shorter, as best suits your program.

Other means of requesting grants—letters, forms, and electronic versions of these— reduce the flexibility while calling more on your ability to make your case creatively, in whatever form the funder wants to receive the proposal.

Letter Proposals

Smaller foundations often ask you to submit your proposal in the form of a letter, frequently specifying the maximum number of pages you can use. I gave you two examples of letter proposals in Chapter 6 in the discussion on proposals to individuals.

When foundation trustees have little or no professional staff to assist them, a letter proposal is a practical means to reduce the amount of materials they must evaluate in their grantmaking. Keeping that in mind, you should scrupulously respect any length restrictions. Don't depend on adding attachments that haven't been requested to get around the length restrictions, because they won't be read.

> **WORDS TO THE WISE**
>
> When a funder asks that you restrict your proposal to a set number of pages, don't employ formatting tricks, such as smaller margins and fonts, to squeeze in more words. You won't help your proposal, and in fact, you might have your proposal rejected out of hand because it's too hard to read.

That's not to say letter proposals shouldn't have any enclosures. Funders requiring a letter proposal usually ask for a program budget and proof of nonprofit status to be attached at minimum. Enclosing an organizational brochure along with the proposal provides the funder with additional background without adding much in the way of bulk to the proposal. But remember that everything you need the funder to understand must appear within the letter itself.

A letter proposal must …

- Function as a cover letter by making a connection with the reader on a personal level and tying the proposal to the funder's interests.

- Act as an executive summary by presenting the critical points of the proposal in condensed form.

- Include all the parts of a full proposal such as the statement of need, process, goals and objectives, key personnel, and evaluation procedure.

- Provide a context for and references to the budget.

If you look back at the sample letters in Chapter 6, you'll see that those very short letter proposals do all these things:

- Establish the personal connection by reference to the donor's friend and include his past support to show why the proposal is being sent to him. If this had been a foundation proposal, an extra sentence or two would have been used to tie the proposal to the foundation's interests.

- Demonstrate the need for the new animal shelter in a series of bullet points in executive summary fashion, with the objectives for the new shelter in a parallel series of bullet points.

- Mention only the fundraising goal for the program. But had the letters been longer, details on the costs of the building could have been added.

The letter proposal enables you to make a more personal appeal because the format encourages a "me and you" tone. I prefer this type of application to all others because of the personal touch, even though it requires greater discipline to keep the length down while making all the important points.

Form Proposals

The degree to which funders use forms varies widely. In many cases, the only form involved is a cover sheet that collects the basic contact information and gives broad strokes about the budget (such as a total for expenses and a total for income). These forms are just an adjunct to your full proposal. The forms I discuss here do, in large part, substitute for a full proposal.

Forms give funders a means to ensure that they receive information in a uniform format from every applicant. This can make evaluating the proposals easier. Forms can also serve to decrease the distinctions between proposals submitted by large organizations with considerable fundraising resources and smaller ones with just one grant writer.

PHILANTHROPY FACT

You're most likely to encounter form proposals when applying for government grants that will provide limited space for each section of the proposal. But even these forms might allow a few additional pages for the program narrative.

When formatting and presentation are made uniform, the quality of the writing, of course, comes to the forefront. This means you have to do an even better job when preparing a grant application form. Having restricted space to make all your points requires everyone who edits your proposal to exercise restraint so it doesn't exceed the allowable length.

A number of regional associations of grantmakers provide a standardized application that many of its members accept. In most cases, these are little more than a cover sheet, an outline to follow when developing your proposal, and a budget form.

The forms likely will be PDF or MS Word files. The more sophisticated forms will be downloadable with empty fields you fill in. Others will require you to fill in the fields using a typewriter, but these are, fortunately, disappearing as fast as typewriters. Saving your work in a PDF fill-in-the-blanks form usually requires additional software.

Regional associations intend their common applications to make it simpler for the grantseeker as well as the grantmaker. No matter how common the application requirements, you must still take all the care described in this book to customize your proposal for each funder. To their credit, the instructions for the regional associations remind you of this. In the end, I'm not sure how much time the forms save anyone, but the outlines each association offers are useful in organizing your proposal.

Chicago Area Grant Application Form

Working collaboratively, representatives from Chicago's foundations and corporate giving programs and a broad range of nonprofit organizations designed this form in order to streamline the grantseeking process.

Be strategic. Make sure that the goals, objectives, and amount requested in your proposal match the criteria of the funder you are approaching. A cover letter should be included with each proposal which introduces your organization and your request, and makes a strategic link between your proposal and the funder's mission and grantmaking interests. Information about many individual grant programs is available from each funder at the Library of the Donors Forum of Chicago.

Important notes

1. Please keep in mind that different funders have different guidelines, priorities, deadlines and timetables. In addition, funders who accept this form may require a preliminary concept paper or request additional information at any stage in the proposal process.

   Know each funder's grantmaking philosophy, program interests, and criteria.

   It is important to follow specific instructions from the funder.

   Be aware of each funder's application process, including timetable and preferred method of initial contact.

2. Include a cover letter that outlines the strategic link between your proposal and the funder's mission.

3. This form must be completed in its entirety.

4. Develop your proposal using the format on page 3.

Resources

Call or write each funder to obtain a copy of funding guidelines and/or annual report.

Use the Donors Forum of Chicago's Grantseekers Toolbox (at http://www.donorsforum.org/resource/gstoolbox1.html), Illinois Funding Source (at http://ifs.donorsforum.org), the *Directory of Illinois Foundations* and other local and national directories as a starting point to your research.

Visit the Donors Forum Library to conduct research on private grantmakers. The Library is open to the public and is located at 208 South LaSalle, Suite 735, Chicago, IL 60604. Regular hours are from 9:00 a.m. to 4:00 p.m. Monday through Friday and until 6:00 p.m. on the second and fourth Wednesday of each month. The Library's telephone number is (312) 578-0175; TDD 578-0159.

Foundations/Corporate Giving Programs that accept the Chicago Area Grant Application Form

Alphawood Foundation (fka WPWR-TV Channel 50 Foundation)	Circle of Service	GATX Corporation	C. Louis Meyer Family Foundation	Retirement Research Foundation
Aon Foundation	Community Memorial Foundation	Harris Bank Foundation	Michael Reese Health Trust	Hulda B. & Maurice L. Rothschild Foundation
The Baxter Allegiance Foundation	R.R. Donnelley & Sons Company	Hartmarx Charitable Foundation	The Elizabeth Morse Charitable Trust	SBC (fka Ameritech)
BP (fka Amoco Foundation)	EVEREN Foundation	IBM Corporation	ONDEO-Nalco Foundation	Sears Roebuck & Co.
The Bufka Foundation	Exelon Corporation/ Commonwealth Edison Company	ITW Foundation (fka Illinois Tool Works)	New Prospect Foundation	Albert J. Speh, Jr. and Claire R. Speh Foundation
Elizabeth F. Cheney Foundation	Jamee and Marshall Field Foundation	Mayer and Morris Kaplan Family Foundation	Northern Trust Co.	Irvin Stern Foundation
Chicago Bar Foundation	First United Church of Oak Park	John D. and Catherine T. MacArthur Foundation	Peoples Energy Co.	TCF National Bank
Chicago Tribune Foundation	Lloyd A. Fry Foundation	The McCall Family Foundation	Relations Foundation	VNA Foundation
				Washington Square Health Foundation

Chicago Area Grant Application Form
rev. 02/03

Donors Forum *of* Chicago

This form from the Chicago Donors Forum (donorsforum.org) collects much of the information you'd include in a proposal, but note that apart from the form, you create the narrative using their outline.

Chicago Area Grant Application Form

Grant Request

Amount requested: $ _____

This request is for: ☐ General operating support   ☐ Capital   ☐ Other: _____

☐ Program/project title: _____

Organizational Information

Organization name _____

Address, city, state, zip _____

Telephone _____ Fax _____ E-mail _____

Executive director _____ Telephone _____

Name/title of contact person _____ Telephone _____

Total organization budget for current year $ _____ United Way funded? ☐ Member ☐ Grant ☐ No

Date of incorporation _____ FEIN number (or equivalent) _____

Is your organization tax exempt under Section 501(c)(3)? ☐ Yes ☐ No   Section 509(a)? ☐ Yes ☐ No

If not, do you have a fiscal agent? *(please identify organization, contact person, and telephone number)* _____

_____

Primary service category of organization *(check only one)*

☐ Arts & culture   ☐ Human services   ☐ Education   ☐ Environment

☐ Health   ☐ Civic / economic development   ☐ Other *(specify)* _____

Summarize the organizationís mission *(2-3 sentences)* _____

_____

_____

_____

_____

Geographic service area(s)

☐ City of Chicago   ☐ Northwest Indiana   ☐ Regional/national

☐ County *(specify)* _____   ☐ Suburbs *(specify)* _____

☐ Chicago neighborhood(s) *(specify)* _____

☐ Other *(specify)* _____

Provide percentages and/or descriptions of the populations your organization serves.

Race/ethnicity (if applicable)

____ African American	____ Asian American/Pacific Islander
____ Caucasian	____ Hispanic/Latino
____ Native American	____ Other _____

Sex ____ Female   ____ Male

Other (i.e. disabled, age, gay/lesbian, etc.)

_____

Staff composition in numbers

	Professional	Support
Paid full-time	_____	_____
Paid part-time	_____	_____
Volunteers	_____	_____
Interns	_____	_____
Other	_____	_____
Totals	_____	_____

Donors Forum *of* **Chicago**

Grant Request *(continued)*

Summarize the purpose of your request *(5 sentences or fewer)*

_____

_____

_____

_____

_____

_____

_____

_____

_____

_____

Time frame in which the funds will be used: From _____ To _____

List other private and public funding sources for this particular request.

(If this is a request for general operating support, please see Attachment A6 on page 3.)

Funding sources—to date	*Amount*	*Date received*
_____	_____	_____
_____	_____	_____
_____	_____	_____
_____	_____	_____
_____	_____	_____

Funding sources—pending	*Amount*	*Anticipated receipt date*
_____	_____	_____
_____	_____	_____
_____	_____	_____
_____	_____	_____
_____	_____	_____

Organizational Budget *(last fiscal year)* Expenses $ _____ Revenues $ _____

Program/project Budget *(if applicable)* $ _____

Signature of authorized official _____ Date _____

Name/Title _____

Chicago Area Grant Application Form Page 2

Donors Forum *of* **Chicago**

Proposal Narrative *Please provide the following information in this order. Do not use more than 5 single-spaced pages, exclusive of attachments. Please staple; do not bind your application.*

A. Background

1. Organizationís mission, history, overall goals and/or objectives.

2. Description of current programs and activities. Please emphasize major achievements of the past two years.

3. Description of formal and informal relationships with other organizations.

B. Purpose of funding request

1. If applying for general operating support, briefly state how this grant will be used.

2. If your request is for a specific project or capital campaign, please provide the following information:

   The community and/or agency needs or problems that this effort will address, including population served.

   Describe how the project addresses these identified needs.

   Program or Capital Campaign description to include strategies employed to implement the proposed project: (1) goals and objectives, (2) timetable for accomplishing stated goals and objectives, (3) program methodology (program only), (4) staffing, and (5) collaboration with other agencies.

   If this is a collaboration, briefly describe the partners.

   If this request is for a specific program, explain how it will be supported after termination of the grant.

C. Evaluation

1. Explain how you will measure the effectiveness of your activities.

2. Describe your criteria for success.

3. Describe the results you expect to have achieved by the end of the funding period.

Required Attachments *Please provide in the following order.*

A. Finances

1. Audited financial statements for the last fiscal year, if available, or Form 990. If neither document is available, include unaudited financial statement.

2. Current yearís operating budget to include both projected expenses and revenues. Categorize expenses under program, general and administrative, and fundraising.

3. Program budget (with narrative, if applicable).

4. If request is for a multi-year grant, include multi-year program budget.

5. Capital budget and a list of Campaign Committee members (if applicable).

6. A list of foundations, corporations, or governmental agencies which funded the organization in the last fiscal year, including amounts contributed ($1,000 and above).

7. Itemization of use of requested funds (if requested by funder).

B. Other Supporting Materials

1. Verification of the organizationís or fiscal agentís tax-exempt status under Section 501(c) 3 and 509(a) of the IRS code. If using a fiscal agent, please include Letter of Authorization.

2. Grantee report (if previously funded).

3. Latest annual report or a summary of the organizationís prior yearís activities.

4. Current board list with related employment affiliation.

5. A description of ethnic and minority representation of Board of Directors in percentages (if requested by funder).

6. Qualifications of professional program staff (if applicable).

7. If the project for which funding is sought is a collaboration with other agencies, include letters of agreement from the collaborating agencies.

8. Letters of support and/or reviews (if applicable).

PHILANTHROPY FACT

The Foundation Center (foundationcenter.org), GrantStation (grantstation.com), and other organizations offer access to many of the application forms accepted in different regions.

Online Applications

Online grant applications are becoming the norm, with paper submission either discouraged or eliminated. Online applications usually involve a form that prompts you to enter information one piece at a time. In some cases, you're able to view all the questions before beginning so you know what's around the corner, but some funders aren't so accommodating.

On the face of it, online submission might sound like a great thing for the grant writer: you don't have to worry about getting it in on time (just press the "submit" button), and there are no decisions to make about paper, stamps, or other bothersome details.

Presentation, in fact, ceases to be a factor because every application appears identically formatted. And that's the reason I don't like electronic submissions. They make it much more difficult to give your proposal personality that would make it stand out in the crowd.

And don't be surprised if some online applications have more than a few bugs. One of the most common problems is that the application only works properly with Microsoft Internet Explorer and no other browser.

With all the cosmetics of the proposal removed, the grant writer's talents become even more important. You must do everything with words alone.

If possible, download and save or print the application and all instructions so you can work through various drafts using the actual form. More than likely, you'll have to work on each section separately in your word-processing program, pasting it into the form after all edits have been made. This gives you the advantage of spell-checking each section but makes it hard for anyone else to review what you've written in the context in which it will finally appear. Remember, too, that you'll probably lose formatting such as boldface, underlining, and bullet points when you paste text into the online form.

As you proceed through the online application, save as you go to prevent losing your hard work by an interrupted Internet connection or glitch when going to the next page.

> **WORDS TO THE WISE**
>
> Many online applications (especially those of government agencies) require you to register before you can begin work on the application. The registration process can take a few minutes or several weeks. Check ahead of time so you don't get stuck in the registration process and miss the grant deadline.

Online applications differ significantly depending on the sophistication of the programming. Some consist of forms identical to ones you would submit through regular mail. These are the easiest to complete because they're most like traditional printed forms. For examples of basic online applications, check out The Meadows Foundation (mfi.org) or the W. K. Kellogg Foundation (wkkf.org).

Some online applications are now structured so you're asked a series of questions that then determines the additional questions you'll be asked and sections you'll be asked to complete. These can be frustrating because they don't allow you to see the entire form at one time. At other times, this process can break down into manageable steps what might seem overwhelming when presented all at once. If you've applied to the funder before, consult the offline paper form you used in the past. The online form is probably very similar.

The New York State Council on the Arts' online application (introduced in 2003) uses the step-by-step procedure with the formerly fearsome budget form. Now, it asks you for each budget category one at a time, which feels less intimidating. The programming assembles all your figures into a completed form and even does the math for you. Of course, you must be prepared to answer each of the budget questions as they're asked, which requires prior knowledge of what they want to know.

Before pressing the "submit" button with any online application, print out a copy of the completed form for proofing and for your files. If possible, save an electronic copy, too.

Even if you registered well ahead of schedule, don't wait until the last minute to complete the online applications. The flurry of people completing last-minute applications can overload the funder's server and prevent you from submitting your application.

E-Mail Submissions

Many funders have taken only the first baby step into the electronic age, requiring you to submit your traditional application by e-mail. This gives you the advantage of formatting and reviewing your application just as if you were submitting it on paper. E-mail submission makes it easy for the program officer to cut and paste from your proposal when preparing for a panel or trustee's meeting.

When submitting a proposal by e-mail, you might want to save the different parts (cover letter, proposal, budget, etc.) as separate files. Make your nonprofit's name part of the name of each file (such as "LiteraryWorks-budget.xls") to help the funder find them later. Use the message of the e-mail to reinforce something in the cover letter and thank them for reviewing your proposal, but keep it very short. Put the name of your nonprofit and what you're sending (proposal, letter of inquiry, etc.) in the e-mail subject line.

If you are e-mailing a spreadsheet, don't unintentionally give the funder access to details about your budget process you might prefer they not know. Before submitting a budget by e-mail, I always copy the entire spreadsheet to a new one using "Edit/ Paste Special/Values Only" series of commands. That way, your formulas and cell comments don't get e-mailed along with the numbers. Even better, paste your spreadsheet into the document with your other grant materials using "Edit/Paste Special/ Picture" series of commands.

The Least You Need to Know

- A letter proposal must contain all the main elements of a full proposal but in condensed form.

- You must customize common applications for each funder, just as if you were preparing a proposal from scratch.

- Access common applications, and find out what funders accept them, from your regional grantmakers association or the Foundation Center's website (foundationcenter.org).

- Always save or print online applications before beginning work to see how the sections fit together.

- Carefully print and proof an application you plan to submit online or by e-mail; after you press the "submit" button, that's it.

Everything Else You Need to Know

Waiting just might be the hardest part of the grant-writing process. It can take months. What should you do in the meanwhile? I discuss what can improve (and what can sink) your chances of receiving the grant while you're waiting.

And then the letter arrives! Whether the answer is yes or no, you still have work to do to develop your relationship with the funder. Reporting back to the funder is critical if you hope to receive a second grant, so I take you through the steps in creating a good report, including what to do if the project has not progressed as you planned.

Individuals face special challenges in getting grants, so I've included a chapter on different research options for individuals and how to create a professional resumé and statement of purpose.

Finally, I've included some advice on how to become a successful freelance grant writer. Before you open for business, you need to examine the legal hurdles you must surmount, gather all the tools you'll need to succeed, learn how to set your fee, and know what to look for in clients.

Waiting for and Receiving the Verdict

In This Chapter

- What to do after you've submitted a proposal
- Making the most of a rejection
- Making the most of an acceptance

You've spent months preparing your grant proposal—researching, cultivating, writing, editing, and formatting. Now comes the really hard part: waiting for the verdict. And there can be considerable waiting involved. Some funders might take eight or nine months to inform you of their decision, but most will let you know in one to four months.

You won't just be waiting during that time: there are things you can do to help your application, and also things that can hurt your chances. In this chapter, I give you some guidelines so you know which are which.

No matter what the funder's verdict, you'll need to respond in a way that makes the best of either situation. Receiving the money doesn't mean you can ignore the funder. And having your proposal declined doesn't mean you give up. I cover both possibilities in this chapter.

Don't Be a Nudge

If you submitted your proposal well in advance of the funder's deadline, wait a week before calling to be sure he received it. The funder's program officer might have a suggestion for additional information that will help your proposal or even suggest you rework a section. Most often, he'll simply acknowledge it was received.

Always ask when you should expect to hear the result of their consideration of your proposal. Mark this date on your calendar, and follow up again somewhat after that date if you haven't heard from them. You might want to call earlier, but don't. The funder's staff has much more to do than keep you posted on the progress of your proposal.

These two calls are the only ones you should make while your proposal is under consideration, unless you have substantive information that could update your proposal.

What's a substantive update? It's not information that your chorus will be performing the fifth Bach cantata rather than the fourth one or the new soccer uniforms will be red instead of maroon. If, however, you have engaged a famous conductor to conduct one of the choral concerts or the soccer team has made it to the state semifinals, these bits of information would be worth passing on to the funder.

> **WORDS TO THE WISE**
>
> Send good news about your program or other grants received for it to the funder without delay. Not only can this strengthen your proposal, but it also reminds them of what you're doing. Don't report bad news unless it's so bad (such as all your funding falling through) that you need to withdraw the proposal, or so public that you know the funder will discover the information on his own. In the latter case, contacting the funder allows you to try to put a positive spin on the issue.

You should report any changes that positively affect the funding of the program under consideration. This would include a grant you'd listed as "pending" coming through. (I wouldn't contact a funder to tell them a grant didn't come through. You can always deal with this kind of bad news later.) In-kind donations of space or materials might also be worth reporting, depending on the degree to which they affect your ability to carry out a program.

There might be times when you must withdraw a proposal. This has to be one of the hardest things you'll ever have to do as a grant writer. If major funding from another source falls through, making it impossible for you to carry out the program, you have no choice but to withdraw the proposal. It's also feasible that your charity could decide to postpone or cancel a program between the time you submit the proposal and when you expect a decision from the funder.

Withdrawing your proposal in cases such as these allows for a better long-term relationship with the funder. You never want to be in the position of sending back a check, which would be disrespectful of the time the funder spent in evaluating your proposal. Of course, programs can also change after you receive a grant, but I discuss that situation in Chapter 21.

Handling Rejection

After carefully preparing a proposal that perfectly matched the funder's interests and was beautifully crafted, you receive a two-paragraph letter telling you your proposal has been declined. Funders employ widely differing levels of tact and courtesy in their rejection letters.

The best letter—if there can be a "best" rejection letter—tells you some specifics about why they didn't fund your program. Other letters make general excuses about previous commitments to other charities and limited funds.

Then again, you might receive a letter like the one a colleague recently received that said they weren't being funded again (after 10 continuous years!) and shouldn't call to ask why because the funder wouldn't tell them. That message got through loud and clear.

No matter what kind of rejection letter you receive, you'll be disappointed, but how you deal with rejection is a sign of maturity. Unless the funder expressly tells you not to contact them, it's wise and perfectly acceptable to call them to try to determine more than what you were told in the letter.

If one of your board members tried to help you get a grant, tell him of the rejection. When informing him that the grant was not approved, be sure to thank him for helping. You don't want the board member to feel powerless because a grant didn't come through. That same board member might be able to help you get another one later.

Where Did You Go Wrong?

In most cases, a phone call is the best way to follow up on a rejection. Asking the funder to write you an explanation creates more work for them, and if they had wanted to tell you in a letter, they already would have. The rejection follow-up call can either improve your chances the next time you approach a funder or burn your bridges forever.

WORDS TO THE WISE

The comments you receive as a result of a rejected proposal can be many times more valuable than information you get from a funder before applying. The rejection comments focus directly on your program and can present a blueprint for your next proposal.

When making these calls, keep the following points in mind:

- Make the call to your contact at the funder. Don't try to go to the head of the foundation just because that's who signed the letter.

- Be polite, no matter what you might be feeling. If you're particularly disappointed by a rejection, wait a few days before calling.

- Respect whatever your contact tells you. If he or she says your proposal didn't meet the funder's criteria (even though you know they've made similar grants), ask how you might have modified your proposal to fit better with their interests. Never argue.

- Be open to using this conversation to mention other programs your charity conducts. Perhaps your program wasn't successful because they only fund after-school programs and your proposal was for activities that were part of the regular curriculum. Introduce the alternate program now to get feedback to use in preparing that proposal at a later time.

- Ask if the trustees responded positively to any parts of your program.

- If there's a possibility of receiving a grant from this funder in the future, ask how long you should wait before reapplying.

- Take careful notes of your call to use when preparing the next proposal.

- Review your notes with program and administrative staff so everyone understands what might be done to receive funding in the future (or why you've removed the funder from the prospect list).

If a program officer has been helpful to you concerning why your grant application was not approved, a short note thanking him or her for speaking with you is a nice touch. Even if you were told there was no point in reapplying, the note will help build your personal relationship with someone who, a year later, might be working at a different foundation and be in a position to help you.

WORDS TO THE WISE

Try not to look at an unsuccessful proposal as a failure—you'll have many of them. Instead, make it a growth experience by opening communications with a funder and getting feedback about the specifics of your proposal.

The Freedom of Information Act requires that federal government funders give you the reasons for a grant decision. Some agencies require that you submit a request in writing and then make you wait some time before you receive the reasons. Others simply tell you over the phone what you need to know. Private funders are under no such obligation, but many, if not most, will share with you what they can within the funder's policies.

Persistence

"Three strikes and you're out" has many connotations these days, but I also use it as my general gauge as to how often to apply to a funder unsuccessfully before giving up on them. I figure that the first time I approach a funder, the "we're already committed to other charities" excuse is probably genuine. If I've subsequently done a decent job to cultivate them, the second time that excuse begins to ring a little hollow. By the third time, I know they're just being polite.

In the best cases, you'll receive comments from the funder that either allow you to modify your proposal the second (or third) time to increase your chances of being funded or allow you to eliminate them from your prospect list. In other cases, you won't know what went wrong. If your research tells you a funder should be open to your proposal, you should try more than once to give them the opportunity to fund your charity.

WORDS TO THE WISE

Never submit a rejected proposal to the same funder a second time. It's a waste of time, not to mention disrespectful of the funder's time and of your charity's investment in paying you to create proposals.

Acceptance

Congratulations! You received a grant! Now you're done, right? Wrong. Things just got more complicated.

Calling to say thank you to your contact at the funder is a courteous practice and a great first step in developing a relationship. The funder's program officer will remember you did this. Also, even when you are successful, it's a good idea to ask for comments from the trustees or grant panel. Knowing what parts of your proposal appealed to this funder might help you focus proposals to others.

If you received the amount you requested (which is fairly rare), and other funding has been coming in, your program will be fully funded and can proceed as planned. It's still advisable to review proposals with program staff when the money arrives so you can find out if they've already modified the program and take appropriate actions with the funders if needed.

In some cases, reduced funding might make it impossible to carry out the program as described in your proposal. If this is so, the sooner you let all funders know about changes to the program, the better.

In my experience, funders are understanding about changes to programs. If a program will still be able to accomplish its mission and goals (even if it's conducted in a different manner and serves fewer people), it's unlikely you'll encounter a problem. Some funders ask you to send them a letter noting the changes. It's important you do this so your reports will be based on the modified proposal rather than the original.

Remember: a grant is a contract between your charity and the funder. You've accepted the funder's money on the condition that your charity will carry out a certain program in a particular way in a specified amount of time. The funder has a right to know if any conditions of the contract won't be met.

A Prompt, Simple Thank You

Within a day of receiving a grant award letter, someone in authority at your charity should sign and send a letter acknowledging receipt of the grant and thanking the funder. Ideally, the same person who signed the cover letter that accompanied the proposal will sign the acknowledgment letter. The executive director, board president, or even the director of development can sign the acknowledgment letter. The important thing is that it be sent promptly.

HOW TO SAY IT

The thank you letter is the first step in developing a long-term relationship with a funder. Take care to make these letters personal, specific to the grant, and free of boilerplate text (except for the required IRS language).

An acknowledgment letter should contain ...

- A thank you.

- A statement that the grant money will be used as stated in the proposal.

- A brief restatement of how the grant will assist your charity and its clients.

- A statement that the funder is receiving no benefit by making the grant (to satisfy IRS regulations).

Here's a general acknowledgment letter:

Dear Ms. Sterling:

The Community Clinic's staff faces an enormous challenge every day to meet clients' needs within the clinic's limited means. That challenge just got easier, thanks to your generous $6,000 grant. We will use your grant to support the mobile unit that provides free blood pressure and blood tests in neighborhoods throughout the city. We will specifically use it to extend the number of hours the mobile unit operates, as described in our proposal to you.

Since we applied to the Sterling Family Foundation, Lifeline Pharmaceutical, Inc., has made a grant of both cash and equipment that will allow us to update the mobile unit. The better equipment, along with the extended hours made possible by your grant, will make a significant difference in the number of people with heart disease we can identify early and treat.

Your support of this program is greatly appreciated, and we look forward to reporting to you on the execution of the expanded program in due course.

Sincerely,

Herbert Washington, M.D.

Herbert Washington, M.D.

P.S. As you received no goods or services in connection with this grant, it is fully tax-deductible under IRS regulations.

I like to put the legalistic IRS language in the postscript so it doesn't spoil the flow of the letter, but I just as easily could have inserted it before the last paragraph.

If one of your board members helped pave the way for a successful grant, you should write her a thank you, too. Depending on your relationship with the board member involved, an e-mail or phone call might do. If the grant is particularly large, a letter or call from your board president to the helpful board member would also be in order.

No, I Really Mean Thank You

You can never say thank you too often. Especially with large grants or grants of any size from a new funder, it's a good idea to send a second thank you a few days later from someone else at your charity. This is especially important if, in order to get the acknowledgment letter out quickly, it didn't have the same signer as the proposal cover letter.

The second thank you should not repeat any language in the first one. Only the acknowledgment letter should have the IRS language, so you have more freedom creating the second letter. And yes, it might be you writing all the thank you letters, no matter who signs them.

Really, Really Thank You!

A handwritten note from one of your charity's board members is a nice follow-up to the letters from staff. These are particularly important when you use a board contact to help get the grant. Use the signer's personal stationery or note cards. These notes can be very short, something like this:

Dear Mary,

I was thrilled to hear that the Sterling Family Foundation has made a grant to the Community Clinic. I know we have you to thank for this. It will mean a great deal to our clients to have the extended service, and it means a great deal to me personally to know we have your support. Thanks so much.

Best wishes,

Cindi

HOW TO SAY IT

Keep a supply of plain note cards on hand for your executive director or board president to use when sending handwritten thank you notes to funders. If he or she has terrible handwriting, the note can be typed, but have someone with good handwriting address the envelope by hand, and use a stamp—not metered postage—on important thank you letters.

The Least You Need to Know

- Limit your contact with a funder after submitting a proposal to one call to check on receipt and one to check on the result (only if they're late in responding to you).
- Accept rejections graciously, but call to see if your contact is free to share information about why you weren't successful.
- Gather as much information as possible in a rejection follow-up call to help you craft the next proposal.
- Don't give up on a funder with the first rejection unless you're told flat out not to try again.
- Acknowledge grants received immediately, including the required IRS language about tax-deductibility.
- Follow the acknowledgment with one or more additional thank you letters from different people at your charity.

Chapter 21

Reporting on Success

In This Chapter

- Cultivating a funder beyond the thank you letter
- Communicating with the funder about problems with a program
- Preparing financial reports
- Modifying a grant contract
- Reporting on successful and unsuccessful programs

In Chapter 10, I wrote about the importance of cultivating funders before asking for money. But cultivation doesn't end when you receive a check. In many ways, it's just begun.

Funders' reporting requirements on how their money was spent vary, but all at least ask for a report a year from when they awarded the grant. You could wait 12 months before communicating with the funder, but in doing so, you would be passing up golden opportunities to make the funder a long-term friend of your charity. In this chapter, I show you how you can integrate the funder's reporting requirements with other communications to cement a relationship.

Developing a Relationship

The thank you letter, discussed in Chapter 20, represents the first step in cultivating the funder into a friend. If you send two or more thank you letters, you've established multiple lines of communication and possibilities for a relationship.

In working to develop a relationship with a funder, you're not just manipulating them to your own ends. In many cases, the funder will want to establish a relationship with your agency. By furthering your work, they accomplish their goals as well. So don't be shy or hesitant about contacting funders after you've received the grant. True, some will want to remain distant and uninvolved, and they'll let you know that pretty soon, but you owe it to your charity to try to establish a lasting relationship.

When the funder believes they can work with you on any project related to your common mission, you'll find that they will contact you about new initiatives they plan to fund before the RFP ever goes out. They'll also work closely with you to craft future proposals that get funded. This chapter is devoted to the various ways to cultivate and communicate with funders to give you the best possible chance at developing this kind of relationship.

Giving Credit Where Credit's Due

Publicly acknowledging the contribution you've received follows closely on the heels of the thank you letter in establishing good karma at the beginning of the funder/grantee relationship. To start with, you'll want to add the funder's name to the list of donors on your website or anywhere else you publish a list of donors. This can be your next concert program, a donor recognition wall, or any publication. On your website, you can also provide a link to the funder's website.

WORDS TO THE WISE

Out-of-date donor lists on websites occur far too often. Leaving out a current donor shows a disregard for the importance of their gift, and I believe leaving a donor on long after their gift can discourage subsequent gifts.

Carefully note the spelling of the funder's name on its letterhead, and use that form in all acknowledgments (unless the funder instructs you otherwise). Is it "The Smith Foundation" or just "Smith Foundation"? These little things can matter a great deal.

Occasionally, a funder will ask in the award letter that their grant remain anonymous. Always scrupulously honor this request. Mark their database record, and let program and development staff know about their request. If the letter says nothing about anonymity, you can assume the funder won't mind being listed, but if you intend to do anything else to publicize the gift, always ask for permission.

Your donor lists make your donors known largely to an internal audience (even if on your website) because only those seeking your services (or your colleagues at other charities looking for prospects) will be likely to read them. If you have received a major grant, you'll also want to let the world know about it by issuing a press release. Always get the funder's permission before issuing a press release. You'll want a quote from them for the release anyway, but also give them the option of seeing the press release draft before you issue it.

You can do a press release for an anonymous gift, but unless you've received a really large gift, the press won't be interested because one of the major facts (the donor's name) isn't available to them. And if you receive a really major gift (say, in the millions), some reporter will try to ferret out the identity of the donor and probably will succeed.

Keeping in Touch

As your program progresses, you'll want to keep your funders informed. It's critical to the development of a long-term relationship that you do this, but you don't want to overdo it and put them off.

To keep funders informed about your project and your charity, consider sending them the following:

- Invitations to events related to the program they funded. These could range from formal events (such as a concert or dinner) to sessions for clients (when the privacy of clients is not an issue).

- Copies of positive news coverage of the program. If you receive negative coverage, you might need to inform the funder with an explanation of why the coverage was negative and possibly a copy of a letter to the editor you have written, whether published or not.

- Copies of your publications that report on the program, such as your newsletter or new information posted on your website.

- Copies of any special publications created for or by the program, such as application forms, catalogs, or books created by clients.

The funder will probably expect to receive these things from you. Sending them in advance of formal reports helps keep the relationship going.

> **WORDS TO THE WISE**
>
> Scandals have rocked several charities in the last few years, which have led to greater scrutiny and public suspicion. Should there ever be even a hint in the press about a problem in your charity, contact your funders right away. You might not be able to turn a story around, but you can assure funders that you share their concerns about how their grant money is spent.

You might be tempted to share with the funder thankful letters you receive from clients, but I'd save these to include with a formal report.

Your charity might have other publications and events not related to the funded program. Be judicious in sending these to the funder. Just as with the proposal, you want to keep the funder's focus on the project they have funded. You want to keep your charity in the forefront of the funder's mind, but don't go too far and be a pest. If the funder receives too much unrelated information, they might stop reading anything you send them.

Gathering Information

The grant writer acts as the pivot point between the funder and the program staff. You can't do a good job of keeping the funder informed unless you know how programs are progressing. Attend meetings where program staff discuss programs. Ask questions. Attend program activities whenever possible. There's nothing quite like firsthand experience of a project to make your next report or grant proposal take on a whole new personal tone.

You'll also find it helpful to let program staff know what kinds of information you need to report to the funder. That way, they can gather the information you need as the project progresses, rather than trying to make it up at the end. The information you'll need relates directly to the goals and objectives stated in the grant proposal.

Progress Reports

Some funders require that you submit a progress or interim report at a time they specify, typically six months. If a project started slowly, that doesn't mean you can delay or skip the interim report. Send it in on time, explaining any delays with the program.

Usually, the narrative portion of an interim report is in letter form. Prepare these reports with great care. Anything stated in the progress report forms the basis for the final report. For example, don't get yourself in trouble by overstating the progress that's been made in the interim report.

If the grant was to make possible 1,200 free meals and after six months you've only served 300, you should explain why. Perhaps the program's start was delayed or the health department closed down your kitchen or bad weather kept away clients. It's better to take advantage of the interim report to explain why things aren't going as planned than to find yourself at the end of the grant period telling the funder the program failed. If you need to make adjustments in the goals, request them in an interim report.

WORDS TO THE WISE

Writing the funder to modify a grant proposal, although not something you want to do often, is critical when a program does not go as planned. By modifying your proposal, your program's final results will be judged against the revised one rather than the original, allowing you to report successful completion of your program.

An interim report also includes a financial report contrasting the proposal budget with actual expenses. Again, if it looks as if there might be a discrepancy at the end of the program, it's better to inform the funder in advance.

Funders realize that in an imperfect world, conditions affecting your charity change. Asking to modify the grant contract should not be a big deal. Going all the way to the end of a program and then telling the funder the project was unsuccessful *is* a big deal. Never let your charity get in that situation.

If a funder does not require an interim report, it would still be a good idea to send something before the end of the grant period. In this case, it can be a feel-good letter of two or three pages reporting on progress that's been made. Of course, if problems are accumulating with the project, inform all funders as well as those requiring a report.

Here's an abbreviated interim report for the internship program for curators described in Chapter 14.

Dear Ms. Brown:

It is my pleasure to report to the Brown Trust on the Curatorial Internship Program since the awarding of your generous grant in September 2010. The program has thus far met or exceeded all our expectations and brought to us three very talented young curators.

City Art Museum conducted outreach for this program through letters sent to the career development offices at three local colleges with large minority populations and to six local galleries that are known for presenting the work of minority artists. We widely publicized the program through press releases, on our website, and on a number of Internet job-posting services. We also held a meeting for interested applicants at State College, which 60 potential applicants attended.

We received a record 30 applications as a direct result of these outreach efforts, which made it very difficult to select only three. The City Art Museum curators along with Sara Bright, curator of contemporary art at the Asian Art Museum, served as the panel to select the interns.

The panel selected five applicants. Because of the intense working relationship between the curators and interns, it was not possible for us to accept all five, even if funding had permitted this expansion. When approached, one applicant had already accepted another offer, so we invited the next three in the panel's ranking to join the program, and all three accepted. We encouraged the fifth candidate to apply again next year.

The interns have since been working directly with the curators assigned to them on upcoming exhibitions. This has so far mostly included research using the museum's library and other resources. The curators are very pleased with the interns' enthusiasm and resourcefulness.

We look forward to reporting to you again at the end of the program year, by which time the interns will have begun preparations for the exhibitions they will curate at the end of their second year. Should you have any questions about this report, I can be reached at (414) 555-1234 or schin@cartmuseum.org.

Sincerely,

Susan Chin

Susan Chin
Head Curator

Note that the report comes from the head curator, not the museum director, who most likely would have signed the grant proposal, nor from someone in the development office. Having a curator sign the report emphasizes the curators' direct involvement with the interns, from selection through their two-year term and beyond. Needless to say, the grant writer actually wrote the letter.

Because the program just got started, the report of necessity concentrates on the selection of the interns rather than what they've done. Now let's look at the financial report that would accompany this letter.

Note that this budget covers two years, reflecting the program's two-year time frame. Because this report comes after six months, exactly half of all personnel costs for the first year have been included in the *Actuals* column at the far right. Other expense items are not evenly distributed. For example, virtually all the outreach costs have already been incurred, but no exhibition costs are claimed because that part of the program takes place in the second year.

HOW TO SAY IT

You might well include a budget narrative with interim reports to explain the rationale behind the allocation of expenses. Even pointing out the obvious (such as the exhibition being part of the program's second year) might save the funder time in figuring it out for themselves.

Income for this program came from a variety of funders, most of which made two-year commitments. Because most are making the grant in equal installments, the surplus in year one will balance an equal deficit in year two.

For an interim report, it would have been acceptable to delete the columns for the second year and the total project costs. This would have made a simpler presentation, but I thought it would be more helpful for you to see the full presentation.

Curatorial Internship Program

	Year 1	Year 2	Total	6-Month Interim Report Actuals
Expenses				
Personnel				
Curators (3 @ 12%)	$27,000	$27,000	$54,000	$13,548
Registrar @ 5%	$3,500	$3,500	$7,000	$1,600
Librarian @ 5%	$3,000	$3,000	$6,000	$1,500
Fringe benefits	$6,365	$6,365	$12,730	$3,163
Subtotal salaried personnel	*$39,865*	*$39,865*	*$79,730*	*$19,811*
Intern Stipends (3)	$66,000	$66,000	$132,000	$33,000
Total Personnel	**$105,865**	**$105,865**	**$211,730**	**$52,811**
Program Expenses				
Marketing/outreach	$5,000	$500	$5,500	$4,921
Supplies	$600	$1,000	$1,600	$302
Travel	$1,000	$2,000	$3,000	$98
Photocopying	$800	$1,900	$2,700	$110
Telephone	$100	$400	$500	$30
Postage/Delivery	$400	$400	$800	$338
Exhibition expenses	0	$40,000	$40,000	0
Contingency	$300	$1,200	$1,500	$15
Subtotal direct expenses	*$8,200*	*$47,400*	*$55,600*	*$5,814*
Indirect costs @ 15%	$17,160	$23,010	$40,170	$8,794
Total Expenses	**$131,225**	**$176,275**	**$307,500**	**$67,419**
Income				
Consolidated Arts Fund	$75,000	$75,000	$150,000	$75,000
Brown Trust	$50,000	$50,000	$100,000	$50,000
Bankers Bank	$10,000	$10,000	$20,000	$10,000
Community Trust	$8,000	$12,000	$20,000	$8,000
Jones Family Foundation	$7,500	0	$7,500	$7,500
Adams Family Trust (pending)	0	$10,000	$10,000	0
Total Income	**$150,500**	**$157,000**	**$307,500**	**$150,500**
Surplus/(Deficit)	**$19,275**	**–$19,275**	**0**	**$83,081**

Spending the Money

It seems obvious that your charity would spend the money received from grants in the manner the funder agreed to. But I've seen many cases where this hasn't happened. Those running programs sometimes don't understand that the funder didn't just make a $15,000 grant—the funder made a grant of $10,000 to be spent on personnel, $500 to be spent on telephone service, $2,500 to be spent on travel, $2,000 to be spent on printing, and so on.

If it turns out you incurred no travel expenses, that doesn't mean you can spend that $2,500 on something else. Small amounts (like $100 or $200) don't need clearance, but it doesn't hurt to keep the funder informed and involved with major changes. This might be an unrealistically strict interpretation of the use of grant money, but if you're not spending the money as planned, the program probably hasn't been conducted as planned, either, and that can present problems when reporting the program's results to the funder. A gentle inquiry of program staff as a program progresses about how the budgeted expenses compare to actual expenses might help avoid misunderstandings or at least nip them in the bud.

Grant Extensions and Exceptions

There will be times—other than when making an interim or final report—when you will need to communicate with a funder, especially if the program has experienced problems. It's not uncommon to ask that a grant's time period be extended because it began late, it took longer to organize, unforeseen complications arose, or everything has simply taken longer than expected.

If it appears your program will need more time, ask for it. Submit a time extension request two months or more before the end of the grant period. Discovering the need for more time later than this would be unusual, so submitting a request only a few weeks before the end looks sloppy at best.

When asking for an extension, be sure to ask for *all* the time you'll need to complete the program. Not only will asking for a second extension make it appear that you're running the program carelessly, but funders will also be much less likely to grant a second extension.

When submitting a request for a grant extension or modification, be scrupulous in the financial reporting. After you've reported an expenditure, you're stuck with it. Having to footnote your final financial report to point out discrepancies with the interim report does not present the picture of professionalism you want to cultivate with the funder.

Deal with other requests to modify a grant proposal as soon as the need arises. This isn't something you want to do often, but it's much better than reporting to the funder at the end of the grant period that you've failed to achieve the program's goals or you have spent the funder's money in ways not given in the proposal budget.

The Final Report

The final report should set the stage for your next grant request to a funder as well as reporting on the current project. But because reporting on the present grant is the primary purpose of the final report, let's look at that first.

Rarely will everything you outlined in your proposal have gone exactly as planned in the execution of a program. That's only to be expected, but the final report must give reasons for successes, failures, and near misses. Quotes from thankful clients sprinkled judiciously throughout the report will make it more real.

> **WORDS TO THE WISE**
>
> A published annual report makes a great marketing tool with funders, sponsors, individuals, and all kinds of other people you want to understand and appreciate your charity's work. You should send a copy to every funder, but this doesn't relieve you of creating a final report on your project or even your general operations. The details in an annual report usually fall short of what a funder wants to know about how their money was spent.

If you did a good job in your proposal of stating goals (results) and objectives (measurable accomplishments toward the goals), the report will be a snap. Your final report narrative should include, in relation to each goal and objective, …

- A statement of the original goal or objective.

- A description of who was served in reaching this objective, providing metrics whenever possible.

- An explanation of why and what the new objective was and how you achieved it, if the objective changed.

And in relationship to the program as a whole, the narrative should include …

- Any challenges you encountered and how you overcame them.

- The method you used to evaluate the program.

- The major lessons learned from conducting this program.

- Future challenges for this program and the problem it sought to solve.

- Any plans for continuation or adaptation of the program, including any funding received for a future period.

Funders have a vested interest in knowing of any problems or obstacles you encountered along the way and how you overcame them (or didn't). From your answers, they can gain knowledge that will assist them in evaluating similar proposals they might receive and in advising future applicants. Be frank about what it took to carry out the program. Who knows: if it was much harder than expected to carry out the program, the funder could see that as a reason to give you a larger grant the next time.

The tone of your report should be enthusiastic, positive, and thankful. Receiving this grant was one of the greatest things to ever happen for your clients, and carrying out the program was a learning experience and a joy for everyone at your charity. Remember: *you are still selling your program.*

HOW TO SAY IT

Always make reports upbeat, and say something positive, even about a disappointing program. The staff at the funder must present your report to the trustees, and they don't want to look as if they made a bad decision in recommending your charity for a grant.

The interim report was probably formatted as a letter. Because of its relative brevity, this was an acceptable means of conveying the information. Because your final report will be more in-depth (and closer in length to the proposal), a cover letter is appropriate, followed by the formal report.

The cover letter in this case should thank the funder one more time, point out one or two of the major outcomes of the program, summarize how the program did financially, and close with a statement that leaves the door open for submitting another application. An anecdote about one client's experience of your program in your cover letter will put a human face on your program and engage the funder like nothing else.

You'll find a full final report with cover letter, narrative, and financial report in Appendix H. This excerpt from a different final report (based on the program described in an executive summary that appears in Chapter 16) illustrates what I described earlier.

Final Report to the James and Mary Brush Family Foundation on a $10,000 Grant to the African American Literary Council

The James and Mary Brush Family Foundation's $10,000 grant to the African American Literary Council had a significant effect on the council's ability to sustain the publication of *Black American Voices* and to serve a wider public. We are pleased to report on how we achieved this goal.

In August, we hired direct-mail consultant Mark Jacobs to revamp the subscription appeal we had been using for several years. Mr. Jacobs was able to suggest a number of simple changes in the cover letter and subscription form that resulted in dramatic increases in income.

One of his suggestions was to decrease the number of choices offered on the subscription form. Fewer choices result in a higher percentage return. He also suggested we add one new option: to become a "Friend of *Black American Voices*" for an additional $10. He also taught us how to re-mail to the best names, thus further increasing the return with very little additional expense. The 50,000-piece mailing went out in late October.

The combined effect of the changes in the subscription package was a higher percentage return and higher net income. In fact, the mailing nearly paid for itself. Our subscribers now number 7,200, nearly a 10 percent increase in only one year. Just as important, 176 of the new subscribers paid the higher "friends" fee. We will work to cultivate these friends as donors with appeals to increase their contributions over the years.

In addition, we saw a slight increase in newsstand sales shortly after we launched the direct-mail campaign. We attribute this to more people knowing about our magazine and buying a single copy rather than taking out a subscription. Time will tell if some of these readers later become subscribers.

As a result of this direct-mail campaign ...

- Subscriptions are up nearly 10 percent, providing a firmer financial basis for our magazine.

- We have 176 new names in our donor database.

- An additional 700 people per issue (including newsstand sales) read the work of our writers.

Your grant made all this possible. Yet much remains to be done. In the magazine business 30 to 50 percent of new subscribers typically do not renew, so to maintain the number of subscribers, and to hopefully increase it, we must institutionalize an annual direct-mail campaign. In addition, if advertising remains at its present level, we still need 10,000 subscribers for the magazine to be self-supporting.

Encouraged by the success of this new direct-mail campaign, we believe we can reach the magical 10,000-subscriber figure in three years. We have set ourselves a higher goal, however, of 12,000 subscribers so the magazine can begin to subsidize the local literary activities.

We would welcome a meeting to review this report with you and discuss the details of our future plans.

This report was pretty easy because the scope of the program was narrow. It's also shorter than an actual report would have been, where we would have included more details on the changes in the mailing that resulted in so dramatic a change in return. We also would have enclosed a financial report and sample copies of the mailing along with this narrative. The cover letter would have been brief and enthusiastic about the dramatic results of the mailing.

Combined Final Report and Renewal Request

In Chapter 14, I showed you how a proposal for general operating support using the outcomes method might consist of a list of notable accomplishments from the past year accompanied by plans for the coming year. With a little more attention to details about what you did in the past year, this same format works as a combined final report and request for renewed funding. You can do this in cases where you have a close relationship with a funder, but sending a separate report before asking for the renewal will serve you better in developing a relationship with a new funder. If you're seeking a large increase in support, you can set the stage for the increased request in a report, saving the asking for a new proposal that would follow it soon afterward.

You can take the same approach to submit a combined report and proposal for a program grant as well, assuming the program runs year after year with little change, the funder has a real commitment to the program, and you're not seeking a major increase.

With some larger (and more bureaucratic) foundations, combining the report with the new request won't work because of the particular ways they want to receive reports. In that case, you'll file your final report and submit a new request a few weeks later.

> **WORDS TO THE WISE**
>
> When submitting your report and new request separately, use the intervening time to call the funder and ask for comments on your report. This will help you shape the new proposal.

Educating and cultivating the funders, thanking them, keeping in touch, and giving them timely reports are all parts of good donor stewardship. If you take good care of your funders, they'll be more likely to continue to support your charity.

The Least You Need to Know

- All your communications with the funder—from thank you letter to final report—should focus on the funded project and work toward developing an ongoing relationship.
- Sending an interim report (including a financial report), is a good idea, even if not required by the funder.
- If a program doesn't go as planned, consider asking the funder to modify the terms of the grant.
- If you need more time to complete the program, request an extension at least two months before the end of the grant period.
- Use the final report to set the stage for your next application by including information on areas not yet resolved or the need for continued similar activities.
- In a final report, include information on each goal and objective listed in the proposal.

Advice for Individual Grant Seekers

In This Chapter

- Searching for grants for individuals
- Making yourself eligible for a grant
- Preparing a professional resumé and statement
- Covering your time and expenses in a proposal

Individual grant seekers have additional hurdles to overcome when seeking a grant, such as lack of nonprofit status and finding information on available grants. As if that weren't bad enough, far fewer funders make grants to individuals.

One thing to keep in mind before starting your grant search: grants to individuals are usually considered taxable income. Exceptions are made for some scholarship aid, but be aware of your possible tax liability, and plan accordingly.

In this chapter, I show you how to find grants that support what you do and how to become eligible for those grants, sometimes even when a funder states it doesn't fund individuals. I also go over the items in a grant proposal for an individual that parallel items I've discussed for organizations. Finally, I explore how to include money to cover your time and living costs in a grant proposal.

Research Is Still the First Step

Fewer than 10 percent of foundations make grants to individuals, but that's still a lot of possible funders—some 8,300! And that means research is equally important for individual grant seekers as it is for everyone else.

As an individual grant seeker, you'll want to develop a network of colleagues to share information about grants (and much else). Yes, you may end up competing for the same pot of gold, but you're likely to get more leads that way, too.

The relatively small number of foundations making grants to individuals is supplemented by a large number of nonprofit organizations that raise money each year just so they can give it away. These organizations fund most anything you can think of and then some. The following examples show the range of these programs.

The American Educational Research Association (aera.net) provides small grants, fellowships, and training for researchers who conduct studies of education policy and practice.

American Academy in Rome (aarome.org) offers support for independent study and advanced research in the fine arts and the humanities in Rome.

Golf Course Superintendents Association of America (gcsaa.org) administers a number of different scholarships for students pursuing careers in the golf course industry, future turf grass researchers, and educators.

> **WORDS TO THE WISE**
>
> Applying for a scholarship usually involves an application form, part of which will be some sort of essay. You'll find using the elements of a grant proposal will serve you well in writing that essay.

Web Portals for Individual Grant Seekers

The variety of opportunities is nearly endless. Fortunately, a few places online are available for individuals seeking grants to discover opportunities just right for them.

The Foundation Center's directory of grants to individuals (gtionline.fdncenter.org) covers scholarships, research grants, and other means of support in all areas. The online version is less than $20 per month, which may be all the time you'll need to research a project.

Researchers at Michigan State University (staff.lib.msu.edu/harris23/grants/prospect. htm) have compiled an extensive list of websites, interactive databases, and books pertaining to grants for individuals. Because it's a university, the site is particularly rich in sources for scholarships.

The Medical University of South Carolina (research.musc.edu/ord/granttips.htm) has compiled a page of links to grant-writing guides, focusing on medical research proposals.

The Community of Science (cos.com) offers information for the "global research and development community." You can sign up for a free weekly e-mail alert of new opportunities.

In the arts, NYFA Source (nyfa.org/source) is the one-stop resource for artists in all disciplines. Created and maintained by the New York Foundation for the Arts, this database contains information on nearly 4,200 organizations and nearly 8,000 opportunities for artists. It's free and updated daily. You'll find that it's more comprehensive in opportunities for creative artists (such as composers, choreographers, and painters) than it is for performing artists (such as actors, dancers, and musicians).

Writers might also want to search *Grants and Awards Available to American Writers* (pen.org). PEN's directory is widely recognized as the most comprehensive resource for opportunities of all kinds for writers, from grants to writing contests to artist colonies. An online database is available with only a small access fee. The Writers Union of Canada (writersunion.ca) offers a similar resource for Canadian writers for free.

Books for Individual Grant Seekers

Because so few foundations make grants to individuals, most foundation directories are of limited use to individual grant seekers. The Foundation Center publishes one of the best, which covers all possible sectors including scholarships. *Foundation Grants to Individuals* (2010) contains similar information as the online guide, as well as a bibliography of other resources (books and websites) for individuals similar to the free one you can find on its website.

Service organizations and grantmaking public charities not only make many grants to individuals, they also publish helpful books and newsletters for finding other opportunities. Newsletters and magazines published by sector service organizations provide more useful information than many books on grants for individuals. These periodicals have the advantage of always being up-to-date, although few are comprehensive.

PHILANTHROPY FACT

A large number of grants to individuals are chosen by nomination by experts. Frequently, foundations keep the list of nominators top secret until the grants are announced. Others allow nominations from anyone working in a particular field.

The following publications cover individual grants in the arts:

The comprehensive *Dramatists Sourcebook 2010 Edition: Complete Opportunities for Playwrights, Translators, Composers, Lyricists, and Librettists* (New York, NY: Theatre Communications Group, 2010) lists more than 1,100 opportunities, including 150 prizes. It also offers a guide to submitting scripts and other helpful information.

Opportunity Updates, a monthly newsletter for members of the American Music Center, gives mostly one-time opportunities such as calls for scores and competitions. An online database at amc.net gives information on ongoing programs that benefit composers.

The bimonthly *Poets & Writers Magazine* lists both recipients of recent grants and awards as well as upcoming opportunities. It includes many paid advertisements of additional opportunities.

In *Directory of Grants for Crafts and How to Write a Winning Proposal* (Torreon, NM: Warm Snow Publishers, 2000), author James Dillehay brings together a directory of grant resources and a guide to writing grants, all with the crafts artist in mind. Although somewhat out of date, it still contains useful information. Just be sure to verify funding sources before applying for a grant.

The following publications cover individual grants in the sciences:

The *Directory of Biomedical and Health Care Grants 2010* (Schafer, Louis S., and Anita Schafer, eds. Nashville, IN: Schoolhouse Partners, 2009) includes more than 3,500 programs offered by some 2,000 sponsors.

Financial Aid for Research and Creative Activities Abroad, by Gail Ann Schlachter and R. David Weber (El Dorado Hills, CA: Reference Service Press, 2010) covers more than 1,200 opportunities for Americans seeking funds to study abroad, from high school to postgraduate levels. It's organized by the country or area in which the grant allows you to study.

The Internet offers many more resources in the sciences, which are covered in Chapter 7 and Appendix C.

For a general guide to grants for individuals, take a look at Judith Margolin's *The Individual's Guide to Grants*. Margolin is on the staff of the Foundation Center in New York and also wrote a book similar to this one for grant seekers of all kinds.

How Does "Me.org" Sound?

Everything I wrote in Chapter 2 about becoming a nonprofit applies to individuals as well as groups. Some filmmakers, in particular, find it helpful to establish a nonprofit organization to finance their projects. But do think seriously and get good legal advice before going down this road. You'll find books and Internet resources in Appendixes B and C, respectively, to help you decide if nonprofit status is right for your project.

PHILANTHROPY FACT

Filing for nonprofit status is not to be done lightly. It takes months (or longer) to get a ruling and even then you only have provisional status, pending further review.

An alternative to becoming a nonprofit is fiscal sponsorship, which I also discussed in Chapter 2. *Umbrella organization* and *conduit* are terms sometimes used to mean "fiscal sponsorship." Those terms, however, do not imply the legal responsibility of a fiscal sponsor and really shouldn't be used. You can find a good online directory of fiscal sponsors at fiscalsponsordirectory.org.

Where individuals are concerned, fiscal sponsorship is becoming a less-viable alternative because of increasing pressures on nonprofits by funders and government regulators. Already, some government grants won't allow fiscal sponsorship unless the nonprofit certifies it has total control over the project. If funders require control over an individual's project, fewer nonprofits will be willing to take on individuals under fiscal sponsorship—and do you really want to give up control of your project? Nonprofits that continue to offer fiscal sponsorship to organizations will usually work with individuals, too.

Grant Proposals for Individuals

The main parts of a grant proposal for an individual are largely identical to those for organizations. You'll still need a cover letter, executive summary, program description, and project budget. The support materials you'll include, however, are quite different.

The Professional Resumé

Rather than a description of an organization's history or background, a proposal for an individual grant seeker requires a professional resumé. This is different from a resumé you'd use to find a job. A professional resumé should emphasize professional accomplishments such as these:

- Scholarly papers presented at conferences

- Publications

- Exhibitions at galleries or museums

You might also list anything published *about* you and your work, such as book or art reviews or peer reviews of scientific work.

Only after listing professional accomplishments should you list your education. Hobbies and outside interests have no place on a professional resumé. Keep the resumé related to the purpose of the grant, and list everything in reverse chronological order—that is, put your most recent accomplishments first. Plan to revise the resumé for nearly every proposal to emphasize your accomplishments most closely related to the funder's interests. Following is an example of a professional resumé for an historian.

Note the main organization of the resumé is in order of importance of achievements and then in reverse chronological order within sections. Hence, books, articles, reviews by other people of her work come first, and finally education.

Don't risk killing your chances by getting artistic in your formatting. Keep your formatting plain and simple and in 12-point type to focus those reviewing your work *on the work* and not on your mastery of MS Word or graphic design.

Susan Parks
456 Broadway
Smalltown, VT 06000
(555) 555-5555
sparks@thecollege.edu

Publications

Parks, Susan. *Maize Cultivation as a Civilizing Factor.* New York, NY: Obscure History Press, 2004.

"Crop Rotation in the Antebellum South," *Journal of Farming History,* November 2005.

"Wheat, Maize, and Barley: Grains in Colonial America," *New England History Review*, June 2004.

"Agrarian Economics in the 1820s," *New England History Review*, February 2001.

Reviews of *Maize Cultivation as a Civilizing Factor*

"More Than You Thought You Could Know About Maize," *New York Review of Books*, September 2004.

"The Corn Lady," *History of Food Quarterly*, August 2004.

Professional Experience

Senior Lecturer, Culinary Institute of Vermont, 2005–present

Adjunct Professor of American History, Iowa State University, 2002–2005

Education

Ph.D., American Studies, Iowa State University, May 2002

M.A., American History, Iowa State University, August 1999

B.S., History and Culture, Brown University, May 1997

Statement of Purpose

Even a grant application that involves a lengthy application form still requires you to write something that describes the work you do. Your use of language is just as important in a statement of purpose as in your proposal narrative. If a professional panel will review your grant request, you may need to include some of the latest buzzwords; but if foundation staff and board will review your work, it pays to use common English. (You might want to reread "Buzz, Buzz, Buzzwords" in Chapter 14 before moving on.)

Here's a simple formula for creating such a statement and keeping it short. First, remember your statement must relate to the project or work you're seeking funding for and to whatever samples of your work that are part of the application, whether scholarly articles, reviews, or slides of paintings. Keeping this in mind, write one to three sentences (no more!) on each of the following points.

- What did you seek to accomplish in the work samples?

- How did you do it? Note any technical issues you encountered in producing the work sample (and in the case of visual art work, the medium and size of your art).

- What were any influences on your work that may help the person reviewing your grant proposal put your work in a context that helps them understand it?

That last point is definitely optional, but it can be helpful for someone unfamiliar with your work. For example, are you approaching mathematical theory in a manner similar to Turing or Russell? If you're a painter, were you influenced by the Dada or Fluxus artists, or does some more recent artist share your *zeitgeist?* Here's a statement of purpose a painter might write.

> Representational painting remains a contemporary medium for me, through the subject matter I choose and through the varied types of paints I employ in my work. The accompanying digital files show paintings, all approximately 40×18 inches, of industrial landscapes.
>
> Each painting was created using specially formulated paint that creates a crackled finish within hours after exposure to the air. This makes it necessary to work quickly with little time for reworking, which gives the work a spontaneity that is at odds with the aged appearance created by the crackling. Charles Sheeler's paintings of industrial buildings first showed me the beauty that can be found there. The narrative qualities of Frederic Church's paintings have also influenced my work.

WORDS TO THE WISE

I've seen a foundation president be totally put off an artist's work by a pretentious, obscure statement of purpose, even though the work itself was initially of interest. Know the type of person who will review your proposal, and write everything accordingly.

Expressing Yourself in Numbers

Budgets seem to hold the most terror for individual grant seekers, who have a tendency to leave out expenses and get totally flummoxed in deciding how to get some money for their own time and labor into a grant budget. If you claim expenses related to your independent work on your federal tax return, you already have an idea of the kinds of things to include in a grant budget. Everything that goes on that form can go into your grant budget: a portion of your rent or mortgage for a home studio or office, office or art supplies, computers, postage stamps, any special furniture you had to purchase, and so on.

It's especially easy to leave out the cost of supplies you already have on hand. If you will use film that's stored in the back of your refrigerator to document your project, include the cost of that film as part of your budget; you'll have to replace it, after all. Just because you bought that ream of paper before you started work on your book doesn't mean you can't include its cost in your budget.

I like to suggest that grant seekers imagine they're going shopping for absolutely everything they need to carry out their project. Put every item into an imaginary shopping cart, and add up the costs. That's the cost of your project.

If you need major new equipment, like a computer, to carry out your project, you should include a portion of its cost in your project budget, usually a third to a fifth of the cost. Taking part of the cost is similar to the depreciation cost you'd use in preparing your tax return.

Money for Your Time

Finally, we come to the really important part—money for *you*. Don't agonize over this; work it out. If the project will consume 100 percent of your normal working hours for a year, then 100 percent of an appropriate salary for you can be part of the budget. If you're going to work on the project on average a day each week, include 20 percent of a salary. Notice that this is just how we figured personnel costs for project budgets in Chapter 15.

"But what," you might well ask, "is an appropriate salary?" To answer that, you'll have to get very realistic with yourself. Sure, you think you should be making at least as much as a minor movie star, but no foundation is going to pay you a million or two for your time. So think about what's a typical salary in your community for other professionals—and don't just think about top surgeons and lawyers, even if they live next door to you. Also take into account where you are in your career. Someone with 20 years' experience can expect to earn more than a recent college graduate.

Rather than putting a "salary" line in your budget, try calling it a "stipend," which implies a subsidy for living expenses. If you're paying helpers or assistants only a token amount, "honorarium" is a good word to indicate that the fee is a token one and that the labor is really worth much more.

Keep in mind that you want the funder to look at the number and think, "Sure, that makes sense." A salary or fee for the artist in the $30,000 to $70,000 range probably won't raise eyebrows in most instances. But you have to relate the amount to the time you'll spend on the project, where you are in your career, and the amount other successful professionals in your community make.

> **WORDS TO THE WISE**
>
> According to the 2008 census, the median household income in the United States was $50,221, with Maryland the highest at $69,272 and Mississippi the lowest at $36,636. Consider using these numbers as guides when determining an appropriate salary to include in your budget.

You can download a sample budget for an individual artist project at idiotsguides.com under "Book Extras."

Literally millions of dollars in grant money are available to individuals. You just have to know where to look for it and how to approach the funders.

The Least You Need to Know

- Fewer funders make grants to individuals, so there's more competition for fewer dollars.
- Fiscal sponsorship or incorporation as a nonprofit can make new sources of funding available to you.
- Use Internet and book resources specifically for individuals to research grants.
- The structure of a grant proposal will serve you well even with scholarship application essays.
- Determine how much of your time and labor to include in a grant budget using the method for determining personnel allocations for an organization's budget.
- Don't underestimate costs for a project just because you have some supplies already on hand.

Working as a Freelance Grant Writer

In This Chapter

- What it takes to be a freelance grant writer
- Developing a grant-writing portfolio
- Creating a professional resumé
- What makes a good client
- Assembling your tools of the trade

Starting a business of your own is a major decision involving many factors, including how much you'll need to live on until you start making a profit, how much profit you must make to maintain your standard of living, what support (financial and emotional) you can count on from your family in the meantime, and the local market for your skills. I can't go into all those factors here (you can read about them in *The Complete Idiot's Guide to Starting Your Own Business*), but I will look at the specific things you need to know to run your own grant-writing business.

The Makings of a Freelance Grant Writer

The fact that you've made it to Chapter 23 of this book demonstrates you have a strong interest in grant writing. That's a great first step.

I hope you also have a high level of curiosity because that will make learning about the work of all of your clients a pleasure rather than a chore. A love of writing and language will also serve you well. You're going to find yourself spending many hours in front of the computer trying different ways to explain an issue to different funders.

And if you're preparing similar proposals for different clients, you may find you need every ounce of creativity to say essentially the same thing in different ways.

The reward, of course, is doing well for yourself while doing good for the community. How's that for a win-win situation!

Developing a Portfolio

You'll need at least two samples of past work to be seriously considered for any grant-writing assignment. A writing sample such as a published newspaper or magazine article demonstrates whether or not you can write clearly and compellingly, but before someone pays you to write a grant, they want to know you also understand the grant process and how to write in a way that appeals to funders.

> **WORDS TO THE WISE**
>
> Assemble your grants portfolio with the same care you put into a grant proposal. Check and recheck for completeness and accuracy. One misspelled word can sink your chances of employment.

The best way to build your portfolio is to create a proposal as a volunteer helping a small nonprofit. This could be for your house of worship, kids' soccer team, community chorus, hospital auxiliary, friends of the public library, or any community group. You'll have the advantage of access to any past grants and descriptive materials they have on hand and be able to interview the people in charge and those who run the specific programs. You may even be able to talk to program participants (like your kids who are on the soccer team or your sister who is in the local chorus) for great quotes that will enhance your proposal. Additionally, this is a proposal you'll submit and get a result—hopefully a positive one!

Other opportunities to create your grant samples might lie with friends who need to fund a personal project. Artists are always looking for support to cover their time and materials, and people starting a new business might need help securing start-up money. A good business plan, after all, has all the elements of a grant proposal.

Two sample proposals are the minimum you'll need for your portfolio, but you'll ideally have as many as five, written for different projects or organizations. Potential employers seldom review more than two proposals, but with more to choose from, you can include proposals that most nearly match what your potential new client wants you to do for them.

All your sample proposals should at minimum include the cover letter, program description, and a budget. Do get permission from the people for whom you wrote the proposals before using them as samples. In some cases, an organization may not want its materials (especially its budget) shown to its peer organizations.

Creating a Resumé

You've now written three or four grants as a volunteer for one or more groups, some of which were successful, and you have a couple of other writing samples in your portfolio. Now you need a nonprofit-friendly resumé.

How do you present your experience to potential clients? You start listing your most recent work first (including freelance, volunteer, and staff positions). Put your education at the end. Be sure to include any experience you've had working with nonprofit organizations, even if your job or volunteer position was not in grant writing. All nonprofit experience shows your interest in and dedication to a cause, and nonprofits like to see that.

HOW TO SAY IT

If you've done a lot of volunteer work over the years, group it together on your resumé for maximum effect and call it "Nonprofit Experience" to get the attention of your nonprofit client.

In addition to the grants you've written, include a list of articles you've published. You might include a Master's thesis if the subject relates to the grant work you're seeking, but don't include term papers. For example, if your thesis was on literacy education in immigrant communities and you're seeking work to write grants about literacy or education, this would be a good addition. (A thesis on the use of adverbs in the works of John Donne would not support your application for the job, unless, of course, you're creating a proposal related to English literature.)

Be sure to list any other professional writing you've done, whether for a newspaper, professional journal, press releases, or position papers for a politician. Any writing that demonstrates the story-telling and organizing abilities critical to writing successful grants shows that you can do well as a grant writer.

Do not apply for grant-writing jobs with *only* journalistic or public relations writing samples. These kinds of writing reinforce your writing ability, but someone who wants to hire a grant writer wants to see a grant sample.

Bragging Rights

Whether in a cover letter or in the resumé, some fundraisers like to make bold statements about how much they've raised. Avoid making this kind of statement. Fundraising is a joint activity that depends on many factors, including what cause the nonprofit serves, past success in raising money, standing in the community, and connections the nonprofit's staff and board have with funders. The artful creation of grant proposals is, alas, not the most important factor—although without it, the other factors might be meaningless. The person deciding if she should hire you knows this and will consider sweeping statements plain old boasting and of little value.

Similarly, quoting your success rate can be misleading. Someone writing proposals for a major nonprofit with deep community roots and a long history of service will have a very different success rate than a grant writer raising funds for a brand-new organization serving an unpopular cause.

So what glowing things can you say about your work in your cover letter? You can objectively state how many proposals you've written and definitely highlight one or two successful ones if you have them. You can also write about what challenges you overcame in creating a proposal. For example …

- The nonprofit had not previously sought grant support and you had to start from square one to create everything.

- A major scandal about the nonprofit had been in the headlines, and you had to create a positive take on that controversy while making the case for support.

- The nonprofit called you two days before the grant deadline, and you completed the proposal on time.

Writing about a great relationship you had with a client is, of course, very positive. Be careful not to sound negative about anyone or any nonprofit you worked with! Just as in any job interview, you never want to be negative lest the person interviewing you wonder what awful things you might say about them one day.

Valerie Clarkson
Fundraising Counsel and Grant Writer
_____

2867 Broadway
Putnam Valley, NY 10557
845-555-9087
valerie.clarkson@putnamv.com

Grant Writing Experience

Happy Valley Humane Society, Putnam Valley, NY, 2010
General operating proposals for Putnam Valley Community Foundation, Helmsley Foundation,
Frederickson Charitable Fund, Entergy Cor., and many others
Services proposal for county government

Mid-County Animal Shelter, Rhinebeck, NY, 2009–2010
General operating proposals for Smith Family Foundation, Helmsley Foundation, Jones Brothers Action
Fund, and General Electric Fund, among others
Sponsorship proposals for Dutchess Country Savings Bank and Hudson Valley Concrete

Hardscrapple Road Animal Shelter, Salem, NY, 2008–2010
General operating proposals for Westchester Community Foundation, Smith Family Foundation,
Omnimedia Inc., Putnam County Savings Bank, and others

Other Writing Experience

"Unconditional Love on Hardscrapple Road," *Putnam Country Ledger*, November 2008

"Lyme Disease and Your Pet," *Westchester Today*, September 2008

"Shakespeare in Sylvan Glades," review in *Westchester Today*, August 2008

Other Work Experience

Hardscrapple Road Animal Shelter, Salem, NY, volunteer adoption counselor, 2006–2008

The Reader's Companion, Purdys, NY, assistant editor, 2002–2007

Putnam Health Services, Carmel, NY, office manager, 2000–2002

Education

B.M. in American Literature, State University of New York at Purchase

"Introduction to Grant Writing" and "Budgets for Grant Writers" seminars at The Foundation Center,
New York, NY

Grant writing samples are available on request.

A professional grant writer's resumé stresses experience over training.

Working with Clients

I'm a great believer in the idea that how you begin a relationship sets the tone for how it will continue. Be sure to get off on the right foot by presenting yourself as confident and professional. Be on time for all meetings, dress professionally, and always check and recheck your work before sending it to a potential client. Keep in mind that when you interview for a grant-writing assignment, you're there to judge the nonprofit's grant-worthiness as much as they're assessing your qualifications.

Do your homework before the interview. Go to GuideStar (guidestar.org) and study everything it has on the charity, including looking over its last few years of 990 forms. (These also tell you what they pay their top people and help you judge how much you can charge them.) Use your favorite Internet search engine to see if the charity has been in the news lately, and go over the charity's website carefully. Come prepared with several questions about the charity's programs. Listen carefully to the answers, and take notes.

Clients to Avoid

Most of your clients will be thankful to have your help, supply you with the information you need, and pay you on time. Some clients, however, you'd best avoid.

Charity cases: They expect you to postpone payment until after the grant money arrives. That's not much different from working on commission (or maybe for free, if the grant doesn't come in).

Stealth clients: They want you to work on a grant without access to other people in their organization. Both staff and board should be aware you're preparing grant proposals for the nonprofit and be prepared to cooperate with you as needed.

High hopes: The worst kind of client is looking for a miracle worker whose grant-writing skills will create a sudden shower of money for their cause. You'll chiefly find these clients among those with little or no fundraising background. Run the other way when you suspect the client's expectations far exceed reality.

Don't Overpromise

Managing clients' expectations is an important part of the grant writer's job, and one you'd be wise not to ignore. Overpromising is the number one worst thing you can do. You'll only disappoint your client, and they'll only blame you. As you know by now, your skills at grant writing, while important, are only one of several factors in whether a grant will be made.

Don't promise the client that three out of four or even one out of six proposals you create will be funded. You have absolutely no way of predicting that, no matter how many years of experience you have. (Which is why I am immediately suspicious of fundraisers who boast of their success rate, and you should be, too.)

PHILANTHROPY FACTS

The acceptance rate for grant proposals is sobering. It's not unusual for a major foundation to receive as many as 20,000 applications in a year and to make fewer than 500 grants! Smaller foundations might receive several hundred applications and award a dozen or so grants.

Do Provide Your Honest Estimation

Even though you cannot predict the results of the grant proposals you create, you will be expected to give your client your honest estimation of the likely success of the grant proposals you prepare. This is not a contradiction. This is an evaluation of the client's program's readiness for funding and an evaluation of the types of funding available in your area. For example:

- If the client's education program works with only one school, major funders and government agencies seeking to reach high numbers of students won't be interested in the program.

- If your client is a church that restricts access to its food bank to the church's members, few funders outside the church will be willing to fund it.

- If your client has run a program for several years but has never done an objective evaluation of its effect on the people it serves, funders who require evaluations and specific metrics probably won't want to fund this project.

I once interviewed with a potential client that had a terrific music education program. It was very small in scale but had global ambitions. I loved what they were doing, but because I knew the many restrictions of the local education funders, I could not come up with a single strong prospect for them. I had to decline them as a client, even though I thought I could have written a passionate proposal describing their work.

It is also important that you be sure your client understands the outside factors influencing the decision about grant applications:

- The economy has a direct influence on how much grant money is available. Everyone holds back during recessionary times, and foundations in particular don't ramp up their giving until after a few years of a good economy.

- The competition for every grant awarded is fierce. Nonprofits far outnumber funders.

- Sometimes, unfortunately, it's all about whom you know, not what you know or do.

> **WORDS TO THE WISE**
>
> As the saying goes, "Success has many parents, but failure is an orphan." You can bet this will be true in your grant-writing career, but by avoiding overpromising results and involving your client with the process of creating the grant, you'll minimize the blame game.

Finding Work

As a new freelance grant writer, you might spend as much time seeking work as writing grants. This would be true no matter what freelance field you're in. It may help you in your search to think of the process from the nonprofit's point of view. Check out the article on how to hire a fundraising consultant at grassrootsfundraising.org.

Recommendations

Nothing will go further toward landing a grant-writing job than a strong recommendation. I wouldn't hire anyone without first speaking with someone the applicant had worked for previously. I want to know if the working relationship went smoothly as well as if the proposal was successful.

If the reference tells me you listened carefully, incorporated everything she thought was important in the proposal, met all your deadlines, and were a joy to work with, the success of the proposal will be a nonissue (assuming it was well crafted).

Resources for Finding Work

Just as if you were seeking a full-time job, mobilize all your connections to help you find freelance work. Use your social networks (online and offline). Create a professional profile on LinkedIn or a similar website. Also check free job listings on nonprofit websites such as The Chronicle of Philanthropy (philanthropy.com) or Idealist (idealist.org). Organizations looking to fill a full-time position may hire you to do grants while they search for a permanent replacement.

And don't forget to offer your services to other consultants. They may have more work than they can handle and can send some work your way.

The Efficient Practice

Whether you've decided to get paid by the hour or the job, you want to perform your tasks efficiently, taking no more of your time than necessary and providing your clients with good value for their money.

To get started, you'll need a computer with word processing and spreadsheet programs, as well as a program that allows you to create, edit, and save PDF files. Many funders require you to complete PDF application forms. The free Adobe Reader software allows you only to read, and in some cases type into, PDF files, but it won't allow you to create or save them. You'll need Adobe Acrobat or a similar program to do that. Some open source programs of this type are available free. Just search the Internet.

And speaking of the Internet ... you'll need a high-speed connection to do research and a subscription to one of the online foundation databases. (Review Chapter 7 to decide which one suits your work best.)

Because you'll be handling confidential and *proprietary* information from each of your clients, structure your computer directory to keep each client's files separate. Avoid naming files "cover letter" or "after-school budget." Start each file name with the client's name followed by something descriptive, like "NewTownMiddleSchool-computer budget," to be sure you keep everything straight. Keep your paper files equally organized. Be sure to keep copies of everything you give to a client.

DEFINITION

Proprietary is defined as "privately owned and controlled." You should consider all materials a client supplies you about its programs and operations *and* all materials you create for that client proprietary, or belonging to, the client. Proprietary materials cannot be shared with anyone else without permission.

You can easily find a wonderful machine that functions as printer, copier, scanner, and even fax machine for under $200. You'll find yourself frequently doing all those things, so minimize equipment clutter with one machine that does it all.

Once you've taken care of practical matters, your thoughts must turn to how much you'll charge, how much of your hard-earned cash will go to the state, and what kind of working agreements to use—all of which is covered in the next chapter.

The Least You Need to Know

- You'll need a minimum of two complete grant proposals as writing samples.
- Your professional resumé should include all relevant nonprofit and writing experience.
- Use examples of other professional writing to reinforce your grant-writing credentials.
- Avoid overly needy or unrealistic clients.
- Subscribe to an online funder database.
- Use social networks and job listings to find freelance assignments.
- Equip your home office with a computer, a multifunctional printer/scanner/fax machine, and software for creating PDF files.

The Business Side of Freelancing

In This Chapter

- Incorporating yourself
- Registering as a grant writer
- Determining your rate
- Working with clients

After putting together your proposal portfolio, creating a resumé, organizing your office, and marketing your services, you still have a few legal hoops to jump through before you can be a freelance grant writer. In this chapter, I explain how to deal with the legal issues and how to handle your clients once you have them.

To Incorporate or Not?

In Chapter 22, I mentioned the advantages of incorporation as a nonprofit to make yourself eligible for grants. Incorporation as a for-profit company might make sense for your grant-writing business as well. Different forms of corporate structures offer advantages and disadvantages, including possibly insulating your personal assets in case of a lawsuit or bankruptcy. For most grant-writing freelancers, incorporation isn't necessary, but you should talk this over with your tax and legal advisers.

Whether or not you decide to incorporate, you might want to open a separate checking account and have a separate credit card to keep your personal and business finances separate.

Caution: Red Tape Ahead!

It varies significantly from state to state, but most states now require anyone who fundraises for a charity (or helps a charity fundraise) to register with the attorney general of the state in which the fundraiser and the charity are located.

> **WORDS TO THE WISE**
>
> If you get a client in a different state, build that state's registration fee into the fee you charge your client.

State registration is not particularly time-consuming, but it can be quite expensive, especially for someone just getting started. New York State requires an $800 annual registration fee for a grant writer who is considered a fundraising counsel (as opposed to a fundraiser, who is defined as someone who personally solicits and collects money). Illinois charges only $100 to register, but then has additional fees each time you send them a copy of a contract. Of course, these fees and regulations may change at any time, but don't expect them to become cheaper or less restrictive. Because the fees are a mandatory business expense, you'll be able to use them as tax deductions, but it's still hard to hand over to the state what may be most or all of your first grant-writing check.

Unfortunately, no central website or other resource currently exists where you can find the requirements for every state. Search online for "registration requirement for fundraisers" and add the name of your state, or go to your state's attorney general's website and search for regulations relating to charities.

The one good thing about registration requirements for some states is that you don't have to register when you start seeking work, only when you have your first contract. Of course, potential employers may ask if you're registered and be more comfortable employing you if you are.

You're probably thinking, *I'm just going to write a grant for the local Girl Scout troop, so the attorney general will never notice me.* Don't count on it. Fines for not registering make the registration fees seem miniscule.

Setting Your Fee

Soon after you start talking to someone about hiring you to write grants, you'll be asked the tough question—How much will you charge? Many grant writers treat this issue as a trade secret, but setting your fee really is just common sense. You want to be paid fairly for your time and expertise, and the best way to achieve those goals is to bill by the project or on an hourly basis.

Percentage or Fixed Rate?

Professional fundraising associations all discourage or forbid grant writing based on a percentage of the grant. There are good reasons for this. First, funders wouldn't make the grant if they knew that was how you were being compensated. They're making a grant to fund a program, not the charity's fundraising efforts.

Also, professionals get paid for their knowledge, skill, and time. As I explained earlier in this book, your skill in crafting the proposal is only one reason among many for a proposal's success or failure.

Finally, it's usually no harder to write a grant for $50,000 than one for $5,000, and there's no reason you should be paid differently for proposals requiring equal effort.

I strongly encourage you to work for a fixed fee rather than on an hourly basis. This will serve you and your client best. The client will know up front what your services will cost, and you'll know how much time you can devote to the project based on how much you know you'll receive.

To figure out how much to charge, take into account an estimate of the number of hours it will take to complete the project. This is based on who the potential funders are and what each requires in an application. Another consideration is the condition of the nonprofit's grant readiness—that is, does it have the existing documentation you'll need to work with. Before bidding on a project, be sure to find out if …

- The charity has the necessary legal certification (proof of nonprofit status with federal or state governments).
- The program director will be available to you.
- The charity has an up-to-date audited financial statement. (This may not always be necessary, but some funders require it.)
- There's an existing proposal to work from.
- Documentation on the program (program evaluations, press recognition, client testimonials) is available.
- The program budget is clear and complete.
- There is a current operating budget in good order.
- The charity has a history with any funders.

> **WORDS TO THE WISE**
>
> You can charge the client for nearly everything you do for it except for the initial interview and the time spent calculating your fee and preparing a contract.

If the charity cannot provide the first two items, you don't want them as a client. Grants are made, with few exceptions, only to recognized 501(c)(3) organizations. And no matter how good the existing documentation may be, without access to the person who runs the program, you won't be able to produce a convincing proposal.

If items 5 through 7 are missing, factor in the time it will take you to create them. Item 8 is important, because charities with established relationships require less research on your part. Not only will you know that those particular funders have an interest in the charity, but this will lead you to other funders with similar interests.

Be clear with the client up front how many iterations of the proposal your price includes. If you encounter a compulsive editor, you'll be doing endless rewrites. Three drafts—that is, two drafts and the final version—should be your maximum.

Charging for the research phase should not be based on coming back with "X" strong prospects. There might be fewer than "X" strong prospects for a particular client or program. Instead lay out for the client how you'll research all possible funders, including their current ones, funders to similar organizations, and other funders with an interest in the client's area of service.

Calculating Your Fee

After deciding how many hours it will take me to do the project, I tack on a couple more hours for profit and a hedge against it taking more time than expected. Then, I multiply that number by my hourly rate to get the fixed fee.

What, you might ask, should your hourly rate be? That's determined by your level of experience and what the market will bear. Few grant writers work for less than $25 an hour, and the most experienced charge as much as $150 an hour. With that range of rates and the range of hours required to complete different proposals, a grant proposal can cost a client from a couple hundred dollars to several thousand dollars. For more about fees, see the article at The Grantsmanship Center at tgci.com. (Type "fees" in the search box, and the article you want will pop right up.)

Chances are, you'll submit nearly identical proposals to several funders. You can't charge the client for creating the same proposal for each funder, but you can tack on a charge for customizing existing proposals for a new funder. If you charged $500 for the template proposal, maybe you'll need $75 to $100 to customize it for the second funder. (Because you, of course, having read Chapter 14, know you cannot submit identical proposals to different funders.)

The client doesn't need to see your entire fee calculation, but do break down the fee enough so the client can see what different parts of the process will cost.

Good Contracts Make for Good Clients

Just as "good fences make good neighbors," a good contract establishes boundaries, helps you maintain a professional relationship, and articulates reasonable expectations for your work for the client. You may prefer to create a simple letter of understanding that states what you will do and for how much, rather than getting into the "whys" and "therefores" of a legalese contract.

Your contracts or agreements should include the following:

- Your fee for the project and the basis for that fee. Are you working for a flat fee? What's included in that fee (for example, research results, two drafts of the proposal, creation of a budget, etc.)? What else will the client need? If you're working for an hourly rate, what's that rate and what's your estimate of the hours you'll need to complete the project?

- What you will do for the fee. How many proposals will you complete? How many will be sent out?

- What the client will provide, including documents and access to those who are running programs.

- A schedule of payments or what action on your part requires a payment. For example, you should request partial payment in advance to start work. The second payment might be due when you've presented the first draft. Be sure to be clear about when full payment is due to you, which usually will be when you present the completed proposal—not when they hear if they received the grant.

- An end date, even if the contract is for ongoing work for the client rather than a specific project. That gives you an easy way to renegotiate the terms if needed or to end the relationship gracefully. (And some states require a start and end date in *every* contract.)

- What expenses must be reimbursed, such as photocopying, postage, and transportation.

- Any conditions required by the charity bureau in your state. You'll find these with the registration information on the attorney general's site for your state.

- A disclaimer that you make no guarantees about what funds your client may gain from the proposals you prepare.

You can find sample service contracts on the Internet you can adapt for your use. There's a good one at raise-funds.com. Although that sample is for an annual fund campaign, you might use it as a model. If you have a lawyer friend who can review your first contract before presenting it to the client, you may save yourself time, money, and grief later on.

The following table illustrates how I calculate a fixed fee based on the number of hours I estimate it will take. Note that the client needs to see only the condensed table at the bottom.

My Fee Worksheet

	Est. Hours
Prospect Phase:	
Review previous funders for renewal potential	1
Search online directory for grants to similar orgs	2
Search online directory for new prospects	4
Evaluate prospects and prepare research report	1
Total Prospect Phase	**8**
Proposal Phase:	
Create missing backup materials	3
Reformat budgets	1
Write first draft	7
Revisions to first draft	3
Customizing proposal for two additional funders	2
Padding for just in case/profit	2
Total Proposal Phase	**18**

	Est. Hours
Meetings:	
To review research	1
To interview program officers	1.5
To visit site and see program in action	3
To review first draft	1
Total Meetings	**6.5**
Total Hours	**32.5**
Hourly Fee	$65
Total Fee	**$2,112.50**
What I give the client:	
Research	$520.00
Proposal and backup materials preparation	$1,170.00
Note: includes 2 drafts. Additional drafts will be billed at $65/hour	
Meetings and site visits	$422.50
Total Fee	**$2,112.50**

Reimbursable expenses will include:

Transportation

Postage

Any additional state-mandated registration fees

You'll find this calculation in an easy-to-use worksheet at idiotsguides.com under "Book Extras."

Maintain an Ethical Practice

You should check out the ethical guidelines of the two principal organizations for grant writers: the Association of Fundraising Professionals (afpnet.org) and the American Grant Writers' Association (agwa.us). Both organizations offer guidelines and standards that will guide you as you work with clients, including explaining why you do not work on commission, how you work with more than one client, and how you avoid conflicts of interest.

The number of potential funders is limited no matter what the charitable purpose of your client. This means that if you decide to specialize in raising funds for after-school programs, you may find yourself preparing proposals for several schools to submit to the *same funder*. As tempting as it may be, you cannot use any boilerplate writing you develop for one school in the proposal of another. Remember that the same people will read them! This will make both schools, and especially you, look amateurish and foolish.

WORDS TO THE WISE

One way to avoid conflicts of interest is to be up front with each nonprofit, letting them know what other nonprofits you have as clients.

You can find yourself with a different kind of conflict if you contact funders on behalf of a client. If you need to call a funder just for clarification about a submission guideline, you don't have to identify your client, and there's no conflict. If, however, you call to get the program officer's read on whether your client's project fits the funder's guidelines and then a week later you call to ask about a different client's program, the lines start to blur. If you advocate with a funder for a particular client, you've done a disservice to your other client and have a real conflict of interest. Additionally, in some states your registration as a fundraiser varies depending on whether you work in the background or actually solicit money on your clients' behalf.

If you specialize in one nonprofit area, you're more likely to find yourself in such sticky situations. Following the ethical guidelines of one of the professional associations provides you a basis for many decisions that arise in working with clients.

The Least You Need to Know

- Incorporating your business provides legal protections but may be unnecessary for many consultants.
- State registration requirements for fundraisers must be researched before you sign a contract.
- A fixed fee guarantees you a reasonable fee and lets the nonprofit know what it's obligated to pay up front.
- A contract provides both grant writer and nonprofit with an outline of the work to be done and the fees involved.
- Avoid conflicts of interest when approaching funders on behalf of a client by not advocating for any one client and not using one client's materials or research to profit another client.

501(c)(3) status   A reference to the paragraph in the tax code that defines which types of organizations are recognized to be free from federal income taxes, defined as "organized and operated exclusively for religious, charitable, scientific, testing for public safety, literary, or educational purposes ...." *See also* tax-exempt status.

990 form   An informational return required by the Internal Revenue Service for all nonprofits with incomes of $25,000 or more and for all foundations. Foundations file a special version of the form, the 990-PF.

ask   As in "the ask," the actual request for a specific amount of money in a grant cover letter or proposal.

board of directors   The governing body of a nonprofit organization or foundation. *See also* trustee.

budget   A statement of a program's or organization's expenses and sources of revenue (income).

budget narrative   An explanation of key expenses or income items in a budget used to highlight particular expenses critical to the program, explain any exceptionally high or low expenses a funder might question, and describe how additional income for a program will be raised.

buzzword   A term in fashion for a time typically used to describe an approach or technique. In an attempt to seem current, users frequently obfuscate, rather than elucidate, the issue.

capital support   Grant for a major project that will have a long-term effect on a charity, usually for a building or endowment.

case statement   The essential part of any funding request. It engages the reader, explains why the project or organization is worthy and needs support, and demonstrates the urgency with which funding is needed.

challenge grant   A grant made by a funder to encourage additional contributions toward a program. The challenger's grant is made conditional on a specific amount being raised to match it.

community foundation   A public foundation receiving contributions from a wide segment of the population to support charitable purposes in a specific geographic area.

competitive grant   A grant awarded on merit rather than financial need. All grants referred to in this book are competitive grants.

corporate foundation   A foundation set up and administered by a corporation, but legally no different from other private foundations and governed by the same IRS regulations.

corporate giving office   The office in a company responsible for making grants without the legal restrictions borne by the corporate foundation. It's frequently the source for gifts of products, or in-kind gifts.

corporate sponsorship   *See* sponsorship.

cover letter   A letter accompanying a grant proposal to introduce the proposal and the organization to the funder.

cross-tabs   Tabulations used in evaluation data whereby one set of data is counted in relationship to another set of data, such as counting the number of people from large charities rating the workshop excellent and comparing it to the number from small charities giving it an excellent rating to see which group was better served by the workshop.

cultivation   A means of educating a funder or donor about a charity in preparation for a solicitation. This can be done through events, meetings, newsletters, and other methods of contact.

development   *See* fundraising.

discretionary grant   A trustee-designated grant that might lie outside the funder's guidelines.

earned income   Revenue not dependent on grants. Popular with funders because more earned income means less dependence on grants. Earned income can come from service fees, products sold, or even interest income.

executive summary   A section of a grant proposal that puts forth the major reasons for the grant request with references to the budget and all major aspects of the proposal.

fair market value   That part of a contribution that's not tax-deductible because the donor has received something of value in return (such as a meal at a benefit dinner).

family foundation   A foundation controlled by family members of its primary donor.

final report   A report required by most funders at the end of the grant period describing the results and how the program was conducted, along with a budget showing how the funder's grant was spent.

fiscal sponsorship   A formal relationship between a nonprofit organization and an individual or an organization that's unincorporated or in the process of seeking nonprofit status. The relationship is formed so the organization or person without nonprofit status has access to contributions from foundations, corporations, individuals, and government agencies.

formula grant   A type of government grant used to reimburse your charity for services you've already performed based on a mathematical formula that, for example, might multiply the number of your clients by the average cost of providing a service in your city by some percentage the government has decided on.

foundation   A private organization formed to make grants or carry out specific programs. *See also* operating foundation.

funders   A generic term used to refer to foundation, corporation, and government grantmakers as a group.

fundraiser   A generic term for anyone who raises money for a nonprofit organization, political candidate, or other cause. By law in some states, it refers specifically to someone who personally solicits money from someone and who may receive donations directly on behalf of the nonprofit or other cause. *See also* fundraising counsel.

fundraising The practice of soliciting money from a wide variety of sources for use by a nonprofit organization in pursuit of its mission. One aspect of fundraising is grant writing, but it also includes membership, direct mail, special events, and planned giving.

fundraising counsel Defined by law in some states as someone who aids a non-profit in raising money but does not personally ask anyone for money and does not receive contributions on behalf of a nonprofit. Most freelance grant writers fall into this definition.

general operating support (GOS) A grant to pay for the everyday expenses all organizations have, such as rent, utilities, and insurance and also for personnel who are not involved in programs (like the grant writer). GOS can also help pay for programs, which is sometimes necessary when a program is just getting started.

goals Accomplishments that will have been achieved at the end of a program. *See also* objectives.

grant writing The skill or practice of asking for money in the form of a grant from a foundation, corporation, government agency, or individual by crafting a well-considered document (the proposal) that outlines how the money will be used, what receiving the money will accomplish, and who will undertake the tasks described in the proposal. Grant writing is one aspect of fundraising.

in-kind gifts Free goods or services donated by a funder in lieu of or in addition to a cash grant.

indirect expenses A portion of a charity's general operating expenses that, although not a direct result of a program, is necessary to maintain the organization so it can run the program. Indirect expenses include rent, utilities, insurance, payroll charges, and administrative and fundraising personnel.

indirect rate A percentage that expresses the relationship between the total costs of running a charity and the portion of those expenses allocated to a particular program.

informational meeting A meeting with funders to pave the way for a grant proposal while pretending simply to be gathering information.

inquiry letter A letter written to a funder to see if a program would be of interest. This usually precedes a grant proposal and is required by some funders.

interim report   A progress report required by some funders before the end of the grant period. It's usually required when asking that a grant period be extended.

jargon   *See* buzzwords.

matching grant   A grant made to help meet a challenge grant. *See also* challenge grant.

metrics   A term common in the corporate world meaning the *measurable* outcomes of a project.

need   What a nonprofit's program seeks to satisfy, which is the justification for seeking a grant.

need-based grants   *See* formula grant.

nongovernmental organization (NGO)   A nonprofit organization outside the United States.

nonprofit   A term used to describe an organization "organized and operated exclusively for religious, charitable, scientific, testing for public safety, literary, or educational purposes" by the IRS. A nonprofit can make a profit (called a budget surplus); it's just that profit is not the motivating factor. (Note that *non-profit* is also an acceptable spelling.)

objectives   The measurable steps taken to reach a program's goals or achieve the intended results. *See also* goals.

operating foundation   A foundation that exists to carry out its own programs, usually making few if any grants.

organizational budgets   A charity's total operations, including all personnel and expenses and all sources of income.

outcomes method   A means of organizing a grant proposal that focuses on the results anticipated at the end of the program. *See also* process method.

process method   A means of organizing a grant proposal that focuses on the way a program will be carried out. *See also* outcomes method.

program   Activities carried out to achieve a limited set of goals and objectives within a set period of time.

program budget   All expenses directly related to a program and all income raised specifically for it.

program or **project grant**   A competitive grant to support a particular program.

program officer (foundation)   An employee of a foundation whose job is to answer questions from potential and current grantees, conduct initial proposal reviews, and prepare acceptable proposals for consideration by the foundation's trustees. The responsibilities of the job vary by foundation.

program officer (nonprofit)   An employee of a charity whose purpose is to carry out programs. These might be service providers from librarians to doctors to research assistants, but the term can also refer to a choral director or soccer coach.

program-related investment (PRI)   A means of funding used by foundations that allows them to "invest" in a nonprofit endeavor in hopes of the funds being returned to the foundation at some point with interest.

proposal   A document prepared to solicit a grant from any source. See Chapter 13 for the parts of a proposal.

proprietary   A term that means "privately owned and controlled." You should consider all materials a client supplies you about its programs and operations *and* all materials you create for that client proprietary, or belonging to, the client. Proprietary materials cannot be shared with anyone else without permission.

regrant   A grant made by a charity with funds it has raised for that purpose. When seeking a grant to support regrants, be sure the funder allows this—many don't, including many federal grants.

renewal grant   A grant from the same funder to continue the same program. This can be a loaded phrase. On the one hand, it signifies a continuing relationship with your charity, which is a good thing to remind them about. On the other, it might imply to a funder that you expect them to continue supporting your charity and maybe even take their continued support for granted.

request for proposal (RFP)   A proactive means funders employ to encourage proposals for a program established by the funder.

social responsibility   A corporate euphemism for a corporate contributions program.

sponsorship A grant made usually by a corporation to a nonprofit or a for-profit in return for tangible benefits to the corporation, usually through marketing.

stewardship A term usually used to mean the practice of looking after a group of people or managing affairs, but in our parlance, it refers to looking after donors to ensure their continued interest (and donations).

tax-exempt status A designation by some level of government that an organization is a charity and is not subject to taxes imposed by that government body. *See also* 501(c)(3) status.

trustee An official at a foundation or at a nonprofit organization who holds the assets of the organization in trust for the public good; also sometimes known as a member of the board of directors. At a foundation, the trustees hold the authority to make grants and determine policy.

venture philanthropy A form of grantmaking that usually involves greater reporting requirements and greater involvement by the funder in the charity's program.

Offline Resources

A few publishers specialize in books dealing with fundraising and nonprofit management. In addition to the books listed here, you might also check the catalogs of the Allworth Press, Aspen Publishers, Foundation Center, Oryx Press, The Taft Group, and John Wiley & Sons.

Funder and People Directories

Clark, David L., ed. *National Directory of Corporate Giving.* New York, NY: The Foundation Center, 2009.

Foundation Center. *The Foundation Directory.* New York, NY: The Foundation Center, 2010.

———. *Grant Guides.* New York, NY: The Foundation Center, 2009. (Twelve volumes based on sector offered as digital downloads.)

Goddard, Mollie Mudd, ed. *Grants for At-Risk Youth, 2003 Edition.* New York, NY: Aspen Publishers, 2003.

Marquis Who's Who. *Who's Who in America.* New Providence, NJ: Marquis Who's Who, 2010.

Martindale-Hubbell. *Martindale-Hubbell Law Directory.* New Providence, NJ: Martindale-Hubbell, 2010.

Miner, Jeremy T., and Lynn E. Miner. *Funding Sources for Community and Economic Development 2006/7.* Westport, CT: Oryx Press, 2005.

Oryx Press. *Funding Sources for K–12 Education.* Westport, CT: Oryx Press, 2005.

The Social Register Association. *Social Register.* New York, NY: Forbes, 2010. (Updated semiannually.)

Writing Guides

Heath, Chip, and Dan Heath. *Made to Stick: Why Some Ideas Survive and Others Die.* New York, NY: Random House, 2007.

Proscio, Tony. *In Other Words.* New York, NY: Edna McConnell Clark Foundation, 2000. (Available free at comnetwork.org/Jargon_Finder.)

Strunk Jr., William, and E. B. White. *The Elements of Style, Fourth Edition.* Needham Heights, MA: Allyn & Bacon, 2009.

The University of Chicago Press. *The Chicago Manual of Style, 16th Edition.* Chicago, IL: The University of Chicago Press, 2010.

Research and Grant Writing Guides

Blum, Laurie. *Complete Guide to Getting a Grant.* New York, NY: John Wiley and Sons, 1996.

Colvin, Gregory L. *Fiscal Sponsorship: 6 Ways to Do It Right, Second Edition.* San Francisco, CA: Study Center Press, 2006.

Dropkin, Murray, and Bill LaTouche. *The Budget-Building Book for Nonprofits.* San Francisco, CA: Jossey-Bass, 2007.

Geever, Jane C. *The Foundation Center's Guide to Proposal Writing, Fifth Edition.* New York, NY: Foundation Center, 2007.

Quick, James Aaron, and Cheryl Carter New. *Grant Seeker's Budget Toolkit.* New York: NY: John Wiley and Sons, 2001.

Seymour, Harold J. *Designs for Fund-Raising.* New York, NY: McGraw-Hill, 1966.

Teitel, Martin. *"Thank You for Submitting Your Proposal."* Medfield, MA: Emerson & Church, 2006.

Resources for Individual Grant Seekers

Brogan, Kathryn Struckel, ed. *2010 Writer's Market.* Cincinnati, OH: Writer's Digest Books, 2009. (Updated annually.)

Foundation Center. *Foundation Grants to Individuals.* New York, NY: Foundation Center, 2010.

Goodwin, Ariane. *Writing the Artist Statement: Revealing the True Spirit of Your Work.* Haverford, PA: Infinity Publishing, 2002.

Palgram MacMillan. *The Grants Register 2010: The Complete Guide to Postgraduate Funding Worldwide.* New York, NY: Palgram MacMillan, 2002.

Schafer, Louis S., and Anita Schafer, eds. *Directory of Biomedical and Health Care Grants 2010.* Nashville, IN: Schoolhouse Partners, 2009.

———. *Directory of Grants in the Humanities 2009.* Nashville, IN: Schoolhouse Partners, 2009.

———. *Directory of Research Grants 2010.* Nashville, IN: Schoolhouse Partners, 2009.

Theatre Communications Group. *Dramatists Sourcebook 2010 Edition: Complete Opportunities for Playwrights, Translators, Composers, Lyricists, and Librettists.* New York, NY: Theatre Communications Group, 2010.

Forming a Nonprofit Organization

Hopkins, Bruce R. *Starting and Managing a Nonprofit Organization: A Legal Guide.* Hoboken, NJ: John Wiley & Sons, 2009.

Mancuso, Anthony. *How to Form a Nonprofit Corporation.* Eagan, MN: Thomson/West, 2009.

Pakroo, Peri H. *Starting and Building a Nonprofit: A Practical Guide.* Berkeley, CA: Nolo Press, 2009.

Consulting

Bacal, Robert. *The Complete Idiot's Guide to Consulting.* Indianapolis, IN: Alpha Books, 2002.

Goldstein, Henry. *So You Want to Be a Consultant!* Arlington, VA: Association of Fundraising Professionals, 2006.

Paulson, Ed. *The Complete Idiot's Guide to Starting Your Own Business, Fifth Edition.* Indianapolis, IN: Alpha Books, 2007.

Weiss, Alan. *Million Dollar Consulting.* New York, NY: McGraw-Hill, 2009.

Useful Organizations in the United States

American Grant Writers Association
PO Box 8481
Seminole, FL 33775
727-366-9334
agwa.us

Association of Fundraising Professionals
4300 Wilson Boulevard, Suite 300
Arlington, VA 22203
1-800-666-3863
afpnet.org

Council on Foundations
2121 Crystal Drive, Suite 7000
Arlington, VA 22202
1-800-673-9036
cof.org

The Foundation Center—Atlanta
50 Hurt Plaza, Suite 150
Atlanta, GA 30303
404-880-0094

The Foundation Center—Cleveland
Kent Smith Library
1422 Euclid Avenue, Suite 1600
Cleveland, OH 44115
216-861-1933

The Foundation Center—New York
79 Fifth Avenue
New York, NY 10003
212-620-4230
foundationcenter.org

The Foundation Center—San Francisco
312 Sutter Street, Suite 606
San Francisco, CA 94108
415-397-0902

The Foundation Center—Washington, D.C.
1627 K Street NW, 3rd Floor
Washington, DC 20006
202-331-1400

Useful Organizations in Canada

Imagine Canada—Calgary
855 2nd Street SW, Suite 1800
East Tower, Bankers Hall
Calgary, AB T2P 2S5
1-800-263-1178

Imagine Canada—Ottawa
130 Albert Street, Suite 1705
Ottawa, ON K1P 5G4
613-238-7555 or 1-800-821-8814

Imagine Canada—Toronto
2 Carlton Street, Suite 600
Toronto, ON M5G 1J3
416-597-2293 or 1-800-263-1178
info@imaginecanada.ca
imaginecanada.ca

Philanthropic Foundations Canada
555 Rene-Levesque Boulevard West
Montreal, QC H2Z 1B1
514-866-5446
pfc.ca

Internet Resources

Websites change every day. In the course of my research, I found that some sites I'd used recently no longer existed. Others were still there, but URLs of specific pages had changed.

If you're unable to find a page where I have given an address for an inner page (such as gpoaccess.gov/fr/index.html), try searching again by taking off the letters after one or more backslashes (for example, try gpoaccess.gov/fr or gpoaccess.gov) until you get the correct website. Then, use the site search or site map to locate the topic you need. Of course, if all else fails, you can also use any general web search site like Google or Yahoo! to find the organization.

General Information on Grant Writing and Research

Association of College and Research Libraries
ala.org
The ACRL—a division of the American Library Association—provides grant resource links in a number of disciplines.

Chronicle of Philanthropy
philanthropy.com
This is the nonprofit world's newspaper of record. Issued biweekly, it includes articles on trends in philanthropy. It also reports on recent grants by foundations and companies. Skimming this listing is a great way to pick up some prospects for further research, but you'll have to subscribe to the paper edition to access all of them.

Corporation for Public Broadcasting
cpb.org/grants/grantwriting.html
This site provides a grant-writing guide from beginning to end in seven pages.

The Foundation Center

foundationcenter.org

In addition to an excellent foundation database, The Foundation Center provides a variety of free and paid instruction in grant writing.

GrantSpace

grantspace.org

The Foundation Center also created this website that offers webcasts, podcasts, and other training opportunities. There are also sector-specific information areas for the arts, education, health, social services, and many other fields.

GrantStation

grantstation.com

GrantStation offers a free funding alert newsletter in addition to fee-based grant-writing instruction and a funder database.

GuideStar

guidestar.org

This database of every nonprofit organization in the United States includes foundations (private and corporate) and provides links and several years of tax returns for each.

Management Assistance for Nonprofits

mapfornonprofits.org

MAP provides much free information on their website, but the section about evaluations titled "Basic Guide to Outcomes-Based Evaluation for Nonprofit Organizations with Very Limited Resources" is particularly useful.

Medical University of South Carolina Grant Guides

research.musc.edu/ord/granttips.htm

The Medical University of South Carolina has compiled these links to grant-writing guides, focusing on medical research proposals.

The NonProfit Times

nptimes.com

The NonProfit Times provides articles about nonprofits beyond fundraising to include management issues.

Society of Research Administrators International

srainternational.org

This site offers information on RFPs and issues in research.

TechFoundation

techfoundation.org

In addition to making technology grants, the TechFoundation also offers information on other funders and a newsletter about grants for technology.

Government Resources

Federal Emergency Management Association

fema.gov

FEMA assists in the recovery from natural disasters like floods and hurricanes, and these days, unnatural disasters like terrorist attacks. FEMA has an office in every state, the address of which you can find on the website.

Federal Register

gpoaccess.gov/fr/index.html

Use this site for new grant opportunities and every minute thing your federal government does every day.

GovSpot

govspot.com

GovSpot is an exhaustive set of links to state agencies plus subject listings for federal agencies.

Grants.gov

grants.gov

You can search here for information on more than $400 million in federal grants. You'll also find information on the multistep process required to apply online (which is your only option in many cases).

National Endowment for the Arts

arts.gov

Most grants are for organizations, not individual artists.

National Endowment for the Humanities

neh.gov

The NEH funds research of all kinds in the arts and humanities, including documentary films.

National Science Foundation

nsf.gov

This is a portal for locating government grants in science and engineering.

Small Business Administration

sba.gov

Most programs are for for-profits.

StateLocalGov.Net

statelocalgov.net

Use this site to find websites of state and local government agencies nationwide.

U.S. Department of Education

ed.gov

The Department of Education makes thousands of grants, but many are to state agencies only. Read the eligibility requirements first when reviewing these RFPs.

U.S. Department of Health and Human Services

dhhs.gov

The U.S. Department of Health and Human Services is one of the government's largest grantmakers.

U.S. Environmental Protection Agency

epa.gov

Information on grants and links to regional resources.

USA.gov

usa.gov

Provides links to grants; nonprofit registration; tax information; and to state, local, and tribal governments.

For state websites, try the state name and ".gov"; for example, oregon.gov or illinois.gov.

Foundation Resources

The Council on Foundations

cof.org

This site has links to many foundations and other associations. Convention information is worth a quick scan for buzzwords of the moment.

The Foundation Center

foundationcenter.org

This site should be your first stop when researching foundations (private or corporate). Extensive online databases and reference materials are available.

FoundationSearch

foundationsearch.com

The Foundation Center's major competitor offers similar features, plus a few others to help you build your prospect list and research connections among foundation trustees. It provides databases for funders in the United States, Canada, the United Kingdom, and Australia.

The Giving Forum

givingforum.org

This site provides you with links to the numerous regional associations and their standardized application forms.

Grantmakers Concerned with Immigrants and Refugees

gcir.org

This site provides links to foundations and tips on grant writing.

Grantmakers in Health

gih.org

Links to funders and to studies that might provide backup for your proposal's assertions.

Grantmakers in the Arts

giarts.org

Grantmakers in the Arts provides all types of funders from foundations to corporate giving programs and grantmaking public charities in a listing with links.

GrantStation

grantstation.com

Many fewer foundations are included here than in the Foundation Center's databases, but more complete information is given for most of the foundations that might help you.

GuideStar

guidestar.org

This free database of every nonprofit organization in the United States includes foundations (private and corporate) and provides links and several years of tax returns for each.

Michigan State University Research Links

staff.lib.msu.edu/harris23/grants/prospect.htm

Part of the Michigan State University's excellent links pages for grants, this section lists many sources of funding for programs for children and youth.

Major Foundation Sites

The Dana Foundation (New York, NY)
dana.org
Principal interests are in improved teaching of the performing arts in public schools
and in health, particularly neuroscience and immunology.

The James Irvine Foundation (San Francisco, CA)
irvine.org
They give in California, primarily for higher education; workforce development; civic
culture; sustainable communities; and children, youth, and families.

The Joyce Foundation (Chicago, IL)
joycefdn.org
They make grants for urban issues in Chicago; improvement of schools in Chicago,
Cleveland, Detroit, and Milwaukee; poverty in the Midwest; the natural environment
of the Great Lakes; election finance reform; and gun control. They also make grants
to individuals whose work falls within these areas.

Robert W. Woodruff Foundation, Inc. (Atlanta, GA)
woodruff.org
Interests of this foundation include K–college education; health care and education;
human services, particularly for children; economic development; art and cultural
activities; and the environment. They prefer one-time capital projects of established
private charitable organizations.

The Rockefeller Foundation (New York, NY)
rockfound.org
Their wide-ranging interests include the arts; civil society; feeding and employing
the poor; medical research, training, and distribution of services; revitalization of the
African continent; and more. They also run a conference center in Italy for scholars,
scientists, artists, writers, policymakers, and others to conduct creative and scholarly
work.

W. K. Kellogg Foundation (Battle Creek, MI)
wkkf.org
Their primary interests lie in health; food systems and rural development; youth and
education; and philanthropy and voluntarism. They also make special grants in their
local community.

The William Randolph Hearst Foundations (New York, NY, and San Francisco, CA)

hearstfdn.org

They fund nationally, but with an emphasis on the two cities where they have the strongest corporate presence. The website gives details on each grant and links to grantees.

Family Foundation Sites

The Arthur M. Blank Family Foundation (Atlanta, GA)

blankfoundation.org

The founder of Home Depot gives to arts and culture, athletics and fitness, education enhancement, environment (including outdoor activities), fostering understanding, and organizational effectiveness in Georgia; Maricopa County, Arizona; Coastal South Carolina; Park and Gallatin Counties, Montana; and New York City.

The Brown Foundation, Inc. (Houston, TX)

brownfoundation.org

They support public primary and secondary education in Texas; services for children, especially in the Houston area; and the visual and performing arts.

The Milken Family Foundation (Santa Monica, CA)

mff.org

Although a number of family members are among the trustees, several nonfamily members are also on the board. Grants are made mostly in education and medical research (especially cancer research) and mostly in California. They make a large part of their grants through awards and fellowships.

Community Foundation Sites

New York Community Trust (New York, NY)

nycommunitytrust.org

With $1.7 billion in assets in 2009, this trust is one of the largest in the country. It serves New York City but is affiliated with community foundations serving Westchester County and Long Island.

Silicon Valley Community Foundation (Santa Clara, CA)
siliconvalley.org
This is one of the fastest-growing community foundations in the United States, with assets of $1.7 billion in 2009. The founders of eBay are among its donors. It serves Santa Clara and San Mateo Counties in California.

Operating Foundation Sites

Carnegie Endowment for International Peace (Washington, D.C.)
ceip.org
International affairs and U.S. foreign policy are pursued through research, discussion, education, and publications by this beneficiary of Andrew Carnegie.

KnowledgeWorks Foundation (Cincinnati, OH)
kwfdn.org
Educational initiatives in Ohio are the sole concerns of this foundation, which does, however, make grants.

Russell Sage Foundation (New York, NY)
russellsage.org
This foundation is devoted to research in the social sciences, supporting scholars who study at their facility or at other institutions. They also publish books and hold seminars.

Venture Philanthropy Foundation

Robin Hood Foundation (New York, NY)
robinhood.org
This foundation focuses mainly on children.

Corporate Resources

The Council for the Advancement and Support of Education (CASE)
case.org
This site maintains the most complete and up-to-date information on corporate matching gift programs.

EDGAR Database

sec.gov/edgar.shtml

Although the information in the Securities and Exchange Commission's EDGAR database is probably more esoteric than you'll need, you should be aware that you can gain access to all SEC filings.

The Foundation Center

foundationcenter.org

The fee-based database includes information on corporate foundations and their parent companies.

FoundationSearch

foundationsearch.com

Provides information on corporate foundations and companies. Its "Director Connections" provides information on corporate directors *and* foundation directors and the links among them.

Gifts In Kind

giftsinkind.org

This site provides a catalog of donated products of all kinds.

GuideStar

guidestar.org

This database of every nonprofit organization in the United States includes foundations (private and corporate) and provides links and several years of tax returns for each.

The International Events Group

sponsorship.com

IEG provides the most complete information on corporate sponsorship. They publish a newsletter, have a helpful website, and hold seminars across the United States.

LexisNexis

lexisnexis.com

This is a very expensive tool that provides access to a database with information on some 200 million households and 700 million phone numbers, among other information. You might be able to gain free access at some business and academic libraries.

Tech Soup

techsoup.org

This site handles the software donations for a number of software companies, in addition to many other services.

Company Sites

American Express Foundation

home3.americanexpress.com/corp/giving_back.asp
This corporate site provides clear directions on how to apply and the areas they fund. Also included are lists of grants they've made.

The Gap Foundation

gapinc.com
Most of the foundation's grantmaking is aimed at programs that assist young people, although they also make some grants in health, human services, the arts, and the environment. Grants are made worldwide, according to their website. Click on "Social Responsibility" to find the information on their grants.

Sears, Roebuck and Co. Contributions Program

sears.com/community
"Cause-related marketing" and sponsorships come from this office, as well as huge donations in products. Local organizations can apply directly to local stores for contributions. Note that the Sears Foundation does not have a website.

People Research

American Medical Association

ama-assn.org
The American Medical Association will give you doctors by name or specialty with office addresses and educational background if they are AMA members.

AnyWho

anywho.com
Based on AT&T information, AnyWho offers free national online telephone directories. Search results will usually return a complete address as well as the phone number.

EDGAR Database

sec.gov/edgar.shtml
Although the information in the Securities and Exchange Commission's EDGAR database is probably more esoteric than you need, you should be aware that you can gain access to all SEC filings.

Google

google.com

Google is one of the best general search engines on the Internet. Google Finance (google.org/finance) offers a wealth of information about corporate officers.

Highbeam

highbeam.com

This site enables you to search on periodicals and corporate press releases. Retrieving the full text of articles will cost you, however.

LexisNexis

lexisnexis.com

This is a very expensive tool that provides access to a database with information on some 200 million households and 700 million phone numbers, among other information. You might be able to gain free access at some business and academic libraries.

Martindale Directory of Lawyers

martindale.com

This site includes business addresses, areas of practice, and the law schools each lawyer graduated from.

Who's Who

marquiswhoswho.com

Who's Who (a pay site) has a long history of compiling biographical data on millions of people worldwide, according to their website. Marquis is the publisher of the most comprehensive *Who's Who*.

Yippy

search.yippy.com

This all-purpose search engine clusters results by subcategory. For example, if there is a doctor, a writer, and a journalist all with the same name, Yippy will group the search results in those categories, allowing you to select to see only the results you need.

Individual Grantseeker Resources

American Music Center, Opportunities for Composers

amc.net

This database, accessible for a small fee, contains information on ongoing grant programs, competitions, and other opportunities for composers.

Community of Science

cos.com

The Community of Science offers information for the "global research and development community." You can sign up for a free weekly e-mail alert of new opportunities.

Grants and Awards Available to American Writers

pen.org

PEN American Center's directory is widely recognized as the most comprehensive resource for opportunities of all kinds for writers, from grants to writing contests to artist colonies. It is updated biennially and now exists as an online database with only a token fee for access.

Grants for Individuals Online

gtionline.fdncenter.org

This is the Foundation Center's online directory of grants for individuals in all areas. This is an inexpensive pay service.

Michigan State University Research Links

staff.lib.msu.edu/harris23/grants/prospect.htm

Researchers at Michigan State University have compiled this extensive list of links for grants for individuals. Because it's a university, it's not surprising it's concentrated on scholarships.

NYFA Source

nyfa.org/source

This free database of more than 8,000 opportunities for artists in all disciplines includes dance, film, music, theater, literature, and visual arts.

OPERA America

operaamerica.org

The Career Guide database provides details on opportunities for opera artists (such as composers, librettists, and singers) including grants and competitions. A fee-based service.

Poets & Writers

pw.org

This site lists recent grants and awards as well as classified ads and limited free access to *Poets & Writers Magazine*.

Society of Research Administrators International
srainternational.org
The Society of Research Administrators International offers information on RFPs and issues in research.

Writer's Digest
writersdigest.com
This site is full of information on the publishing business, although it's better for commercial (as opposed to literary) publishing.

Fiscal Sponsors

Film Arts Foundation (San Francisco, CA)
filmarts.org
This organization offers sponsorship for film projects. Click on "Services" and follow the links to information on sponsorship.

Fiscal Sponsor Directory
fiscalsponsordirectory.org
National directory of fiscal sponsors created by the San Francisco Study Center.

Fractured Atlas
fracturedatlas.org
Service organization for artists specializing in fiscal sponsorship.

New York Foundation for the Arts (New York, NY)
nyfa.org/fs
Here you'll find information on NYFA's sponsorship of emerging arts organizations and artist projects in all artistic disciplines. NYFA also offers an extensive list of other arts fiscal sponsors at nyfa.org/files_uploaded/OtherFSPrograms.pdf.

The Rose Foundation (Oakland, CA)
rosefdn.org
The Rose Foundation sponsors environmental protection and community regeneration projects.

NEWARK PUBLIC LIBRARY
121 HIGH ST.
NEWARK, NY 14513

Third Sector New England (Boston, MA)

tsne.org

Sponsorship for community coalitions and regional or national projects that share their mission of creating healthy, sustainable communities and active democracy can be found at this site. Information on sponsorship can be found under "Program Services."

Forming a Nonprofit Organization

Management Help

managementhelp.org/strt_org/strt_np/strt_np.htm

This free reference library was created by Authenticity Consulting and offers articles on a wide range of subjects. The link takes you to a guide to the whys and why nots of forming a nonprofit.

Also look for information specific to your state under the secretary of state or attorney general departments.

Consulting

American Grant Writers' Association

agwa.us

Look to this professional association for guidance in ethics, contracts, and everything else dealing with being a professional grant writer.

Association of Fundraising Professionals

afpnet.org

The primary professional association for fundraisers provides most of its services to members only, but you can browse its bookstore.

Grassroots Fundraising

grassrootsfundraising.org

Check out the article on how to hire a fundraising consultant to learn how employers will consider hiring you.

Tony Poderis: Fundraising Forum Library

raise-funds.com/090706forum.html

Consultant Tony Poderis offers a wealth of free information, including an article on becoming a consultant.

Canadian Resources

Canadian Customs and Revenue Agency

cra-arc.gc.ca/chrts-gvng

This is the agency that certifies Canadian Charitable Registration.

Canadian Environmental Grantmakers Network

cegn.org

This site provides a database of funders to environmental causes in Canada, all with links to their websites. Membership in the network gives you access to additional information.

Canadian Government Departments and Agencies

canada.gc.ca/depts/major/depind-eng.html

A listing of numerous government agencies, many of which offer grants.

Imagine Canada

imaginecanada.ca

Imagine Canada provides many services similar to those of the U.S.'s Foundation Center, including a searchable database of funders and grants for a fee. Imagine Canada also researches issues in the nonprofit sector and acts to develop public policy favorable to nonprofits and donors.

Philanthropic Foundations Canada

pfc.ca

This site provides a series of links to member foundation sites and to sites covering various aspects of philanthropy from a national membership organization for Canada's independent, grantmaking foundations.

Writers Union of Canada

writersunion.ca

The literary links section will guide you to other writers groups in Canada, as well as information on residencies and other opportunities.

Sample Foundation Grant Proposal

The proposal that follows was sent to a large corporate foundation that had not previously funded us. Before we sent the proposal, a board member called her contact at the foundation to ask for a meeting, and the executive director subsequently met with the foundation's president.

Because this was a new funder, we gave a capsule history of New York Foundation for the Arts (NYFA) and some recent accomplishments in the cover letter. Note that the cover letter and the proposal both seek to provide a context for the grant that extends beyond NYFA's own needs. It expresses how the grant will increase service to its constituencies. It also speaks to how the technology upgrade will provide greater efficiency in operations. There's no "knowing of your interest" phrase in this cover letter, but this foundation's interest was in increasing institutional capacity, so the entire proposal indirectly addresses its interests.

The section headings in the proposal are mostly from the funder's guidelines, but they are similar to what most funders will want.

This foundation awarded us a $25,000 grant.

Ms. Ann Smythe
President
Company Foundation
89 Center Street
Anytown, CT 06400

Dear Ms. Smythe:

On behalf of the New York Foundation for the Arts (NYFA), I am writing to request support from Company Foundation in the amount of $40,000 for a major, organization-wide technology upgrade at the NYFA. This upgrade will increase our organizational capacity and strengthen the long-term effectiveness of our service to artists and arts organizations in New York and beyond.

In recognition of significant support for NYFA's technology upgrade, the Company Foundation would receive logo exposure on our website; recognition in the donor newsletter and in our quarterly arts journal, which is available nationally and has a readership of 70,000; and in our biennial report.

History and Background

Established in 1971 as an arts service organization to facilitate the development of arts activities throughout the state, NYFA serves individual artists, promotes their freedom to develop and create, and provides the broader public with opportunities to experience and understand their work. Throughout its history, NYFA has explored multiple ways of developing and providing grants, technology planning, and informational services to respond to the needs of a diverse and ever-changing arts community.

Entering its thirty-first year of operation, NYFA has firmly established itself as the leading arts service organization in New York and is now poised to enter a critical juncture in its institutional development. Many members of the corporate and foundation community have a long-standing relationship with NYFA and have leveraged their investments on NYFA's success in providing artists with the support and practical assistance they need to move from the initial inspiration to creating art.

Repeatedly, both artists and funders turn to NYFA to help meet the most pressing needs of the arts community. During the past twelve months, there have been three prominent examples of this involving all parts of the arts community:

- *Culture Counts: Strategies for a More Vibrant Cultural Life for New York City*, the culmination of a yearlong study of the impact of arts funding by the NYC Department of Cultural Affairs.

- New York Arts Recovery Fund, a comprehensive effort to address immediate, short-term, and long-term challenges facing New York's artists and arts organizations most affected by the September 11 national tragedy.

- Development of a national information service for artists in collaboration with the Urban Institute.

The first two initiatives required a high degree of cooperation and participation from New York's diverse cultural community. NYFA was able to obtain this and, as a result, has made significant contributions to the cultural life of New York

City. The third project called on NYFA's expertise in providing information to artists in all disciplines to a degree unequalled by any organization in the United States.

Over the past ten years, NYFA's programs and services to the field have expanded and undergone many changes, its organizational budget has grown from $5.5 to $16.7 million, and NYFA's staff has grown by 35 percent. As the next step of NYFA's long-term technology plan, we will be upgrading workstations and software, networking hardware, server, and server software to increase efficiency and aid in communication—all with the aim of more effectively fulfilling our mission to invest in individual artists and the broader arts community.

Technology at NYFA

Although NYFA has been a pioneer in exploring new possibilities enabled by the recent information technology revolution, convening landmark conferences on the intersection of arts and technology, and in providing financial support and services to artists and arts organizations seeking to use the Internet or build organizational capacity, it has never received a significant donation for the sole purpose of upgrading internal technology systems. We have received small donations of second-generation equipment from individual donors and corporations, but the vast majority of our computer workstations, printers, and various file servers have been leased or purchased on an ad-hoc basis with funds from general operating support.

A grant of this magnitude from the Company Foundation would be an investment in the contemporary artists and artist-centered organizations we serve at a key moment in NYFA's institutional history, bringing our infrastructure up to a level more appropriate to our preeminence among arts service organizations.

I am grateful for your kind consideration of this request, and I welcome any questions or suggestions you might have regarding NYFA, its programs, or its goals. Please contact me at 212-555-1212, extension 201, or by e-mail at exec@nyfa.org should you have any questions about this proposal.

Sincerely,

Executive Director

Proposal to the Company Foundation for a grant of $40,000 to Implement NYFA's Technology Plan

Introduction

The New York Foundation for the Arts (NYFA) was established in 1971 as an arts service organization to facilitate the development of arts activities throughout the state. NYFA serves individual artists, promotes their freedom to develop and create, and provides the broader public with opportunities to experience and understand their work. NYFA also collaborates on the development of regional, national, and international initiatives.

As one of the country's preeminent arts-service organizations, much of our work is conducted using computers and information technology. Over the past 10 years, NYFA's programs and services to the field have expanded and undergone many changes, our organizational budget has grown from $5.5 to $16.7 million, and NYFA's staff has grown by 35 percent. We have gone from conducting only a portion of our work on computers to conducting almost all of our programs and internal tasks using various forms of new technology.

NYFA is in a leadership position regarding issues arising from the intersections of arts, arts organizations, and technology. In 1997, NYFA became the first organization in the country to offer Artist Fellowships ($7,000 unrestricted cash grant) in the computer arts. The 1988 Orcas Conference, "Creative Support for the Creative Artist," gave rise to NYFA's Arts Wire program, the first national online network to provide the arts community with a communications network that incorporated the websites of individual artists and community-based cultural groups, and offered technical assistance and information regarding online and computer arts.

In 1998, in partnership with the New York State Council on the Arts (NYSCA), NYFA planned and coordinated the Governor's Conference on Arts and Technology "Circuits @ NYS—the arts in the Digital Age." Our Knowledge In Technology (KIT) program has provided technology planning workshops to groups of arts organizations located in various regions of New York and the greater Northeast (including Arts Boston), and Washington, D.C., and The Arts and Technology Technical Assistance Program (TechTAP) provides subsidies for computer systems consultants, staff training, and professional development.

Technology Planning

As with so many nonprofits that are primarily program-focused, we had never stepped back to make or implement our own comprehensive, organization-wide technology plan. This we did between February and September 2001, working first with a cross-department committee before involving the seasoned expertise of outside consultants and the entire staff in the process. The result was a clear direction and mission for NYFA's technology needs.

The external section of the plan calls for a reassessment of our website and the development of a strategy of employing e-mail effectively, both of which are in progress. The main needs identified in the internal section of NYFA's Technology Plan were to …

- **Unify databases:** Each department maintained separate databases, causing overlaps and inaccuracies.

- **Configure a group calendar:** Keeping all of NYFA's 50 employees current on NYFA activities is difficult at best. An electronic group calendar was a crying need, as was an intranet to post everything from the graphic style manual to the news of the day.

- **Upgrade workstations:** Computers had been added as staff were added, with the newest employees usually receiving the newest machines and (at that time) current basic software. Older machines were seldom upgraded to match, resulting in employees working side by side on similar tasks with greatly varying tools to accomplish them.

Since completion of the plan, three of the five major databases at NYFA have been combined, making a marked change in how those three departments operate and immediately increasing cooperation among them. In addition, an intranet site was begun in December 2001 and continues as a work in progress. The group calendar feature requires new software and hardware that is part of this proposal, as well as the workstation upgrade.

Project Description

With assistance from our network consultants, NYFA has developed a plan for an organization-wide computer equipment and network upgrade. The workstation and file server upgrade is the next—and critical—step in the implementation of the larger technology plan, addressing concerns such as optimizing time management, increasing overall systems efficiency, and standardizing programs and processes.

Currently, 22 out of 48 workstations use the all-but-obsolete Windows 95 operating system, 20 use the later model Windows 98, and the others use the newer Windows 2000. This mix of platforms means various staff members do not have access to the same tools; for example, those with Windows 95 cannot upgrade other software such as Internet Explorer to the current versions. Also, the older machines simply work slower, making it impossible for employees to work at their maximum capabilities. In addition, many older machines lack CD drives, which means they cannot access files sent to them on CD from outside the organization. Perhaps more importantly, this means adding any new software is more laborious because the CD has become the preferred means for new software to be distributed.

Under the IT upgrade, old workstations will be replaced with new, Pentium IV machines operating with Windows XP platforms, along with new Microsoft Office XP software. This organization-wide workstation consistency will make training new employees easier (because everyone will be working with the same system) and allow future upgrades to be done in a consistent and efficient manner.

It is also necessary to upgrade the file server at the same time as the individual workstations. NYFA is now using an IBM NT server leased since 1997. Although it was state of the art computer technology in 1997, it falls significantly short of the capacity and speed needed to run a 48-station network today.

As part of this systems upgrade, NYFA will purchase a new IBM Series 240, Pentium III server, with the complementary software. The new server has the capacity to create a parallel copy of all data on a separate drive. With this facility, should the main hard drive fail, a new one can be installed while the network continues to operate off of the "ghost" drive. In addition, the greater capacity of the server necessitates a new backup drive and tapes. Data security is critical to any system, and particularly at NYFA, which is a national clearinghouse for information and resources artists rely on for their career needs.

Rationale

Strategy: NYFA recently completed a strategic plan for institutional advancement, the primary goals of which are to (1) conduct research and analysis about artists, art making, and arts funders; (2) sustain and create programs of the highest standards; and (3) primarily serve individual artists but always recognize the critical dynamics among art making, arts organizations, donors, and the public perception of artists' value to society. NYFA's Technology Planning Committee took these goals into consideration in prioritizing the implementation process and underscored the primary need for standardized operating systems and increased server capacity.

Tangible results: As mentioned in the previous description, the systems upgrade will:

- Make training new and present employees much quicker and easier, increasing workflow and freeing up time for senior staff.

- Make CD drives standard technology in each workstation, increasing the ease of adding new software or viewing CDs sent from outside the organization.

- Optimize speed and reinforce security of the file server, which not only saves time but often means the difference between having an accessible and reliable archive and being unprepared.

Long-term organizational potential: With more and more artists and others wishing to take advantage of NYFA's services, but with funding relatively static at best, we must work more efficiently to continue to serve our constituencies. The technology upgrade's major long-term benefits will be in optimizing staff time and workflow, increasing service to the field, and enabling efficient time management.

Agenda

Implementation and evaluation of the NYFA computer systems upgrade will take one year to complete:

June to August 2002: inventory/consolidation of organizational file server

August to September: begin purchase and installation of new equipment, staff training

October to December: purchase remaining equipment and assess progress, launch some new program components

March to July 2003: organization-wide, program-wide evaluation of systems upgrade

August 2003: generate final report

Evaluation

To ensure that NYFA's technology equipment upgrade is properly implemented and brought to optimal effectiveness, NYFA will follow a rigorous evaluation procedure throughout the year. We will survey staff on special software needs and inventory all existing hardware to determine if any parts are upgradeable.

We will then refine the purchase documents. We will seek evaluations of all staff following the initial training on the new machines and provide additional training based on those findings. We will again ask staff to evaluate the functionality of their new equipment after two months of use and make adjustments based on that evaluation.

Past Technology Support

Although NYFA has been a pioneer in exploring new possibilities enabled by the recent information technology revolution, convening landmark conferences on the intersection of arts and technology, and in providing financial support and services to artists and arts organizations seeking to use the Internet or build organizational capacity, it has never received a significant donation for the sole purpose of upgrading internal technology systems. We have received small donations of second-generation equipment from individual donors and corporations, but the vast majority of our computer workstations, printers, and various file servers have been leased or purchased on an ad-hoc basis with funds from general operating support.

Attachments [only the Project Budget is included here]:

- Project Budget
- Organizational Profile
- FY01 Audited Financial Statement
- FY02 Organizational Budget
- Funders List
- IRS 501(c)(3) determination letter
- Biennial Report for FY00 and FY01

New York Foundation for the Arts
Information Technology Systems Upgrade Project Budget

EXPENSES	July 02–June 03		
	Hours	Rate	Total
Personnel			
Staff allocation			$22,000
Fringe benefits			$3,960
Server installation and setup (consultants)	32	$135	$4,320
Workstation installation and setup (consultants)	52	$135	$7,020
Subtotal			$37,300
PROJECT COSTS	**Unit**	**Qty.**	**Total**
Workstations			
Pentium 4 processors w/Windows 2000 Professional	$1,104	33	$36,432
E74 17-inch Black CRT Monitor	$194	20	$3,880
Microsoft Office Professional Upgrade	$284	44	$12,496
GHOST Corporate Edition Licensing	$31	33	$1,023
Media kits (CDs) for MS Office and GHOST	$41	1	$41
Subtotal			$53,872
PROJECT COSTS	**Unit**	**Qty.**	**Total**
Server and Networking Hardware			
24-prog HP ProCurve Switch (hardware connect to workstations)	$899	3	$2,697
IBM X Series 240 Pentium 3.1 GHZ Server w/4 36.4 GB hard drives, RAM upgrade	$7,006	1	$7,006
250W HS Redundant Power Supply	$224	1	$224
APC Smart Uninterruptible Power Source	$670	1	$670
Backup Tape Drive (100/200GB LTO Int. SCSI)	$3,035	1	$3,035
Backup LTO Tapes	$107	12	$1,284
Subtotal			$14,916

continues

New York Foundation for the Arts
Information Technology Systems Upgrade Project Budget (continued)

PROJECT COSTS	Unit	Qty.	Total
Server Software and Accessories			
Lotus Notes calendar software and customization for server	$5,200	1	$5,200
Windows 2000 Server License	$704	1	$704
Windows 2000 Server Client Access License and Media	$32	44	$1,408
Backup Exec. NT Windows 2K 8.6 Server, Open File opt.	$935	1	$935
Accessories	$74	1	$222
Subtotal			$8,469
SUB-TOTAL: PROJECT COSTS			$77,257
TOTAL EXPENSES			$114,557
INCOME			
Requested from Company Foundation		$40,000	
Other pending foundation proposals		$40,000	
Allocation from FY02 GOS		$34,557	
TOTAL INCOME		$114,557	
SURPLUS/(DEFICIT)		**$—**	

Sample Corporate Grant Proposal

In this case, a meeting with the funder helped guide what I would apply for to this corporate giving program, which you'll note from the address was in the public affairs department. Like many grant proposals to corporations, this one is an amalgam of techniques used in sponsorship proposal writing and grant writing.

The cover letter reads like we were seeking a sponsorship, but the proposal that follows is more like a grant proposal, except for the prominent section on "public visibility." Note also that the amount requested is a range ($10,000 to $25,000), typical for a sponsorship proposal. This hybrid approach is common when seeking corporate support, particularly if you're applying to an office other than a corporate foundation.

Cover Letter

Ms. Janet Kinard
Manager
Strategic Giving, Public Affairs
Big Corporation, Inc.
987 Main Street
New York, NY 10000

Dear Janet,

Thank you for taking the time to meet with me yesterday to discuss how the New York Artists and Big Corporation, Inc., might work together on a project. Artists in the Branches presents an excellent opportunity for Big Corporation, Inc., to make a significant impact on access to the arts on a grassroots, community level. Furthermore, any grant you make will release an equal amount from the challenge grant we have recently received from the New York City Department of Cultural Affairs.

A full description of the project is enclosed. This project will ...

- Provide increased access to the arts through branch libraries in neighborhoods with limited arts programming.

- Introduce local artists to their surrounding community.

- Help support artists by providing an honorarium and helping them to develop an audience for their work.

- Develop a publicity and marketing kit that will be used for the other artists programs we present with community organizations for years to come.

The pilot program involves ten events (two in each borough) during a six-month period. It will reach an audience of around 1,000. The publicity and marketing kit developed through this pilot will be used annually by as many as 100 community organizations statewide for years to come. Event sponsors include community centers, senior centers, public schools, local arts groups, and groups working with young people. Please see the enclosed list of sponsor organizations from the last two years. Although events take place statewide, 70 percent were held in New York City.

As a major funder to this project, Big Corporation, Inc., will be prominently credited in ...

- The programs prepared for each event.

- Flyers announcing each event distributed to and posted at community arts, education, and social service groups.

- Bookmarks distributed throughout the New York, Brooklyn, and Queens library systems.

- Advertisements taken in neighborhood newspapers, such as the *Amsterdam News*, *The Brooklyn Skyline*, *New York Press*, *Village Voice*, *Bronx Times Reporter*, *Asian-American Times*, and *Queens Times*.

- All press releases.

- Announcements and reports on the project in New York Artists' quarterly newsletter, with a subscription base of more than 24,000 statewide and a readership of nearly 80,000.

- New York Artists' annual report.

- New York Artists' website.

A publicist will be working with us to get the word out for each event and help develop the publicity and marketing kit. *Big Corporation, Inc.,'s support for this pilot program would also be prominently acknowledged on this kit*, which we expect more than 200 community groups to use within the following three years.

We must raise $24,500 by June 1 to meet the challenge grant requirements, and we hope that Big Corporation, Inc., will join us in this project with a contribution of $10,000 to $25,000.

Should you have any questions or need any additional details about the pilot project, you can reach me at 212-555-6900, extension 211, or via e-mail at wt@nya.org. Your kind consideration of this proposal is greatly appreciated.

Sincerely,

Waddy Thompson

Waddy Thompson
Director of External Affairs

Enclosed:

- Full program description

- Program budget

- Background [not included here, but it consisted of a one-page summary of the organization's history]

- List of sponsor organizations [not included here]

- Copy of 501(c)(3) letter [not included here]

- Audited financial statement [not included here]

Proposal

Proposal to Big Corporation, Inc., to Support Artists in the Branches

The New York Artists respectfully requests a grant from Big Corporation, Inc., in the amount of $10,000–$25,000 to support its Artists in the Branches program. This grant will be applied toward a $24,500 matching grant from the New York City Department of Cultural Affairs to provide free arts events throughout New York City.

One of the conclusions of the recent study *Culture Counts* indicated that a majority of New Yorkers want to attend more cultural events than they currently are able to attend. The greatest impediments to attending cultural events were transportation and price. Our Artists Exchange program surmounts both these obstacles by providing free arts events in local communities.

The Exchange encourages artists to present their work through free public events (readings, workshops, lectures, performances, demonstrations, or other activities) in collaboration with a nonarts, nonprofit host organization to reach audiences who might not seek out arts events.

For Artists in the Branches, we will coordinate and promote 10 events around New York City involving 10 to 28 artists of various disciplines based on the Artists Exchange program. We expect the events to average 100 attendees, giving the program an audience of 1,000. To tie these events to local communities, branch libraries will collaborate with us on selecting and presenting these events. Each will be free and open to the public. Like the Exchange, Artists in the Branches is a crucial means to promote greater awareness and understanding of the artist's craft and creative process, as well as a means to reach out to New York communities with limited exposure and access to the arts. These events differ from other free arts offerings through the inclusion of living creative artists (composers, writers, choreographers, painters, and so on), many of whom live and work in the same communities as those who will attend the events.

Audiences will be able to identify contemporary art as something that is alive and part of their own community. Through this grassroots approach, the minds of the audience will be awakened to the possibilities of art in their lives and the image of the creative artist will be enhanced.

Artists will be chosen through a request for proposals that will be sent to 3,000 artists who have previously presented events for us. In this way, we will be able to choose artists who have demonstrated a desire to work with the community and whose artistic abilities have already been evaluated. After initial review by our program staff, final selection of artists will be coordinated with the events department at each of the three library systems. A program coordinator will oversee the RFP process, selection of artists, and execution of events.

Public Visibility: New York Artists will handle publicity and marketing for the events through means such as press releases to community publications, bookmarks with event information distributed through the libraries and local schools, and guerrilla marketing techniques such as posting flyers on community bulletin boards and in local gathering spots such as bookstores and restaurants.

We normally play a passive role in Exchange events, limited to paying the artist upon confirmation that the event took place. With Artists in the Branches, we will take an active role by connecting artists with communities now lacking free events such as these and will take the lead in publicizing the events—something usually falling to the sponsoring organization. The benefits of this approach are many:

- Underserved areas will have new art events.

- Libraries will be able to market to new audiences.

- Artists will receive additional exposure through greater attendance at these events.

- New York Artists will gain new visibility in these communities.

At the conclusion of this project, we will create a model public relations kit for sponsors to use in future years. The goal of the kit is to improve the publicity of all Exchange events and help local sponsors articulate the value of individual artists to their communities. By developing improved communications mechanisms, this project will indirectly benefit the 150 to 165 artists who participate in Exchange events annually.

Evaluation: A senior staff member will attend each Artists in the Branches event. He or she will also be available to assist libraries in securing any special equipment needed for the presentations. A meeting will be held with the library event coordinators at the conclusion of the project to receive feedback from the libraries. It is hoped that the bonds formed during the execution of this program will lead to branch libraries sponsoring more of the regular Artists Exchange events.

Conclusion: Artists in the Branches is just one of the programs that helps fulfill our mission to serve individual artists, promote their freedom to develop and create, and provide the broader public with opportunities to experience and understand their work. This project allows us to concentrate on the neighborhoods of New York City in which free arts events are not a regular occurrence. It also allows our artists to make their work known to a wider public.

Funding from Big Corporation, Inc., will help us meet the Department of Cultural Affairs' challenge to match their $24,500 award, and in turn, provide communities throughout the city with free access to the arts they might not normally have.

Budget

Artists in the Branches

EXPENSES

Personnel

Project coordinator @ 30%	$11,800
Communications officer @ 5%	$2,000
Fringe @ 18%	$2,484
Subtotal salaried personnel	$16,284
Artist fees	$24,000
Total Personnel	**$40,284**

Direct Expenses

Space rentals/utilities (in-kind by libraries)	$15,000
Equipment rental/supplies	$2,250
Postage	$1,000
Travel/transportation	$750
Advertising/promotion/marketing	$5,200
Printing of model PR kit	$2,000
Total Direct Expenses	**$26,200**
Indirect Expenses @ 12%	**$8,016**
Total Expenses	**$74,500**

INCOME

Requested from Big Corporation, Inc.	$20,000
Department of Cultural Affairs (committed pending a 1:1 match)	$24,500
Library systems in-kind	$15,000
A. Family foundation (pending)	$10,000
H. Family foundation (pending)	<u>$5,000</u>
Total Income	**$74,500**
Surplus/(Deficit)	**$0**

Sample Sponsorship Proposal

Although sponsorship proposals are not really grant proposals, many grant writers are asked to create these proposals as well. I described the differences between the two in Chapter 4.

The following proposal is for a fictional bicycle ride-a-thon to support the local AIDS service organization. Other than this short letter and one page giving the specifics the marketing director will want to know, the only enclosures would be no more than three press reports and one sample of a printed item from a previous year's event showing prominent sponsor credit.

It's particularly important not to bulk up sponsorship proposals with extraneous information. They won't be looked at. There's very little here about this agency's good works because the good works are not the point. The agency's reputation and the audience it can deliver are the selling points.

Note that at the end of the fact sheet I've given the overhead rate for the event. This isn't something you'd ordinarily have to do. Big fundraising events such as this, however, have been criticized in the press for the low percentage returned to the charity (sometimes as low as 20 percent). By letting them know that 75 percent of the money raised goes to the charity, I've averted a potential concern before it's raised. A budget is not enclosed with this initial request but would be supplied on request from the company.

Cover Letter

February 1, 2011

Mr. Martin Doyle
Marketing Director
Anytown Daily News
1 News Square
Anytown, SC 29000

Dear Mr. Doyle:

Thank you for speaking with me this afternoon about *Anytown Daily News*'s sponsoring the AIDS Ride 2011. *Anytown Daily News* has covered this event in the past, attesting to the interest it holds for the entire community. The presence of Morgan Whitney (fresh from her recent box-office-busting film) is sure to attract attention from a wide range of electronic and print media.

The money raised from this event is as important today as it was when we held the first AIDS Ride in 1990, but maintaining the public's interest in conquering this disease has become increasingly difficult. This is why a partnership with *Anytown Daily News* is so important to the success of the event. The pro bono advertising we discussed will be critical in recruiting riders and will also play a role in increasing public awareness of the dangers that risky sexual behavior continues to present.

Community AIDS Services has a constituency we believe *Anytown Daily News* will find very attractive, especially the young demographics advertisers relish. Through signage at the event and press reports (including television and radio), we will showcase *Anytown Daily News* as an important supporter of this worthwhile cause.

On an enclosed sheet, I've outlined the benefits we can offer you, as well as provided specific demographics of the audience based on past events. As we discussed, for status as a category exclusive sponsor, we would be looking for a cash donation of $5,000 to $10,000 in addition to pro bono advertisements of a quarter page or larger in each of the four weeks leading up to the event.

Please consider everything in this letter a point of departure for additional conversations. I look forward to working with you to refine this partnership to our mutual advantage.

Sincerely,

Betty Sanders

Betty Sanders
Director of External Affairs

Benefits and Demographics Sheet

Benefits to Anytown Daily News as Exclusive Media Sponsor of AIDS Ride 2011

1. Exposure to the 11,000 people either participating in or attending the start and finish of the AIDS Ride 2011

2. Exposure to the 4,000 supporters of Community AIDS Services through monthly newsletter

3. Prominent acknowledgment in all press releases, advertisements, and mailings associated with the AIDS Ride 2011

4. Celebrity participation (actress Morgan Whitney) will draw significant press attention

5. Status as sole media sponsor excludes any competitors from participating

6. Opportunity to be associated in the minds of all who hear of the event from the local agency that has done more than any other in Anytown to provide services to people living with HIV and AIDS

Audience Demographics

Riders: average age 31; 60 percent male; household income between $40,000 and $55,000; 80 percent college degree or higher

Starting and finish line audience: average age 29; 70 percent female; household income between $40,000 and $55,000; 80 percent some college

Supporters of Community AIDS Services: average age 42; 65 percent female; household income $55,000 to $75,000; 72 percent some college

Event Details

Date: June 16, 2011

What: Bicycle ride to raise money to fight AIDS

Where: A 13-mile route starting and ending in front of City Hall with a route through the main business district and City Park

Who: 800 riders and an estimated 10,000 spectators

All funds raised will support Community AIDS Services programs for people with AIDS. Donated labor and products allow this event to operate with a low overhead of 25 percent.

Sample Government Grant Proposal

The following sample grant application to a state arts council is typical of government grant forms: it requests some special codes specific to the agency and gives little room for a project description. Note that the application not only asks specifically who will benefit from the project, but also lists the state assembly and senate districts in which the project will take place. This type of information is critical for the council's record-keeping and to justify expenditure of taxpayer money.

Forms such as this one, which was on a council website for download as a Word document, are rapidly becoming historical relics. Government agencies are moving faster than other funders to online grant application submission. The online forms will all be different, but each will require you to describe your organization and project in a limited number of words, fill in contact information, and provide basic information such as total budget and project cost. Many will also allow you to attach a fuller description of your project.

Proposal

Application and Budget Form for Organizations
State Council on the Arts

Please check the program area, type of grant and fill in the amount requested. Fill out a separate application for each grant request. For grants not listed write in grant name next to "Other".

ORGANIZATIONAL SUPPORT PROGRAM

X Organizational Support Project Grant
❑ Cultural Conservation Grant
❑ Cultural Facilities Grant
❑ One-Year Operating Grant

ARTS IN EDUCATION PROGRAM

❑ Artist Residency in Schools Grant

COMMUNITY ARTS PROGRAM

❑ Community Arts Project Grant

TRADITIONAL ARTS PROGRAM

❑ Traditional Arts Project Grant

MULTI-PROGRAM AREAS

❑   Mini-Grants
❑   Peer Mentorship
❑   Other: _____

AMOUNT REQUESTED $ 7,000

---

1. APPLICANT INFORMATION (TYPE OR PRINT CLEARLY)

Official IRS name of applicant or Fiscal Agent:
Folk Arts Collaborative
Authorized Official's Name:
Bettina Maxwell

Mailing Address	City/Town	State	ZIP
999 Park Street	**Middletown**	**CC**	**20000**

Daytime Phone	Fax	E-mail	URL
717-555-1222	**717-555-1230**	**bmax@folkcollab.org**	**folkcollab.org**

Arts Discipline (for *primary* area of applicant's work):   folk arts
Race/Ethnicity of Organization/Individual (Grantee Race):   general population

---

2. PAYMENT (If payment is to be made to someone other than the applicant, please fill in.)

Official IRS name:
Same as above

Mailing Address	City/Town	State	ZIP

Daytime Phone	Fax	E-mail	URL

For Office Use Only: FY   Activity Type   App. #

1

3. APPLICANT NAME: Folk Arts Collaborative

3A. CONTACT PERSON/SITE COORDINATOR

Name **Sarah Kiesinskie**   Title **Curator**

Address (if different from above)   City/Town   State   ZIP
Same as above

Phone   Fax   E-mail   URL

---

4. GRANT REQUEST DATA

Project Summary, one sentence only. Please attach a project description no more than one page.

Folk Arts Collaborative will present an exhibition of pottery made by local craftspeople in a vacant storefront in downtown Middletown for one month in September 2011.

Project Director (if different from Contact Person)   Project Start and End Dates
                                                                January – September 2011
Enter Discipline codes from web site: **45, 6VA**

Arts Discipline (describing this project's activities)   **folk arts**
Project Race   **general population**
International Activity of Project   Yes_____   No **X**_____
Estimate the total number of individuals to benefit from this project: **20 artists + 3,000 visitors**

Number of Towns/Communities to benefit __**1**____   Number of students/youth to benefit__**0**____
State Assembly District of applicant: **23rd**___   State Senate District: **6th**____
Number of Artists to participate __**20**_____   Number of State artists __**20**_____

If you are using any artists registered with the Arts Council for this project, please list names below with register code (PA, FK, PH, etc.):
Henry Folkstone (FK)   **Helen Friendly (CE)**

Marian Kilnning (CE)

---

5. ORGANIZATIONAL DATA

Year Founded: **1982**   Incorporated in State: **1982**   Number of paid staff: Full-time **4** Part-time **2**

Fiscal Summary. *Provide actual figures for last completed fiscal year and estimate figures for current and future fiscal years included in grant proposal.*

Dates of current fiscal year: __**7**__ / __**1**__ / __**10**__ to __**6**__ / **30**___ / **11**___

	Past Year	Present Year	Future Year
Total Income:	**$117,812**	**$120,000**	**$135,000**
Total Expense:	**$117,500**	**$118,000**	**$135,000**

2

APPLICANT NAME: Folk Arts Collaborative

6. FACILITY DATA

Name of facility(ies) where arts activities funded by this grant will take place.
Folk Arts Collaborative's offices (for planning) and a now vacant storefront at 500 Main Street (for the exhibition), both in Middletown.

How long has the facility(ies) been used for arts activities?
The Collaborative's offices have been occupied for 6 years. This will be the first arts activity in the storefront.

Answer "Yes" or "No" to each of the following questions.
Y_____ Is this facility accessible to people with disabilities?
Y_____ Is accessibility part of the organization's long range plan?
Y_____ Has an ADA self-evaluation of the organization's facilities and programs been conducted?
Y_____ Have policies and procedures been established which address nondiscrimination against persons with disabilities?
Y_____ Is this information posted?

N_____ Does applicant own the facility? If no:
Name of Owner: Address:
Middletown Commercial Properties, Inc.   **63 Pine St., Middletown**

Length & Expiration of Lease: **We are in year 6 of a 10-year lease, which expires in July 2013.**

7. CERTIFICATION

(Type in authorized official or artist name below)
I, Bettina Maxwell , do hereby certify that all of the figures, facts, and representations made in this application and its attachments are true and correct to the best of my knowledge. Any grant funds received will be used as described and any changes in the project will be submitted in writing for approval.

Bettina Maxwell   *Executive Director*   *7/3/2010*
Signature of authorized official   Title   Date

Signature of person preparing this application (if different)   Title   Date

Applicant hereby agrees to comply with Title VI of the Civil Rights Act of 1964; Section 504 of the Rehabilitation Act of 1973, as amended; Title IX of the Education Amendments of 1972 (where applicable); Title 29 (Part 505) of the Code of Federal Regulations (governing fair labor practices); the Age Discrimination Act of 1975; the U.S.C. Sec. 1913 regulating lobbying with appropriated monies; the Drug-Free Workplace Act of 1988; and the Americans with Disabilities Act of 1990; as well as all regulations of the National Endowment for the Arts pursuant to these statutes & regulations described in OMB circulars A-102 and A-87, Cost Principles.

3

BUDGET
STATE COUNCIL ON THE ARTS

APPLICANT NAME: Folk Arts Collaborative

EXPENSES (PROJECT ONLY)	CASH	IN-KIND
Salaried Employees (*Prorate wages and fringe benefits to include only time spent on this project. Indicate the # of positions and the % of time each position will spend on the Project.*)		
Administrative: 2 @ 10%	$ 8,760	$
Artistic: 1 @ 80%	$38,400	$
Teachers:	$0	$
Technical/production: 2 (part time) @ 50%	$ 9,000	$
Outside Fees & Services (*independent contractor fees*)		
Registered Artist Fees	$0	$
Other Artist Fees (*specify*): graphic artist/marketing materials	$	$ 4,000
Other (*specify*):	$0	$
	$0	$
Space Rental:	$	$6,000
Travel (*number of travelers, mileage, per diems*)		
In-state: 2, $1.20/mile, $60/day	$ 360	$
Out-of-state:	$0	$
Marketing/Publicity (*specify*):newspaper ads, posters	$ 6,000	$
Remaining Project Expenses (*specify*): paint/repair space	$ 1,800	$
Total Cash Expenses (should equal Total Cash Income)	**$ 64,320**	
Total Value of In-kind Contributions		**$10,000**

4

APPLICANT NAME: Folk Arts Collaborative

INCOME

Revenue *(Earned Income)*

Admissions (# of tickets x av. cost $:   )................................... $0..............................

Contracted Services (specify): .... $0..............................

Other Revenue (specify):20% commission on works sold .... $ 8,000......................

.... $.................................

Support (Unearned Income)

Memberships: (this is an allocation).. $27,820......................

Corporate Contributions *(identify)*:Countywide Bank & Trust grant .... $ 5,000......................

Private Foundations *(identify)*:Middle City Art Foundation.......................... $ 5,000......................

Support organization(s):... $0..............................

Other Private Support *(specify)*: opening night benefit .... $10,000......................

Government Support

Federal: .... $0..............................

State *(other than this request)*: .... $0..............................

Local: .... $ 1,000......................

Sub-Total: ....$56,820......................

Amount Requested from Arts Council: .... $7,500......................

Total Cash Income: (Must equal Total Cash Expenses)............................... $64,320......................

Budget Notes. The grants noted above have been received. The estimated commission from sales of art work is a conservative estimate, based on 80% of the sales in our last such exhibition.

5

Folk Arts Collaborative

Project Description

The Folk Arts Collaborative seeks a grant from the State Arts Council to complete funding for the 2011 juried exhibition of area potters. This will be the third biennial pottery exhibition we have held. Each previous show has been hugely successful in many areas:

- Local artists have received recognition and exposure to the community. Sales of work in the last exhibition slightly exceeded $50,000.

- The public has benefited by being exposed to an array of work in pottery being created my some of the nation's best ceramic artists. All our exhibitions are free to the public and are typically attended by more than 3,000 during the one-month run.

- We have turned our lack of a permanent exhibition space into a virtue, presenting exhibitions in vacant storefronts downtown. Property owners have been more than willing to provide free space for these shows. Downtown Middletown has been plagued with businesses leaving for strip malls. Our exhibitions not only bring life and people into downtown (benefiting existing merchants), but we also turn an eyesore into an attractive space, making it easier for the property owner to show it. The spaces used for both previous biennials were rented to commercial tenants within a month of each show's closing.

The space at 500 Main Street in Middletown chosen for the 2011 exhibition has been vacant for over a year. Given the success other property owners have had renting space after our exhibition, Mr. Frederic Goodman of Middletown Commercial Properties, Inc., has agreed to hold the space for the exhibition.

The exhibitions have also proven artistically successful. Local press have given the shows glowing notices, but more significantly, press from the state capital reviewed the last biennial exhibition, the only statewide coverage for an arts event in Middletown in that entire year. One artist whose work appeared in the 2009 exhibition has had a work purchased by the State Art Museum, and four other artists have gained gallery representation. All the artists have reported to us that they sold more work subsequent to the 2009 exhibition than they had in the previous year.

We are fortunate to have Sarah Kiesinskie as the curator for the 2011 exhibition. Ms. Kiesinskie received her M.A. in art history from Yale University in 1992 and is now an adjunct professor of art at the State University. She has curated exhibitions at the Cincinnati Folk Art Museum, New York's National Museum of Design, and numerous university shows. Her catalog essay for the exhibition *Women Make Pots: Eight Potters of North Carolina* won the prestigious Walter Hinkle Prize for art criticism.

The combination of artistic quality with commercial and community development makes this an ideal project for support by the State Arts Council.

Sample Final Report

This report is for the literacy program described in Chapter 14 for the Ralph Goodson Literacy Project (a fictional organization) that addresses literacy issues in three ways. This funder earmarked its funds for one part of the program. Note that the cover letter highlights several points that are described more fully in the proposal.

Please review the condensed proposal in Chapter 14 before reading the following report.

Cover Letter

Mr. Martin Szebo
President and CEO
Community Trust Company
456 Main Street
Anytown, IL 60000

Dear Mr. Szebo:

We are pleased to enclose a report on the Ralph Goodson Literacy Project's family program. The Community Trust Company's $50,000 grant was instrumental in making it possible for us to continue a program that requires a high degree of personal attention to each client. Although costly, personal attention is key to the program's success.

Over the past year, we have continued to help families help themselves by gaining essential skills in reading and writing. Eighty-five families consisting of 140 children and 118 parents participated in the program for at least 6 months. A full 90 percent of these continued with us for an entire year.

The benefits to the families and the community are striking. Grades in all subjects went up by one to two levels for 90 percent of the children participating. Of the

62 parents who were seeking work at the beginning of the period, 49 have found work. Few other programs of any kind can point to such dramatic results, which attest not only to the Literacy Project's ability to run this program but also to how essential basic literacy skills are to other kinds of success.

A new corporate sponsor (Firetown Tire Company) and a new source of service fees from training teachers working for other agencies will provide some security for the program in future years. As you read this report, we hope you will consider the long-term value of this program and consider becoming an ongoing partner with us in this important effort.

Should you have any questions about the report or the program in general, you can reach me at 312-555-4567 or fgsmith@goodson.org. Thank you again for your generous support.

Sincerely,

Florence Goodson Smith

Florence Goodson Smith
Executive Director

Enclosed:

- Final Report
- Budget
- Program brochure [not included here]

Final Report

Report to the Community Trust Company from the Ralph Goodson Literacy Project

We are pleased to present this report to the Community Trust Company on the $50,000 grant awarded in August 2010. The past year has been a challenging one as we struggled to maintain and expand programs during a period of recession. It was also a time when our services were most needed. Now we would like to report to you the program's many successes and several remaining challenges.

Family Literacy

The family literacy program seeks to improve reading and writing skills in families with multi-generational illiteracy. Your grant helped make possible our family literacy program, which served 85 families in this, its tenth year. Ralph Goodson, our founder, was himself a child of illiterate parents, which is why he founded this organization. Because of the success of this program, it has remained our signature program.

Illiteracy too frequently becomes a tradition handed down from parents to their children. Many adults have learned to function well enough that few people, even those close to them, realize they are illiterate. But illiteracy holds them back and is the major contributor to the poverty in which these families inevitably live.

The Social Thinkers Forum's 2009 report on children in our state with inadequate reading and writing skills found that "in the majority of cases studied, children's literacy problems stem from having illiterate or barely literate parents." The Ralph Goodson Literacy Project's family literacy program seeks to end this cycle of poverty and illiteracy.

Getting to the families who can most benefit from this service requires a number of strategies. Illiteracy is not something adults readily admit to. The Goodson Project seeks to identify and address these families by …

- Working through schools. We hold an orientation meeting for elementary school reading teachers and counselors twice each year to acquaint them with our programs. In addition, we help them understand the signs present when a child might have illiterate parents. By asking parents to attend counseling sessions with a staff member from the school and from the Goodson Project, we are able to broach the topic of the parent's literacy through a discussion of the problems their child is experiencing.

- Working through job training centers. We meet regularly with counselors at major job training sites throughout the county. These counselors are trained to work with illiterate adults, but we ask that they call us in if they discover the adults are parents. Many adults are more comfortable approaching literacy training as another job skill rather than as a shortcoming.

- Working through employers. Twelve of the county's largest employers of unskilled and low-skilled laborers work with us to offer literacy training as a job benefit. When adults see the clear relationship between job advancement and literacy, they are typically more willing to address this problem. We work with other literacy organizations so we can concentrate our efforts on those employees with children.

Through these outreach efforts, we identified 142 families with multigenerational literacy problems last year. Teachers from the Goodson Project began work with each of these families, but the drop-out rate continues to be around 40 percent, which left us with 85 families participating in the program for at least 6 months, a minimum period of time in which to make a significant and permanent difference in their literacy skills.

Goodson Project teachers worked with families in several ways:

- Sessions with the children alone to reinforce what they are being taught in the classroom

- Sessions with the parents to overcome any embarrassment they might feel in front of their children because of their lack of reading and writing skills

- Sessions with parents and children in which they are able to share their skills by reading aloud together and working on family writing projects

The sessions with parents and children are the key to the program's success. By making the activities of reading and writing family activities, the shared skills become an integral part of how the family relates to one another, thus strengthening these skills and family bonds.

Most family sessions are held at the Goodson Literacy Project facilities, although teachers frequently make house calls to families for whom transportation to downtown is a hardship.

One parent participating in the program last year told us that "being able to read with my daughter has brought us closer than ever before." Another parent commented that "My Sara is so bright that I have to stay up late studying to keep up with her, but it's worth it to see her doing so much better in school." The program equally affects the children. Billy, one of three children in a family, let us know that "we all look forward to our weekly session with Ms. Thomas. The new books she brings us are great, and she even finds ones my dad wants to read."

Evaluation

In the past year, of the 140 children participating, the 123 for whom we were able to access school records all recorded significant advancement in their schoolwork. For 90 percent, grades in all subjects went up by one to two levels. Of the 62 parents who were seeking work at the beginning of the period, 49 have found work.

One of the truest measures of the program's success is the length of time families remain in it. As mentioned before, there is a considerable attrition in the first few months. Of the families that participate for six months, 90 percent complete a year in the program.

The Context

This program is complemented by our work with preschool children who come from families representing all economic and educational levels. The preschool program's goal is to make reading a joy and a lifelong occupation. We also work with the after-school programs with the county's elementary schools, providing tutoring in reading and writing. Twenty-nine children were involved in these programs who were also clients of the family literacy program.

Present and Future Challenges

Overcoming the natural reluctance many adults feel in admitting a lack of skill usually possessed by five-year-olds will always be a challenge. Frequently, even in two-parent households, one of the parents refuses to participate in the program. Addressing literacy as a job skill like mechanics or other manual skills has made the greatest inroads to this hard-to-reach group.

The extremely high teacher to client ratio of this program (1:4 per session, and 1:18 overall) provides the dramatic results for which the program is known. It also makes it a very expensive program to run. We believe that, given the higher levels of employment it creates for the present and the next generation and the contribution it makes toward more stable families, the program is actually quite cheap.

Funding will always be a problem, but we are pleased to report that the local factory of Firetown Tire Company has become our first corporate sponsor, making a five-year funding commitment and providing space at the factory for us to meet with clients.

A literacy center in Monroe County has approached us to provide training to its teachers in the family program beginning next month. This will provide us with modest service fees to complement the contributed income.

We hope you share in the pride we feel at the success of the family literacy program and all the programs of the Ralph Goodson Literacy Project. By acquiring literacy skills, the cycle of poverty can be broken, lives are made richer, and children will be allowed to reach their full potential. On behalf of all our clients, we thank you again for your generous support.

Budget Report

Ralph Goodson Literacy Project: Family Literacy Program

Final Report for the Year July 2009 through July 2010

Expenses		Budget	Actual	Variance
Personnel				
Teachers (15)	100%	$570,000	$570,000	$0
Teaching supervisors (3)	75%	$135,000	$135,000	$0
Executive director	5%	$4,000	$4,000	$0
Teaching assistants (4)	72%	$77,760	$77,760	$0
Subtotal salaried personnel		$786,760	$786,760	$0
Fringe benefits	16%	$125,882	$125,882	$0
Total Personnel		**$912,642**	**$912,642**	**$0**
Direct Expenses				
Telephone		$600	$589	–$11
Travel		$950	$1,095	$145
Supplies		$3,000	$3,498	$498
Printing		$1,200	$818	–$382
Postage and delivery		$700	$650	–$50
Mailing costs		$400	$350	–$50
Advertising and marketing		$500	$380	–$120
Website		$500	$500	$0
Membership and subscriptions		$250	$250	$0
Equipment		$600	$800	$200
Contingency		$400	$0	–$400
Total Direct Expenses		**$9,100**	**$8,930**	**–$170**
Indirect Expenses	11%	$98,758	$98,740	–$18
Total Expenses		**$1,020,500**	**$1,020,311**	**–$189**

Income	Budget	Actual	Variance
Community Trust Company	$75,000	$50,000	–$25,000
State Department of Education	$800,000	$800,000	$0
Firetown Tire Company*	$0	$40,000	$40,000
United Charity Drive	$28,000	$22,000	–$6,000
Anytown Community Foundation	$100,000	$100,000	$0
Anytown Legal Association	$2,500	$0	–$2,500
Stars Fund	$15,000	$0	–$15,000
Smith Family Foundation	$0	$3,500	$3,500
Consolidated Electric	$0	$5,000	$5,000
Total Income	**$1,020,500**	**$1,020,500**	**$0**
Program Surplus (Deficit)	**$0**	**$189**	**$189**

Firetown Tire Company grant represents the first installment of a five-year grant.

The Elements of a Grant Proposal

It never hurts to have handy a checklist of everything that goes into a grant proposal. Review this list before you submit each proposal and be assured you've covered all the bases.

Cover letter (1 or 2 pages):

- Introduces the charity and the activity to be funded.
- Provides a reason for funding based on the funder's interests.
- Connects with the funder on a personal letter.
- Asks for the money.

Executive summary (1 page only):

- Briefly introduces the charity and the activity to be funded.
- Summarizes all the key points in the proposal narrative.
- Provides a context for the budget.
- Asks for the money.

Proposal narrative (3 to 15 pages):

- Covers all the areas requested by the funder.
- Presents an orderly, logical argument for funding.

Program budget (1 or 2 pages):

- Lists all main expense categories directly related to the program, including personnel and any expense that wouldn't be incurred if the program didn't take place.

- Shows an allocation of indirect expenses that support the program (such as rent and administrative personnel) but are not directly related to it.

- Lists sources of income for the program, including other grants (received and pending), and any income that will be earned from fees or other activities related to the program.

- Includes footnotes or a narrative highlighting the main expenses and explaining how additional funds will be raised.

Attachments (vary according to funder requirements):

- Proof of tax-exempt status

- Audited financial statement

- List of your board of directors with their professional affiliations

- List of other funders

- Organizational budget

- Organizational history

- Press clippings, client testimonials, programs, brochures, flyers, and so on that directly relate to the proposal

The Hallmarks of a Good Grant Writer

Just as the stamp on the bottom of a silver vase indicates it is of first-class materials, the hallmarks of a good grant writer signal to one and all that you are the real deal—you know the ins and outs of the grant process. Keep these reminders by your side, and you'll produce a professional proposal every time.

Hallmarks of good research:

- Does not rely on one source for information.
- Compares a funder's stated interests with the grants it makes.
- Includes research on the individuals associated with a funder.

Hallmarks of good grant writing:

- Follows all of the funder's instructions.
- Strives for succinctness and to be jargon free.
- Remains focused on who will benefit from the funding, not the charity providing the service.

Hallmarks of good funder stewardship:

- Educates and cultivates a funder before soliciting a grant.
- Keeps the funder informed of the progress of a funded activity.
- Submits a thorough and timely report on every grant.

Index

Numbers

D

CHECK OUT THESE BEST-SELLERS

More than 450 titles available at booksellers and online retailers everywhere!

978-1-59257-115-4

978-1-59257-900-6

978-1-59257-855-9

978-1-59257-222-9

978-1-59257-957-0

978-1-59257-785-9

978-1-59257-471-1

978-1-59257-483-4

978-1-59257-883-2

978-1-59257-966-2

978-1-59257-908-2

978-1-59257-786-6

978-1-59257-954-9

978-1-59257-437-7

978-1-59257-888-7

ALPHA

idiotsguides.com

Find us on

facebook®

facebook.com/completeidiotsguides

Become a fan and get updates on upcoming titles, author book signing events, coupons, and much more!